Parallel Universes

A Memoir from the Edges of Space and Time

Linda Morabito Meyer

HEAVENS

An Imprint of SciRel Publishing
www.lindamorabito.com

FIRST EDITION

ISBN: 978-0615548814

To the great men who have filled my life with meaning,
my husband David, my son Ryan, my brother Gary,
and Gibson Reaves. And for my grandsons
Robert and Nathan and the men they will become.

"Blessed are the pure in heart, for they shall see God." (KJV)

Matthew 5:8

Contents

Note by Ray Bradbury

I've told people that in the future, when I finally pass on, that I'd like to arrive on Mars with my ashes in an empty can of Campbell's Tomato Soup. I hope that Linda Morabito Meyer, alive, will arrive soon after and put a flower on my grave, where the Campbell's soup can lies. My spirit will be there to welcome her.

- Ray Bradbury
September 29, 2009

Forward

I am grateful to God for the way my journey in life unfolded.

Had I known what the reality of my life was at an early age, I could never have achieved the accomplishments in my field of Astronomy, which I love.

Had the mystery of my life as presented on these pages been solved quickly, I would have never been motivated to write this book.

The reality of each, the cold truth and the solution to the great mystery in my life, are too disturbing to base a literary work on, in my opinion, particularly because this is a memoir and all real. As a scientist brimming with love of this universe, I could never have moved forward with my education in science at an early age, and the messages of this book, which are in fact quite positive, if I had known what I do now.

In fact, right up until the moment the abuse that I suffered got the name and the face of a killer, I wrote about the joy of the pursuit of scientific knowledge in the universe and understanding our place within it; the mighty help that is available for people who have suffered trauma; and the Promise that God has for our lives, which I witnessed many times as a child. Not to mention the importance of cherishing children everywhere.

I realize that eventually you will read in these very pages that for a while, a little girl who would go on to become a world renowned scientist spent some time on this Earth as the target of a psychopath, and for that there is no helping her. Otherwise, she has soared in a universe more glorious than anything we as human beings can imagine.

-Linda Morabito Meyer
June 18, 2011

Introduction

I do not contend that my life has been typical. But, I have found the answers to questions I wanted answered for more than fifty years on this planet. The answers were told to me by a precious little girl who had lived only 30 months when she died. She was from a different universe. What follows is what happens when universes collide.

In 1979, working as a NASA Jet Propulsion Laboratory navigation engineer, I discovered the volcanic activity on a moon of the planet Jupiter, called Io. At that time, the Earth was the only known celestial body in our solar system to be volcanically, geologically active. But why would Io be the most fiercely volcanic body in the solar system, far more volcanically active than the Earth, when Earth's own moon is a dead and barren world? Io is no different than the size of Earth's moon and the same distance from its planet Jupiter, as the Earth's moon is from Earth. Astronomers had previously long wondered about the torus of charged particles that surrounded Jupiter. Where did it come from? Astronomers had much longer wondered about the possibility of finding life elsewhere in the universe.

My discovery of active volcanoes on Jupiter's moon Io has been described as the largest discovery of the planetary exploration program. Although plumes of above-surface material have since been found on other moons which orbit the planets of our solar system, such as Saturn's moon Enceladus, and Neptune's moon Triton, no world with visible plumes, in fact no discovery in space from our robotic exploration of other planets has equaled my discovery of volcanic activity on Io in significance and mystique. Jupiter's torus is composed mostly of the violently ejected particles from Io's behemoth eruptions. Io is volcanically active because it is caught in a gravitational tug-of-war between giant Jupiter and Io's sister moons. Our Moon has no sister moons to alter its orbit and flex its surface until its interior becomes hot and molten. The very existence of Io has redefined the possibility of life on other worlds orbiting other stars in our galaxy or any galaxy, as well as the possibility of life beneath the surface of another of Jupiter's moons in our solar system, Europa. Tidal forces, this gravitational tug-of-war between celestial bodies, can produce heat in worlds that orbit dead stars, or orbit objects too far from their star to experience much warmth, such as Jupiter. My discovery on Io redefines the possibilities of life elsewhere, captivates our minds and imaginations about worlds as alien in appearance, and compelling as Io. My discovery solved age-old mysteries about space, and my career in space exploration was only just beginning.

These mysteries in space were not the only mysteries in my life, though. As a young woman, I had wondered about the smallest of many mysteries, such as why when I decorated the home where I lived, my eyes always needed to be cast upon light blues and pinks to feel comforted and in the presence of beauty. I had wondered why after an absence from college after earning my Bachelor's of Science degree in Astronomy from the University of Southern California I found it difficult to want to go back to school there or on any campus, and after working as a Jet Propulsion Laboratory Senior Engineer in Pasadena, California for nine years and taking a break to start my family, I found it difficult to want to go back there, and in fact never did. I wondered too often why I had not been able to protect myself from bad relationships, when there were obvious character flaws in a person I had chosen for a mate. I wondered why one of the clearest memories I had from my childhood was bright red blood on the sand of a beach in Vancouver, Canada.

I was 50 years old when I mentioned to my mother during a telephone conversation that the oddest thing had happened. It had been a typical weekend in Arcadia, California, and I had visited my father-in-law at his apartment in Monrovia on the previous Sunday with my husband. Gene Kelly had terminal cancer. He was an intellectual man who had fathered four sons, and he was dying now of the same disease that had killed the astronomer Carl Sagan. None of his sons had the intellect of their father, none were as extraordinary. One, in particular, David, was an honest and smart and gentle man. The son of Gene's I married, Paul, appeared to be kind and gentle and wise beyond his years. He was actually none of those things.

Gene had lifted a leg of his pajamas to show me a rash on his leg that had set in on his weakened frame. His leg was stick thin. When I woke up the next morning for work, I couldn't catch my breath. I telephoned Paul's and my marriage counselor in Arcadia, Joseph Dickson. I couldn't understand what was happening or that it was the sight of Gene's leg that had opened a door that would never again close. I kept saying something about the way my own father had died.

When Gene Kelly had gathered the family to tell them about his illness, something had been triggered in me months before. In fact the entire year of 2003 had been a struggle. I had faced political trouble at work, which as an everyday occurrence was unusual. A newly hired fundraiser who was not able to raise the necessary funds for the non-profit space interest group, The Planetary Society, where I worked set her path in the organization and made sure I wasn't part of the future there. She balanced the budget for the organization by eliminating my salary. I was vulnerable politically, but in no other way. My career since I was 16 years old had been stellar in the field of space exploration.

Joseph Dickson said he had a cancellation that evening, and to come in and see him. It was a blessing. I knew of no way to stop the hyperventilation and faceless flood of anxiety, and had never suffered from it before. Joseph seemed to understand the symptom to be of a condition that I had never heard of before. When I arrived at my appointment we talked about my family. He asked me what kind of relationship I had with my mother. I said it was wonderful, and always had been. I loved my mother as I had loved my father, and made sure her life in older age was everything that it should be.

My father had died five years before. He had been sent to a nursing home after a fall in which a broken bone had been missed in an X-ray of his hip. He never got out of the nursing home system, and died after months of what seemed like undiagnosed and nonspecific, agonizing pain in the next one he was sent to.

As far as I could tell, I was hyperventilating about the way that Dad died. My father's death was inhumane. Over the interim years, I lamented to anyone I spoke to about his death, "No one should die that way." I had not known over the months my father was terminally ill that my mother had been told in no uncertain terms that he had 6 months to live by the doctor who was treating him; my father died exactly 6 months from the day she had been told. I did not know he was dying, until the conclusion became inescapable. He had been denied palliative care, or end-of-life care to ease his pain. By my mother.

During this phone call to my mother, we talked about Gene's declining health and my work, and I carefully explained that she shouldn't worry about this anomalous anxiety that had happened to me. I told her I was receiving the best of care from Joseph Dickson. I calmly explained that I had learned there are treatments for people who are suffering anxiety from events they haven't quite faced, and that I would be fine, and that it had something to do with the way Dad died. I told her, "I'm sure everything will be okay, Mom. You have a wonderful evening. I love you!" and hung up.

My mother was Narcissistic. At this stage of her life, she often had panic attacks that seemed designed to get my full attention. She carried on with uncontrollable panic during a series of incidences, which got more bizarre with each turn. She said she was bitten by a banana slug as she shopped in Pavilions Market in Pasadena, and reached for the bananas. She claimed she had nearly been pulled into a car by a strange man as she was walking toward downtown on Colorado Street in Pasadena. Whether or not these things actually happened to her and how serious they were, we inevitably ended up in the emergency room at Huntington Hospital in Pasadena. Each time, she would return to her usual self in about a week, once medical tests at the hospital only revealed once again that she was perfectly healthy. But, her Narcissism had grown since my father's death and her ability to be unkind to me seemed to be sharpening with time. It was as if I became her designated supplier of attention once my father died. With that I became the focus of her mental cruelty.

When I ended our conversation, my mother put on her slippers instead of her walking shoes. She went outside onto the sidewalk and crossed diagonally on the nearest street corner. Because she was unaware that she was wearing slippers her feet became tangled. She fell face-first into the pavement, smashing her nose into the ground. Her nose bled on the street.

Onlookers called the paramedics. When the paramedics arrived, she insisted they take her home, instead of addressing her obvious need to seek further care. She bandaged and treated her own nose in secrecy, which looked odd and swollen on her face for at least a month afterward. When I learned what she had done, I could not understand what could have prompted my mother to hang up the phone and walk unaware into the middle of the street and fall. Her desire to play down what had happened was completely inexplicable to me, given her insatiable desire for attention.

It made me begin to wonder how aware she had been of her selfish cruelty toward my father, by refusing to acknowledge he was dying, and then to wonder, for the first time, how aware she was of her escalating cruelty to me. At the time, I dismissed it. But, I knew my mother could not accept blame for anything and responded to any suggestion of blame only with rage.

My mother had once told me that something had happened to her mother when my mother was young; for an extensive period of time, her mother would wail in emotional pain all through the night, every night. I never put this together with what happened to my mother that day, until recently. Because of what I had innocently told my mother during that phone call, she knew exactly what was happening to me.

The concept of parallel universes has always been unsettling to me when I first heard it described as a possible implication of some burgeoning theories of the formation of our universe. As an Astronomer who believes the universe can be known, it is unsettling to know there might be another universe that would be so different than our own that it would be unrecognizable. What kind of truth can be learned about our own universe when the most fundamental aspects of another universe might be completely different than our own? The charge of an electron. The size of an atom. It might also make you believe, you know nothing about the universe at all.

Chapter I

A Parallel Universe

I was 17 years old when I listened to Ray Bradbury, the famed science fiction author speak on campus at the University of Southern California where I was an undergraduate astronomy major in 1972. Ray Bradbury's lecture was widely publicized on campus. His presentation to the audience of students I was in was thrilling me. He spoke my language in the way he felt about the universe. He said the last thing you think about before you fall asleep is what is the most important thing in your life.

For all the years I was in college, just before sleep, I would envision one night in the future at the moment before sleep, when I would know I was scheduled to blast off into space on a mission to explore other worlds at the dawn of the following day. Everything I did in my life up until then was based on getting closer and closer to that goal. Learning about the universe around me was the highest priority of my existence. Knowledge acquired through the exploration of space seemed the key to our very existence on this Earth. In my estimation, human history was filled with examples of prejudice, wars and aggression based on ignorance about other races or cultures. I felt much of it was rooted in too small a perspective of human beings' place in the universe. Space exploration offered humanity a larger perspective by acknowledging the gargantuan size of the universe in which the Earth was less than a speck of dust, that we on this planet, if nothing else, were uniquely related by our place here. Perhaps, I imagined, our differences on this world were less than we imagined.

Missions to space seemed relevant to medical strides here on Earth as well; for example, digital imaging, which revolutionized diagnostic and research techniques, was first used on spacecraft cameras in the exploration of other worlds. My belief about the importance of space exploration to our world didn't stop there. Like all life forms on this planet, humanity daily faced the consequences of an evolving environment from weather, earthquakes, all manner of natural disasters. Knowing where we were in the universe that surrounded us; where we had been as a planet, and where we were going, by studying other like objects in the solar system and beyond, seemed the logical means to me to bettering our chances of survival; to see the fate of other worlds like our own.

Beyond that, if through study of an evolving universe, our place in it would emerge, would it bring our priorities into focus for us; the way we house and feed and educate our people? Would we want to know where our technology is best concentrated for the advancement of the human condition in the fulfillment of that destiny? Who could ignore, I wondered, that the universe is in motion; that we were passengers on board this planet Earth? How much of a clue to the origins of our existence was in that motion?

Earth and the other planets of our Solar System orbit our star, the Sun, and our Sun travels, along with a few hundred billion other stars around the center of our galaxy, and our galaxy is moving away from a hundred billion other galaxies, each filled with millions to billions of stars and potentially planets around those stars, in a universe expanding through space and time; on scales of cosmic proportions. It seemed irresistible, compelling, and mandatory to me in my young life, that on such a journey that I wanted to see out the windshield with every scientific means that was available at this stage of our development, as well as looking into the rear view mirror along the way.

I was 4 years old when I could hear the sound of a foghorn from a ship off the coast in Vancouver, British Columbia, Canada, where I was born November 21, 1953. I lay in bed in my family's apartment on Nelson Street, and in the dark heard the beckoning sound of a ship that I knew was probably far away, but seemed imminently close. It was haunting to me. I felt alone and afraid and yet awed by a world that was so far beyond my window. I wondered where that ship had been. I wondered why the sound it was making was happening now, piercing the stillness of the night and its eerie emptiness. I knew I remembered being in my crib when I was much younger, but otherwise my recollections before then were few.

My father was a shoe salesman, but I had no knowledge of where he worked or how he even got to work. We didn't own a car until I was eight years old and lived in the United States. I didn't know what my mother did. She stayed home with my brother Gary and me and would bake a cake occasionally. At those times, Gary, who was two-and-a-half years older than me, and I would have to tiptoe around the apartment in the residential outskirts of Vancouver, particularly in the kitchen, so that the cake wouldn't fall, as my mother would say. She cooked our meals for us.

I recall soft-boiled eggs in wooden egg cups that were brightly painted with the faces of little boys and girls who had real little knit hats on that mother would remove to place the eggs in so their delicate shells could be cracked with the back of a spoon and the lovely, warm contents could enter our mouths and be devoured. I remembered Cream of Wheat when I was older, with sugar piled in layers that would crunch in each spoonful and make mornings so tolerable. But, when my mother wasn't cooking meals or making cakes that might fall, she was inaccessible, although she was home all day. On a rare occasion, she would talk to us about the wonders of the world as she called them. She had a specific number of wonders that she knew about, such as Niagara Falls in the United States, or the Taj Mahal in India. She once added a sum of figures and turned to me and said, "I bet you wish you could add like that." It turns out, she was right. Mathematics became a passion for me that was second nature, and I came to adore it, all the way through Calculus and beyond.

During a phase of my life that would be a complete departure from anything else I ever did, I became known to high school students in the Corona-Norco Unified School District in Southern California in the United States, as the only substitute teacher who could do the Calculus. Mother was "absent," although Gary and I remained in the same apartment at all times before we were old enough to begin school. When she wasn't cooking or calling us to meals, my mother was in her bedroom at her dressing table, looking in the mirror.

My mother and I walked regularly along a main street, which must have been just off the central area of downtown Vancouver, when I was four years old. My mother had me by the hand and in the store window was a sweater with hand-woven, vividly colored flowers appliquéd on it. We hardly had any money at anytime in my childhood. My mother said she would put a down payment on the sweater and add a little money each time she could, so that I could own it. Watching the bright colors in that sweater for each visit past that store was one of the delights of my early childhood. I hardly remember the day my mother had put enough money toward it, so that I could own it. Owning it didn't matter. Perhaps the gesture that something that was mine and mattered to me is what was so important to me; some acknowledgement that I had a need that my mother was filling. There were only a handful of times in my childhood where such a need was acknowledged, that I existed as a person who might have wants and desires of my own. I cherish the memory of that sweater and the brightness of the colors that represent an early childhood's ideal view of beauty. Otherwise, the memories of early childhood were dark.

Our apartment was dark and confining, in that light from outdoors never seemed to penetrate into the rooms. The day my Uncle Charlie died, the husband of my father's sister, Dorothy, was another such dark day I spent there, but one that stood out in very early memory. Charlie had fought in the Spanish American war, my mother told me. I could tell my Aunt Dot as we called her was suffering. She stayed with us for days to try to recover from her loss. She wasn't the darkest, most depressed person I would ever know from my father's family, yet some quality of her was not right in my eyes, but I couldn't tell what it was. I remember telling her that I wanted to use the phone to call one of my friends. She asked me why. I never used the phone, it wasn't allowed. But, it seemed significant to me that her husband had passed. She seemed so sad, but oddly no gloomier in spirit than she ever was before in all my memories of her.

Aunty Dot held onto some tiny glass animal figurines that I owned when our family left for the United States in 1961. She wrote to me about them too in letters that she would send my mother to read to me, but as much as this should have amounted to a lighthearted and warm personality in my recollection, that wasn't Dot. In the light of her siblings whom I would meet over time, excluding my own father as I knew him from the age of four, though, a very distressed existence of some distant past of theirs was in the ether of my consciousness all my life.

Our neighbor was a young, teenage boy named Chris Grayston. I remember witnessing him torture a young girl who had long hair, who was his age, considerably older than my brother and myself, by pulling her hair until she was completely bent over backwards on a low fence. I remembered thinking how awful it would have been to be her when he did that. I wasn't sure why my brother and I spent so much time with him; he was so much older than we. He had an electric train and a trained parakeet, which would run after the toy cars, beside the toy track, and then hop onto one of the small cars that was designed to carry freight.

Chris Grayston conducted intense comic book fights with Gary in my brother's room in our apartment. There, he and Gary would throw comic books at one another in all-out war, which was akin to a pillow fight. The comic books would fly everywhere and be dismantled by the violence. When he wasn't doing this, Chris Grayston was sitting on top of me. I would get very, very warm, fully dressed under the blue jeans that this large, teenage boy wore.

I remembered this for the first time when I was 24 years old and for just a moment in the room where I made my historic discovery of the volcanic activity on Io on March 9, 1979, at Jet Propulsion Laboratory, in Pasadena, California. It was in the summer of 1978, the year before my discovery. I got a fleeting image of Chris Grayston sitting on top of me when I was a little girl. I was married then to a young man named David Morabito, and grown. I called my mother and asked her about it. In an angry rage, which wasn't her daily characteristic at that time, my mother informed me that never happened. When she did that, I wondered where my mother had been when that was happening to me as a child. Probably, I thought, she was in her room in our apartment in Canada, looking at herself in the mirror.

My mother Marline Craman, was born Merle Bessie Daien on February 21, 1921. She was very beautiful as a young woman, and sang in the background chorus in the opera in Vancouver. As I have always known, my mother liked to share memories about her life. Like all my mother's stories of her interactions with the famous and not so famous, although mother always imbued the people who she associated with in a kind of fame, immortalizing them in their interactions with her, she would cycle through them and any particular story could pop up randomly every now and then. It wasn't until much later life that she would begin to recount some of the stories even multiple times in one day.

There was the story of the man who took her to dinner when my father was ignoring her on one vacation she and my father took to Las Vegas, Nevada. The man told her of his private jets, his wealth, and his desire to simply take her away with him and keep on going. There was the story of the producer of the once very popular television show about a talking horse, *Mr. Ed*, and his sick, ailing mother who was in the same room with my mother at the hospital in Los Angeles, where my mother had a breast biopsy. The story was about how my mother had combed the lovely, elderly lady's white hair and how much that meant to the producer. When she had passed away, my mother told how she and Dad attended the funeral. This story in later years would morph to the producer also wanting to take my mother away from my father for his own.

There were the stories of mother's tea cup readings and how she volunteered to do this for my elementary school in California, McKinley Elementary in Pasadena, during their school fundraiser, and how people lined up and flocked to her to get their fortunes read and screamed and clamored for more when my mother hit on the most important things in their lives and entranced them with their fortunes.

There were stories of her many engagements to men as a young woman, and how the pharmacist in Vancouver who tried to abort my brother with illegal pills he supplied to my mother at my father's request, was eventually killed himself in a boating accident. There was a story of how my mother foretold the death of a man in an airplane accident in Canada, when she had read his tea cup and how she had cautioned him over and over again about safety on the trip, causing her to vow never again to acknowledge anything negative in a tea cup.

There was the story of her voice instructor in Canada, a Mr. Foxwell, and that he was the top voice instructor in Canada at the time. That was the entire story. There was one more story; so far back in its origins that I can't even remember the first time I heard it. My mother would mention it approximately once a year. When we had been vacationing when we lived in Canada, two people, a man and a woman had walked up to my parents and offered to take my brother for a walk. My parents had let them. By the time the two strangers got back, Gary was terribly hurt.

This story had no more meaning to me than the rest. I was never present in any of the stories my mother had. This one was no exception. When she would share it, I would think that probably she was referring to a place I knew only through recollection. I had seen cars on a ferryboat at a very young age, at some location at the ocean near Vancouver. That was an amazing sight to me and memory that I had, that I was once on a boat that was carrying cars too.

Also, I recalled that someone had told me not to jump down some stairs in front of bungalows during a vacation at what seemed to me to be a familiar place. This was among my few memories prior to the age of four. I truly seemed not to give much thought that I had images of blood on sand in my mind and very brightly colored bandages. That image usually reminded me of my family's times on the Canadian beaches when I was slightly older, and someone, maybe my brother got cut or scratched, but this was extremely vague. The memories of the brightly colored bandages and blood seemed stand-alone, almost without any other link to anything except their really overly vivid colors. Perhaps bandages like band-aids were made that way back then.

I could well remember playing in the sand on the beach in Vancouver in a swimsuit that was adorable and was smooth and shiny. As to this story of my mother's that two people had done something wrong to my brother, it had no particular significance to me because it seemed so long ago, in the way my mother recounted it. As the years went by though, especially when I had children of my own, I often wondered why anyone would agree to allow their five year old son to go anywhere with two strangers, who had seemingly come out of nowhere and asked to take my brother for a walk.

My father, Robert Craman, bought gifts for the family on one occasion when I was a very young child, which may have been one of the only times he had any extra money. He bought the family a small, gold portable bar on a trip on a train into Washington State in the U.S., where we crossed over the border, and shopped at the depot. This small bar with a small gold lock on the three bottles of hard liquor (nobody ever used it to drink, although for a time the bottles had liquor in them) was a decoration that my mother kept for all the years she was able to live on her own, into old age. My mother's sister Clare hung on to it when we came to the United States, and when she also moved to the U.S., she brought it with her and returned it to my mother. The gold bar signified the only tiny bit of affluence from my childhood.

My father bought me a pair of clear plastic high heals and a thin, tiny fake mink stole. When my mother would dress up in her mink stole that was old and bit battered, and I would wear those plastic slippers and my mink stole, it would stop traffic when we went into the city in Vancouver. It must have been adorable to be a miniature adult. That, for my father, was the only time I recall he offered anything in my early childhood to let me know he understood that I had any individual identity whatsoever. He did, however, buy all four of us in the family matching Hawaiian print shirts, which we would wear on weekend excursions to Stanley Park in Vancouver. That too, would stop traffic, the family dressed alike.

My brother Gary was a tragic figure in my eyes. He wore thick glasses as a very little boy and seemed distressed in a way that suggested to me he couldn't collect his thoughts about the world around him, although he was quite intelligent in his own way. I was constantly worried that something would happen to him.

Gary and I were taught no formal religion at all by our parents, but I invented religion in the absence of any. I thought through the details of offerings to the gods I invented so that nothing would happen to my brother, so that he could be protected from harm on a daily basis. It is no surprise, as time would tell, that my brother and I are in our mature adulthood, both Christians. My brother, in young adulthood, had a catastrophic mental breakdown that institutionalized him for life.

I remember so long ago in distant childhood, my brother's decision to leave our apartment and run away from home one day in Vancouver. I believe that he actually packed a thing or two in something that resembled the proverbial knapsack on his back. I remember following him to the front door of the apartment in Vancouver and begging him to reconsider. Once that door opened, I thought the world would end, that I would never see him again and that something bad would surely befall him. I remember running to get my father and awakening him on that weekend morning, when my parents would sleep the entire morning away until noon.

My brother and I were often with babysitters in our apartment, because my parents went out in the evenings before we were put to bed. We were put to bed when the sun was still up, which left for endless hours of being alone in our individual rooms. There was a television set in the living room, but we could only watch it on rare occasions.

My father woke up and angrily put a stop to my brother's retreat from our lives. I didn't know why my brother wanted to leave home; I always had the sense he believed he was being treated unfairly at home. In my heart, I knew that too, that my father was an angry and perhaps violent man toward Gary, but, because my father prevented him from leaving, I still had my brother in my very young eyes, and no harm would come to him at least on that day.

Dr. Pidders, the Pediatrician, came to the apartment when my brother was ill one evening. He was forced to chase the frightened, timid, and near-sighted little boy through every room until he caught him, dragging him out from under a bed, to administer a shot of penicillin. This sad and difficult image encapsulated the difficulties I was aware my brother had. My brother could be angry though, as well as frightened.

My grandfather, Charlie Daien, my mother's father, would come to our apartment every Friday night to teach us Hebrew. On one such Friday night, my brother declared angrily that we were not Jewish and should not be learning the language. He ranted and raved and I suspected until recently that he might have picked some aspect of this thinking up from the older Chris Grayston. He made such a scene it was unforgettable. Not only did my grandfather not show up the next Friday night, I never recall seeing him again.

All these years later, I now believe I know why my parents prevented us from seeing my grandfather ever again after that day. They were perhaps afraid of what my brother had said, of what he might have been reminded of in the presence of his grandfather.

Up until recent years, I could only surmise that my grandfather's reason for coming to see us regularly as children to teach us Hebrew was some thin strand that hearkened back to my mother's very primitive past that began in a community called Yorkton, Saskatchewan, Canada. Her family owned a store there, but they were impoverished. My mother told her friends at school that her mother and father were the maid and butler of her wealthy parents. The school children believed my mother. They hoisted her on their shoulders as they carried her in the streets in some form of worship and admiration for her singing and dancing talents, as she would tell us as children.

She danced for the Governor General of Canada as a child, when he visited Yorkton. The town took up a collection to send her to Hollywood as the next Shirley Temple, but she became ill and could not go. She sang in operas in Vancouver later on as a young adult. My mother, who did not finish high school, worked at a department store in Vancouver, and indeed, had a proclivity for picking up marriage proposals. She was attractive and sought after by multiple men to marry her, and received a collection of diamond rings, many of which she gave to her mother. Up until recently, I remembered seeing my Grandmother Rosie only one time, when she was already ailing, and being asked by her to rub her stomach in gentle jest. When my grandmother died, my mother complained bitterly that her two sisters took all the rings.

Before my brother's refusal to learn Hebrew from my grandfather, I recall one of grandfather's teaching sessions that would set the stage for an experience that would repeat throughout my later life. My grandfather had conducted his teaching with a small blue book whose hard cover was encased tightly in thin navy blue fabric. Inside were Hebrew characters, some nearly as large as an entire albeit small page, something akin to a giant letter "A," perhaps, in a teaching book of the English language for small children. I remember one of the first early lessons I had, where I listened carefully to what my grandfather told me.

I recall the exact moment when I was cognizant that if I told him what I had learned from these brief sessions and applied it, he would be amazed. I will never forget the look on his face when he learned how smart the very little girl was who was sitting beside him, when I applied what I had learned. For one brief instant, I could see in his expression he experienced a form of awe at the capacity of the little person's mind he could never have envisioned.

Learning languages easily came in very handy for picking up a plethora of computer programming languages later on. In a computer programming class at USC where I studied astronomy, the professor said to me after I scored one hundred percent on the first exam, "You've had this class before, right?" I hadn't. I'd just rapidly picked up the concepts, and run very, very far right from the beginning.

After my first appointment with Joseph Dickson for my strange anxiety in 2003, I was driving along one evening that week, after stopping at the market. Joseph had informed me that I was not to blame for the horrible way in which my father died. I had done everything I could back then to help my father; wrote the doctors letters, interrogated them, begged the nurses for more cooperation. I had tried everything to make my father more comfortable. Of course, I had probably felt I was to blame for not doing more, but how could I? My mother had not told me my father was terminally ill. I was not to blame.

I felt better and had stopped hyperventilating during the appointment. Joseph asked me to write down anything in the week that came to mind before my next appointment with him. Two irritating songs that signified failed relationships with men (one of whom I had married, Jerry Hyder, and had fathered my son, and the other a boyfriend I had dated after my marriage) kept playing over and over again in my head. I couldn't get the songs out of my mind.

Suddenly, I was asking God to help. I kept repeating, "God help me." "God help me." I had no idea why on Earth I thought I was in any trouble at all. What was the basis of believing I needed to be helped? God help me, why?

The sand at the Canadian beaches was unforgettably white. On excursions where we would take the bus, there were deep family adventures to be had in very early childhood. There was a place where we would vacation, but my only memories of it were a ferry that we used to travel on water that carried cars too, and perhaps some bungalows where we stayed there. A stranger told me not to jump down a stair of a small set of stairs just outside the bungalows there, after I had already jumped. There were large leaves in Stanley Park, as big as I was, it seemed, and totem poles made by the Indians. There was "fish and chips" to be eaten by the sand on Vancouver beaches with the smell of vinegar lingering in the air.

When my parents determined I had a lazy foot that I didn't want to use when going down stairs, they began me in ballet. Of all the students she had, the crippled, aged instructor, a former prima ballerina, who shot her instructions to us children while hitting the ground with her cane from her wheelchair, singled me out for a professional future as a ballerina. I knew even then I had no interest in becoming her protégé, but was good at ballet, very good, particularly at this age. I could emulate instruction and see its essence, derive its meaning, and add my own interpretation. I was always in performances, and selected to model an original child's outfit at the Vancouver fair. My outfit was judged second place. I hadn't attained first place because the outfit did not come with a required matching jacket, the judges explained to the seamstress who had entered me in the competition. I narrowly escaped consideration of jumping from the huge five-foot high stage, when no one had bothered to explain to me what to do after they guided me onto the stage alone.

In hours and hours of endless play to fill the time in my bedroom, I would set up tea parties for my stuffed animals and dolls. I would work so hard to conduct successful parties that I would be exhausted by the start of day for my parents. Organizing my work and following through meticulously with precision was a hallmark of good engineering, and I exercised these skills first in a bedroom tea party in a dark apartment, alone. But, my love for my brother Gary was the hallmark of my early childhood, and it was infinite. We were somehow it seemed one person.

Although I was independent in my own mind, his spirit and who he was even back then, had no boundaries from my own. In very rare excursions into the city, that once included a trip to the Hudson Bay department store, where I rode a pony and owned a tiny gold ring until it was accidentally and immediately washed down a sink in the restroom there, were also trips to a dimly lit and special restaurant made with my parents and my mother's sister, Aunt Clare and her husband, who were of greater means than us. This was also true of my mother's other sister, Nora, who married a dentist and kept a suburban life with her two children, that included her charity work, that was beyond anything I could imagine in my social standing.

Upon leaving this special restaurant, at the location of the cash register, small children were offered the ability to pick out a gift from open toy chests. My brother asked me to combine our individual choices from the toy chests and pick out one of the larger gifts, wrapped as a surprise, that were for exactly that purpose. But, my eye had caught a purse in the girl's chest that had a Scottish plaid print, which suggested multiple compartments inside. I simply had to have it and see how many compartments were inside. My brother was horribly disappointed when I did this.

To my disappointment, as well, there was only one compartment inside that purse. I remember feeling crushed that I had made this selection, but there seemed to be more to it at the time. I wasn't sure why, but I didn't forgive myself for letting Gary down that day, even with the passing of time. It was the singular and only time I could ever remember letting him down, and I never got over it. It would be nearly fifty years before I ever understood why.

———————

My brother suffered corporal punishment at the Lord Roberts School in Vancouver. That was the practice at the time. Such punishment nearly happened to me too. I was told by older students not to step on the wet spots in the flooded basement of the school in the first days I began there at the age of four. The floor itself was slick and shiny and it was very difficult to tell which spots were wet and which were dry. I knew if I erred the children told me, I would end up being hurt with rulers and hit like I had heard my brother often was. The school seemed vast and vacant and terrifying and held children of so many grades. I was so young to begin when I did. When I walked across the freezing playground one morning alone to the reach the office, a cat attacked my legs.

I would fall in the slick and wet snow when it would begin to turn to sleet on my way to school. The walk was far and difficult. Two little boys, classmates, I knew that fell in love with me, would roll in the streets in front of me when the sun would come out to impress me on that long walk.

The school had plenty of resources. There was a pretend kitchen and pretend cars in my classroom, and my mother came to see me in some performance of my class work, when I was told by my teacher to pretend to drive a car that was rather like a gigantic building block, fashioned to be carved from one block of wood. I drove my car in that classroom by the power of my feet. I recognized that there were means here that I did not have elsewhere. School began to speak to me about what it could offer. Early, we learned sophisticated concepts. When I was taking a spelling test at age four, the teacher said the word "wind" like to wind a wristwatch, long before there were batteries in wristwatches, of course. I didn't know how to spell the word and had never seen it in print to my knowledge.

I knew how to spell wind, like the kind that blew my skirts of heavy flannel against my black tights that would keep me warm against the brisk Canadian wind. Such tights protected me too during a fire drill the first day of school there when a little boy held me by the hand and accidentally pulled me down a flight of stairs as we evacuated the building. Without the tights, I would have been far more badly hurt. I wondered to myself in real time if I should put an "e" at the end of the word that represented the Canadian wind, to achieve the word that would wind a wristwatch. I told myself, no, I doubted it.

I wrote down the word that represented brisk breezes. It seemed odd and counter-intuitive, but somehow I knew I was right. My deductive reasoning kicked in, for the first time in my life, and there was no limit to where it would take me.

———————

Joseph Dickson, who was also my marriage counselor during my marriage to Paul Kelly, told me as my sessions continued with him, that when I first arrived with Paul at our counseling sessions, earlier that year, I had been very unhappy with something Paul had done. Rather than be angry, I was accommodating and understanding that maybe Paul would eventually be more aware of the effects of his actions. Joseph shared with me, that that demeanor is a defense mechanism, one that in later life we are able to discard. He was trying to convey that if I were furious, why didn't I simply act furious? I didn't fully understand what he was driving at. It would take me literally years to learn how to identify emotions by the word of the emotion that I was feeling. I could only describe love. When things negatively affected me, I could fully describe what I would think or believe, never what I felt.

In my mind, in Joseph's office, I remembered my father in a fetal position as I had found him in the middle of one night in his nursing home, crying like a baby in complete pain. I knew full well that every night in the middle of the night for those last six months of his life had been that way. I wept violently in Joseph's office over the suffering my father had endured.

I mentioned to Joseph that when in the room at Jet Propulsion Laboratory in the year before I made my discovery, I had what was like a flashback of the young boy Chris Grayston sitting on top of me when I was a very little girl. Joseph's eyes looked sad.

I needed as well to get those haunting, sad songs out of my head and deal with how difficult a final vacation with Jerry Hyder, my son's father, had been that had ended our marriage. Instead, in a very intense session, I remembered my parents. I saw colors, first blue, the blue jeans of the boy Chris Grayston, as though they were real, as I had never seen them since the days when I was a very little girl, and then their blue color broke down into green and yellow and the yellow became the pale pants of the boyfriend I had after my marriage to Jerry. He was walking away from me during a recollection where at the time, I had thought he was in love with me, and then I knew.

This man, and the young Chris Grayston had one thing in common for sure; their complete indifference toward me. Suddenly too, I could see my mother looking in a mirror in her dressing area. Indifference too. That is what she had been doing when the teenager Chris Grayston was taking advantage of her absence with a very little girl. Being indifferent toward me.

I was markedly aware that Gary's and my life got better when we were old enough to navigate the world on our own, when our family came to the United States in 1961. We made it better for ourselves.

I began to recall in these sessions, openly now, that I might have transferred my worrying about my brother all my life to my son Ryan when he was born in 1982 in Riverside, California when I was married to Jerry Hyder. Ryan's father was a mathematician whom I met while working on the NASA Voyager mission to Jupiter and Saturn. Being Ryan's mother is the best and most important thing I have ever done in this world. Ryan is everything I ever hoped my son would be. I only briefly wondered at what I could not remember and that was *when* I began worrying about my brother. That could have been from the moment of any awareness, when I was just a year old, I surmised, since my parents were indifferent. Indifference meant neglect.

But, with Ryan, I had always been overprotective, and I recalled now the moment I had looked at him in infancy, on a day when he resembled my brother Gary, and when I told myself I was going to have to worry about him from then on.

Since Ryan was a grown young man, I could now under Ryan's current situation in young adulthood factor out circumstances when I would worry about Ryan more or less. I would worry more when Ryan was walking in a parking lot he had to pass through to get to work, until his car was repaired, because that was an open area without trees. It was a very stark parking lot that evoked current images of worry about Ryan's safety. Like a vast, open terrain the color of sand.

For just a moment, I thought about images of blood on sand, as I told Joseph this, but they escaped me as they always did. I would worry less about Ryan if he were walking in areas with trees, completely different landscape than anything open and hued uniformly. Trees were good, I associated safety with landscapes that were not open but had green trees. It would be a very long time before I would ever connect any of this to my feelings of being haunted in open areas at the University of Southern California or Jet Propulsion Laboratory.

Later, I told Joseph that I had the funniest thought recently to the point of obsession even before the anxiety that had originally brought me to him. I had been wishing I could live my life again as a child growing up on Mars with colonists. Joseph looked like he would laugh. Because, I went on, I think on Mars, even children's impressions would be important and they would be asked for their feedback on the world that surrounded them. My parents had been indifferent toward me, and Gary. I had a very large intellect locked in a child's body and nobody knew I was in there. My parents never acknowledged us as children as having individual needs. These realizations were painful.

I came home after this latest and helpful session with Joseph. All the songs had stopped playing in my head. I felt like I had learned what I needed to learn. I did some dishes at home. I thought about the colonist idea and sort of realized that I would probably now stop thinking about that obsessive notion of wanting to grow up in a colony on Mars. We all try to make up for things we didn't get as children, it seemed.

I was tired after this last session with Joseph. While putting the dishes in the dishwasher, I suddenly thought something about "Monsters," "Monsters from the Id," from the old science fiction movie *Forbidden Planet*. I tried to dismiss what seemed like such flighty thoughts too. I went into the living room and fell asleep on the sofa for just a few minutes. I opened my eyes startled when my field of vision in my sleep filled up with the stark color of blood.

My father made the decision to leave Canada in 1961. The perception that some aspect of Vancouver was at the very least not allowing our family to flourish came through even to me at the age of six, as he and my mother discussed the choices. We would head to Australia or New Zealand or perhaps California. Perhaps their final decision had something to do with school children at Lord Roberts joining arms and walking across the outdoor playground, when it was not raining most of the time, yelling, "Hey, hey, get out of my way, I just got back from the USA!" that caused them to select California. Also, my father had a sister Ruby in Hollywood, California.

An Uncle of my mother's, Harry Daien, sponsored our exodus to the United States, although he lived in Florida. My mother's side of the family had some highly intelligent people, although I would not include my mother in that category. Although mother had common sense, it was all self-directed in a curious way, and she never had a grasp of actual facts beyond her own world, but at that she was expert and could apply laser-sharp mental power seemingly at will. Her two sisters, my Aunts, were well read and highly functional, with very high IQ's, but were not intellectually wise in my opinion, despite in the case of my Aunt Clare, an avid intellectual appetite. One of my mother's cousins, Bora Laskin, was Chief Justice of the Supreme Court of Canada from 1973 to 1984, when he died.

Once the decision was made, my parents put all of their furniture on sale for a give-away price. An acquaintance of theirs knew someone who wanted to buy it all. Later, when the buyer came to pick up what he had seen displayed, the buyer felt he had been cheated and that there was more the night before when he had seen it. There wasn't. My parents were very honest in that way.

My parents had a rocking chair and had introduced Gary and me to instrumentals of the variety of "Balero." My father's taste in music in later years also ran to Frank Sinatra and Mario Lanza. My mother's tastes were always love ballads and songs dripping with emotion. My brother and I would rock in the chair and listen to the instrumentals for long hours. In far more recent years, I picture Gary and I rocking in that chair and listening to music, in God's hand, on the edges of space and time. Even the records were sold.

My brother and I were told by my parents to give away all our personal belongings. In a yard sale that was definitely earmarked by excitement about adventuring off to the "New World" I sensed we were selling our souls as children; that any security we had in physical possessions was being taken away. The only money my father had once we reached the United States was from the sale of a coin collection my brother had been given. I had prized possessions, a large bride doll that had been given to me, and a smaller pink baby doll in a plastic pink carrier that smelled as delicious as any plastic could, that I knew I would never see again.

Gary and I had been given other gifts by the seemingly wealthy and flamboyant husband of my Aunt Clare, Harry Mason, including two brand new, shining bicycles. Such possessions were beyond our parents' means. Within a day, my father had taken the bicycles away. He thought them dangerous and didn't have any idea of the effect it would have on us to see such items and never be able to own or use them. My father broke our spirits with broken promises too. They were made casually when we might ask for a privilege and when it was withdrawn, there was not a single acknowledgement of how that might affect us. My father was stern.

I had the feeling that if I didn't smuggle something of value to me in a suitcase where no one would see it, that I would have nothing. I sensed my parents didn't want any reminders of the past, apparently. I had two tiny dolls, just over the size of my hand, which I had named Penny and Jenny. Those dolls were my salvation and were hidden. I placed all my value in them, told myself they were everything to me and smuggled them into the luggage.

Gary had no such luck. His prized possession of a Bambi stuffed animal, who when it spoke always said the same thing, through his translation, "Boosha Boosha" which meant whatever was called for at the moment, was taken from him at the train station, while he was screaming to retrieve it. I can still remember the sight of Bambi sitting near a trash can, alone at the station, where no child could love it as it had been loved, and my brother's tears.

––––––––––

I was scheduled to see Joseph Dickson early in the following week. I was getting dressed in my dressing area on Sunday so Paul and I could go to breakfast. I looked in the mirror to apply my makeup and I thought to myself, "Two people took my brother." In the first seconds, it didn't mean anything to me. My mother had talked about this incident when we were vacationing in Vancouver all my life. Then, I realized I had no independent thought of this at anytime in my life until this moment. I didn't know that I was there when this happened. I started gasping and tried to catch my breath. I couldn't. I called Joseph immediately and paged him.

Joseph called me back. I told him what had happened. He warned me not to do anything, not to try to understand anymore of this. To stop this process now, to get distracted, to do yoga, to do work, surely he said you can exercise and can stop thinking about this. He warned me that this is what I was going to have to learn to do in between these sessions. I didn't think I could do it. I didn't know how to stop this, whatever it was. I have never experienced a type of pain that I was soon going to recognize over and over again as a mental agony I never knew existed in this world.

On Paul's last birthday, Ryan and I had taken him to his favorite restaurant. I didn't feel well during dinner and hadn't felt well all day at The Planetary Society. I kept excusing myself to the restroom at the restaurant in the hopes the feeling would pass. It wouldn't. Soon, I told Paul and Ryan I would have to go to the car and wait for them. They found me laying in the back seat in agony. I said, "Get me to the hospital, I think I have a kidney stone."

I had watched my former husband Jerry Hyder suffer through this, years before. People could hear him screaming through the entire emergency room in the hospital in Corona, California back then. I did the same thing, I kept crying for someone to help me as Paul drove steadily to emergency.

When I was in a hallway on a gurney and given pain medication, Paul told the attending physician, "Linda always thinks she knows what's going on. She thinks it's a kidney stone." The doctor said, "She's right, I think so too." Luckily, I passed that very small stone within a few minutes of that, but not before the doctors caught its picture with an x-ray. That pain, worse than my labor pains when I had Ryan, was not as bad as the mental anguish I began to experience as I entered a world that was slowly and excruciatingly coming to the surface.

I had a feeling that I needed to relive the emotions of when my father had agreed to let these strangers take Gary for a walk. When I was finally in the session with Joseph, I was having trouble bringing any images to mind. Joseph told me not to force anything, just to let this happen on its own. I did relive some emotions of perhaps my brother being gone and then me being worried and him coming back? I wasn't sure. My parents were there in fleeting images, but mostly outdoor scenery kept moving by. I thought I may have remembered the arm of the man who took my brother, but it didn't look like a man's arm. I was pleased I had felt anxiety from the event back then; it seemed to fulfill what I needed to get off my chest about this.

I was filled when it was over with a sense of anger at my parents, that their indifference toward us didn't protect my brother from two strangers who hurt him. I recounted to Joseph as I had in the past that my parents had been forbidden from taking Ryan anywhere when he was a little boy when my father kept asserting that Ryan needed to be independent at the age of three, and be left in playgrounds alone as he did once with Ryan. It never made any sense to me and I surmised that probably my father had wanted Gary to be independent, when he let him go for a walk with the strangers. They had hurt Gary, I didn't know exactly how. It made me angry at my parents for their negligence and indifference.

Joseph asked me if I felt okay about things now, and I said that I did and that I had probably made the progress that I needed to. It was as if the way my father died was sort of a porthole into remembering my parents were indifferent parents, and that indifference had hurt me with Chris Grayston sitting on top of me, albeit clothed, and my brother with these strangers.

My attitude toward my mother wasn't enhanced by this experience. When Paul and I married, he asked me why I didn't have a regular time for visiting my mother. My mother loved Paul in the way she loved all people who gave her attention, and he at least pretended to love her. He would call her Gorgeous. Paul enjoyed doing everything on a schedule. He picked Friday nights for us to spend with my mother. When he did this, I had a sense that is something I would never have done on my own. I had a vague sense I did not understand that since my father died, I was backing away from my mother. But after a time, I would always miss her and had always been a devoted and loving daughter. I never at anytime in my life ever let my parents down.

I wanted to remember more about this incident with my brother. But, I assumed I had to give it time. I felt bold one Friday evening and decided I would try to learn a little more, especially when my mother coincidentally brought it up once again on her own. She said, as we were all sitting in my living room, two people took Gary for a walk and when they got back, he was so very, very hurt. Her voice went into the crying thing she did when she expressed emotion like for lost puppy dogs on the TV news, or anything that moved her. So very hurt, rang in my head. Perhaps I had never listened before to her language closely enough. That riveted me.

I took Mother aside. I said, "Mom, tell me a little about what happened to Gary back then. It's okay. It was a long time ago. Nobody's to blame." I was thinking in the context of hers and my father's decision to let Gary go with strangers. Her eyes dropped, not out of embarrassment. She was thinking. She changed the subject. "How old was I, Mother?" I asked. She said, "Two-and-a-half." I repeated what I said to her three times about nobody being to blame, then she said, with laser sharp reasoning, "What do you remember?" I didn't remember anything. I said, "It's okay, you can tell me." She said, quickly, "Well these two people, well Gary had a seizure, but we took him to the doctor and the doctor said he was fine, that can happen when kids get hurt." And she changed the subject again. For whatever reasons at the moment, I didn't want to press further. In my thinking, trusting my own mind was paramount, as it always had been in my life. I didn't want too much help, or maybe I already sensed that there wasn't any point in pressing my mother because only lies would come out, but I am not sure. We rejoined the rest of the family. I was made of solid brick, I was learning. I didn't even react to the fact that now after decades of recounting this she now said my brother had a seizure. She had never under any circumstances said that before.

––––––––––

We waited an entire day at the immigration and naturalization building in Vancouver for our passports to a different world. My brother literally screamed for countless hours that day. You could hear his screams echo through the vast structure of that building. An eyelash had gotten into his eye and he was in pain that no one could diagnose. When my mother finally got to the point of not being able to hear those screams anymore, she grabbed the boy and pulled him toward her, lifted the eyelid of the eye he had been screaming about, finally saw and extracted the offending lash. In retrospect, my brothers screams were like some ominous beacon of the past we left behind and the stark and difficult journey we were about to take.

Fruit in Vancouver was not a plentiful staple of our diets. Oranges certainly weren't grown in that climate. When my mother and father and my brother and I boarded the train to California, we were offered oranges the size of huge baseballs like we had never seen before during the trip. We all ate a lot of them. We all got sick on the journey because of that, and as anyone knows who is sick and traveling, this made the entire trip miserable.

We made our entry into the United States at Blaine, Washington on August 14, 1961. When we arrived at the train depot in Los Angeles, California, and stepped off the train we stepped into one of the strongest heat waves Southern California had ever seen. It felt like a furnace. The blast of heat that hit me was as foreign and shocking as the trees that had no leaves and only a bare trunk that led to some bizarre foliage high on top, which people called Palm trees here. We had never seen anything like them.

My parents had heard stories that the streets in California were paved with gold from people they knew who had visited the United States. My parents must have believed this literally. We boarded a taxicab directly from the depot in our first evening in Los Angeles. My father asked to be driven to a hotel in Hollywood, near where my Aunt lived. My mother timidly and politely requested the taxicab driver please tell her when we got near a freeway so that we could see what it was like. The driver responded, "Lady, you are driving on one." We all looked around. It was just a road we were on; a barren one at that. The fact that we were traveling at a high speed was completely lost on us.

My parents had no idea what was a good or even a safe area in Hollywood where we could stay. On the first night we arrived, a man staying in one of the rooms of the hotel they chose decided to end his life. He turned on the gas in the small stove in the room, waited, and then lit a match. The explosion tore out windows up and down the neighboring streets for blocks. Two old ladies who neighbored our room dropped dead later that day when they went walking from heart attacks or some after-effect of the explosion. We weren't hurt, but this was our introduction to the United States.

Over the days that followed in that California sun, my pale Canadian skin turned brown and I became a strikingly beautiful child. People remarked on me wherever my parents took me. It hurt me that they never said anything about Gary, who cried and agonized in a type of heat we had never before experienced, and which he could not tolerate at all. Each day brought temperatures above the 100 degree mark as did the next day and the next.

We frequented some of the local, colorful stores. My father tried to contact his sister, who was studying on her own for the California state bar exam to become a lawyer, for the umpteenth time, and could not see us, she said. We eventually moved into an apartment that didn't have a bed for me, so I slept on a large upholstered chair with a hard back that mechanically laid back flat just big enough for me. That hard surface of the back lay under my head as I slept on it the first night and I developed neuralgia the next day and could not feel the side of my face for the entire day. I believe this apartment introduced me to the concept of putting wet towels in the refrigerator, and spreading them across my body for temporary relief of oppression from the heat.

Eventually, my Aunt consented to seeing us. She was singularly the darkest person I had ever met, in the sense that, even as a child, I could literally picture a dark cloud on top of her that followed her around even in the blazing sun. She occulted the sunshine with her depressed nature. She was "poison" of some kind, or had been somehow figuratively poisoned, I could sense. But, I didn't know anything more than that to account for her nature.

She had married an Arab man, who had passed away many years ago, and had a daughter named Angela, whom I would later come to be very fond of. Angela, in her early twenties, reached out to my brother and me for a brief, special time when we were just a little older. She would pack her car with amazing gifts for us, and brought us a book of Shakespeare's plays, and wonderful, unique toys. Her own mother's depression infected Angela, however, and probably had all her life. She found her mother dead on Mother's Day one year when she was much older, in her locked apartment in Hollywood, and underwent some extended trauma. We never heard from Angela again. Angela seemed doomed by the dark spirit of her mother. I had sensed that from the beginning.

Gary and I began school in Hollywood at Lockwood Elementary, which was an abomination to us. The children seemed vial and used swear words. In Canada the children we knew were kept under much stricter conditions at school and in the way I was raised, were to be seen and not heard.

My mother always said I never complained to her about anything I wanted as a little girl, and I was the best child she had ever seen. My parents took full advantage of my brother's and my maturity in the regard of our manners around adults we did not know. In later years, we were the only children allowed in several of the apartments where we lived. Lockwood Elementary was light years behind where we had been in Canada. My brother had always come home from school, two grades ahead of me, and taught me everything he learned that day. There was nothing either of us was learning at Lockwood Elementary that we hadn't already learned. We were dying of thirst in an intellectual desert. We spoke differently than other kids did, pronounced long ees in words such as "been" to the store, chesterfields were sofas where we came from, not cigarettes, creemo was milk not something special designed for coffee. As difficult as the world was that we came from, we wanted to go back. We cried nightly and begged our father to take us back to Canada.

In March of 2004, my father-in-law Gene Kelly lost his valiant battle with cancer. I had lost my job at the start of the year with The Planetary Society. When Gene died, my son Ryan was only months away from undergoing emergency surgery at Huntington Hospital in Pasadena in an operation that would be botched by the surgeons, and would over the following years to this very day, change my precious son's life and my life forever.

By September, I took up work at a local proprietary college, Mt. Sierra College, recruiting high school students to attend, patiently waiting until something in astronomy and space exploration came around. It was a difficult time for the space community, and lay-offs of long-time employees at Jet Propulsion Laboratory were taking place.

I was rigorously trained by the college, and it was charming that many, but not all of my co-workers were the ages of my children. They welcomed me within their ranks. One young girl had an amazing effect on all of us who met her and were training with her. She had a dynamic personality and had the demeanor if not the complete appearance of a young child. She was 25 years old, but in many ways, appeared simply child-like. As the days of training went by, she confessed she was under the saddest type of strain. Her mother was dying.

This young woman spoke in a language that was beginning to cause me the type of anxiety I thought I had overcome by now. She talked about being completely unprepared for her mother's illness and impending death. She said things like that she could not deal with or handle what was happening. The vast majority of this type of pain was not knowing or be able to pinpoint its source; the excruciating slowness with which this parallel universe emerged. It showed no mercy in that regard. I did not know why I hurt. My work schedule was too hectic to schedule an appointment with Joseph Dickson, but I did speak with him, and told him I would get in as soon as I could to see him.

All of this may have had something to do with my brother on that beach when two people had taken him for a walk, I told Joseph, but I wasn't sure. I was sure it had something to do with death. Paul's father's impending death had triggered something about my own father's death and that had been the windows in to my anxiety the first time around. Now, it was this child-like girl's mother's death for which she was unprepared. A neighbor of mine who was on the Board of Directors of our condominium complex, as was Paul, was also dying. I believed that my lifelong friend and mentor, Professor Emeritus of Astronomy Gibson Reaves at the University of Southern California, was dying as well. I had so much sensitivity on death, I could barely even think about the prospect of Gibson dying.

As I struggled to find a time to schedule with Joseph to relieve this anguish of not knowing where my anxiety was coming from, I fought depression from simple Christmas music playing in markets. I waited for my chance to find out why this was happening as patiently as any person could. On November 2, 2004, while doing my job for Mt. Sierra College and hauling a heavy laptop computer across a high school campus, I discovered the ball of my right foot was very sore when I came home. I was forced to cancel my projected work the next day. But, by the morning of November 4, 2004, I felt ready to go again. By the end of that hectic day of activity and carrying equipment across another high school campus, I was seriously injured in this same area of my foot. This time it did not get well.

When I saw Joseph Dickson on November 16, 2004, I was limping badly. In the initial weeks after the injury there were times when my foot hurt so badly, I became feverish. I had never had an injury in my life had ever stopped me or slowed me down. This was taking a lot of adjusting to even in the very first days.

When I met with Joseph, I remembered a red rose appliqué on a deep blue nightgown I had. When I had dressed earlier in the week in my dressing area, I had stared at that appliqué as if I was seeing it for the first time. My eyes rushed into the red and then into the deep blue of the nightgown and then this gave way into an ocean and a sky above. There was a dock there that I hadn't ever seen before. I was back on the beach in my recollections where my brother had been hurt. I didn't want to move or change this view of this beach in my mind. The relief was overwhelming. At least my pain had a face. This was still to do with my brother and what happened on that beach. At least I knew.

I remembered my father as he looked back then, from the vantage of me being nearly as tall as a minute as I was at two-and-a-half. My father was angry. I commented he was angry for the wrong reasons. I had suspected this. He was probably disappointed in Gary for being hurt. It reminded me of how he had reacted at the optometrist office at Sears when I was in junior high school, and he was informed I had a retinal hemorrhage. It was as if that made him angry, it seemed, for whatever reason, just like this with Gary now, seeing my father look angry standing there in his bathing suit on that beach. He was young and handsome and wearing a blue shirt.

I had a sense of my brother Gary, for an instant, but not on the beach, in some stand-alone sense. My brother looked normal. My mind didn't want to move from this image; he was beautiful, he was beautiful. I could now see my own feet as I looked down, in little white sandals against the wood of the dock. I'm so little and chubby and my skin is perfectly soft. I told Joseph, "Somebody help my brother, somebody help him! Why won't anybody help him?"

I couldn't remember anything when I was crying this. At the end of the session, I told Joseph, "This is the end of the world. It's the end of the world because my brother is hurt." Joseph, rushed for time, said, "But, you are older now and you know that it is not the end of the world, of course." I didn't have time to collect my thoughts; Joseph's waiting room was full. I dried my tears. Later that night, I felt the compulsion to express what I felt I had learned from what I remembered in a one-page fax to Joseph.

I now knew three things. The first was that it "was the end of the world" when my brother got hurt on the beach by the people who took him away, because Gary was my entire world for the first two-and-a-half years of my life, as he was after, until we were old enough to expand beyond the sphere where we lived with our parents in Vancouver. Next, I knew that it was not only true that my brother changed forever after the incident, but it was also true that he was once normal, not the tragic, timid and frightened figure of a boy I had known in not as early childhood. My parents perpetuated that lie throughout my life, that he was never truly normal. Now I knew that he was normal from the first moments of my life with him, and that I knew him as a normal person for the first two years of my life. The magnitude of the incident, which destroyed his ability to live a normal life, happened apparently without any acknowledgement of the severity from my father.

And my final conclusion was this: It was possible that this incident became my definition of death. The incident took the complete person of my brother away forever. So, in a sense he died. I believed it was possible now that all of the feelings I had toward what happened to my brother when I was two-and-a-half were transferred by me to every incident concerning death in my life. So, superimposed on what any person might feel about death being "a part of life" were these feelings of helplessness and horror from that day in childhood. Another contributing factor over my lifetime, which seemed to join what happened to my brother and death, was my parents' denial of both. Never, at any time in my childhood had my parents ever admitted they were going to die via conversations about wills or anything else. If any subject like that came up, they skirted it in unabashed statements of basically immortality.

My father, who had never completed elementary school, had fought in World War II for the Canadians, alongside the Americans. Whatever he faced back then probably made our family's move to the United States not challenging by comparison. When he was on one of the landing craft that put him on the beach in the second wave of the Invasion on D-Day at Normandy, France, he refused his shot of whisky. He wasn't interested in his last drink before he would die, as nearly every man who was with him on that boat and drank that shot did.

When he went into the water he sunk from his heavy backpack. A very tall American who was broaching the beach at his side picked him up so that he didn't drown, carrying him forward until he got his footing, saying, "Come on, Canada!"

On the beach my father's fellow soldiers got under the landing craft for the only cover from incoming fire they could find. The boats sunk in the sand killing them. Spray from machine guns cut the man beside my father in half. The walking half kept on walking for a while. Throughout his stay on that battlefield near Caen and for days afterward, my father complained about the bees that were buzzing about his head. They were not bees, but bullets that had kept him alive by narrowly missing him again and again and again. His entire command was wiped out in what he said was his only psychic premonition experience of his life. He heard them scream when they died, although he was nowhere around them.

Bad teeth had kept him on one or two occasions from death. As he waited for a plane that would transport him out of that area after his tour was done, an aching tooth pulled him out of line for the flight, which went down in battle killing all aboard. There was something about his calmness that was like some kind of steel. The same calmness that many years later, when two prisoners, who escaped from their guards at the Pasadena, California, courthouse, found him in his car as he waited for my mother in a store parking lot, put a gun to his head and told him to drive. He told them, calmly, "Here are my keys, you take the car and drive yourselves." They did.

Calmly, but like steel, my father found an apartment for us in Pasadena, California, within a short time after we arrived in Hollywood. He told us the night before we saw the apartment, that it had a yard. It didn't, the front yard was filled with vines. It was a duplex that was cockroach infested, but it had a warm feel to it. Pasadena was the home of Jet Propulsion Laboratory and McKinley Elementary School, undergoing experimental educational programs, was located right next to the Board of Education.

In this decision to move to this city, I began to flourish, and began my ascent.

I sat in the office of Dr. David W. Curkendall, Supervisor of the Outer Planet Navigation Development Group in the Tracking and Orbit Determination Section, Section 391 as it was designated, at Jet Propulsion Laboratory, in July of 1973. I made the decision to wear a pink dress to my job interview at JPL that day, because it was a favorite of mine. I was later told by another engineer, that day, my hair looked to be in just one long sheet down my back.

David Curkendall wanted to talk about astronomical plate reduction. We had a very nice and polite conversation about how well I was doing at college, I had just finished my junior year at USC, he had heard, and how nice it would be to have me join JPL for temporary employment over the summer. Then he asked, "So, just how do you reduce a photographic plate?"

I knew because one of the most distinguished men I had ever met, Dr. John Russell, professor of Astronomy, one of only three in the tiny department at USC, gave a class in observation and plate reduction. In this class, in an exhaustive set of hand calculations, which went on for the entire semester, was the reduction of one photographic plate taken of some stars. The object was to go from millimeter locations or simple x and y measurements on the plate, which was just basically a picture of some stars taken by a telescope on Earth, to meaningful celestial coordinates in space.

Of all the astronomy classes I had taken as an undergraduate at USC in the department of Astronomy, I disliked this class. In fact, I received a failing notice at some strategic time during the semester that reminds a student it's time to do something about the situation.

That was totally uncharacteristic for me. Photographic plates were not my "thing." In fact, any observation done from Earth didn't grab me, the way travel into space did.

I later learned that one of fellow astronomy majors at USC reduced the course to programming the transformation equations into a computer – this was a time when computers were only available to students at the college level – and thus reduced the entire course to simply submitting the x and y measurements of the stars on that plate as data to the computer and spitting out the right ascension and declination of the objects, the celestial coordinates, on the other side. So much for spending an entire semester on this exercise! That thought grabbed me! The programming of equations into a computer, the development of those equations would be the frontier and the tools I would thrive on utilizing at JPL.

I deftly answered David Curkendall about his question on reducing a photographic plate. I only thought about my first computer class at USC taken as a sophomore, quite a while after. At the large computing facility at USC, students would turn in their computer programs to operators, who were, themselves, students, who would load the programs on cards into a mainframe computer and produce a printed output from the computer, which each student would receive. The output would show the result of the work or calculations each student had programmed the computer to do. I was just learning the computer language Fortran at the time, which nearly all my work at JPL was conducted in. I had learned a simple print command and had instructed the computer to print out "My name is Linda."

One of the two computer operators at USC opened up my output printout when I came to pick it up, to see what I had instructed the computer to do. He saw that I had successfully had it print out "My name is Linda," which was about as rudimentary a use of a computer as a child reading their first words, see Spot run.

The computer operator asked me why I was taking this programming course at USC. I answered, "Because I wanted to work at JPL." He burst out laughing on the spot, so loud that everyone in the large facility could hear him.

His co-operator smirked at me. The operator said to me, "You can make a computer print out 'My name is Linda' and you think you can get a job at JPL because of that?" Now he seemed angry. "I can do everything with computers that can be done and *I* can't even get a job at JPL!" In some way I cannot comprehend, it was music to my ears.

For whatever reason he said it, I knew he was wrong about my chances of getting a job at JPL, and that in some indefinable way, his comment affirmed exactly where I was. It was like a road sign I had come across on a track that had been pre-set telling me where I wanted to go was just up ahead. I wanted to go into space.

On November 17, 2004, I had a reasonably good day. It came to me in the morning that there was probably one thing left for me to do. I felt inclined to communicate this to Joseph Dickson, via fax, so I was following my instincts. It felt like part of the process. I told Joseph in the fax he didn't have to answer the fax if the process was all that was needed.

I realized that this was the second year where as my birthday approached I was either in the aftermath or in the midst of remembering something about the incident on the beach with my brother. An entire year had passed since I had realized I was present during the incident my mother had described my entire life. I sensed that I would never get to the end of this process until my mind allowed me to see what happened to my brother on that beach, not just the water, the sky, the dock, me and my father.

I expressed that I was now in a peaceful negotiation with my mind to allow me to see what I saw on that day. I was assuring myself that it was time.

I asked Joseph if there was anything else that I could do in that regard. The mysteries of so many things had been unlocked with my new understanding of my confusion that day in childhood with death. Now, what remained was for me to see what locked all this away so long ago, and set my life and interpretations in ways that caused me so much difficulty and created portholes into a place that remained hidden still.

I never made it to my next session with Joseph before I remembered.

On the day before my Birthday, I was watching TV. I always marvel at the way cars are advertised, and I believe what I saw was another car advertisement, but I'm not completely certain. I often wonder what a list would look like of how cars have been represented in advertising over the years. Cars as art, cars as insects, cars driving cut in half, etc.; it would certainly be a list that would make me laugh. But, this commercial was different. It showed a little girl running down a dock on a beach that resembled the one I had already remembered. I felt my heart jump in my chest.

Within a half hour I was looking in the multiple mirrors of my dressing area. A year before I was there when I remembered that two people took my brother. A couple of days prior to my last appointment with Joseph I had stared at the blue in my nightgown and the red flower appliqué, standing just there, as though I were seeing it for the first time. Now, I saw my eyes in that dressing area in the mirror and my eyes did not meet my eyes in the mirror. I watched my own eyes, which were not focusing on what I was seeing in the mirror. I could see my eyes, but as if they were different instruments than what was producing the vision of them in the mirror.

Within an hour I was back downstairs in Paul's and my condominium and suddenly began weeping for Gary from a place inside me I have never experienced before. I could tell I was weeping in "present time," when I was two years old on that beach, not for anything that happened since that day on the beach. It was the greatest sorrow for another human being I have ever known. I could feel my sorrow for Gary in a physical pain in my heart as I called his name again and again. I have never experienced anything like the sadness for the tragedy of what was happening to this human being, and although I could not remember anything specific, I knew I would remember this feeling for the rest of my life. At some point, I became discernibly aware of a lifetime of sorrow I experienced over this.

Paul came home and I told him this would be the last birthday these memories would ever destroy. I was praying this would be over soon, but didn't know for sure when it would come to an end. Since seeing my eyes in the mirror, I could nearly "feel" the point in my body that the memory had arisen to. It was still well below my chest.

By 3:00 PM, I was bathing and told myself that I couldn't do this on a schedule, couldn't release this memory by waiting until my next session with Joseph. I wept and rocked in the bath water, crying and pleading to "give this memory back to God." I said this again and again, with my eyes tightly shut crying.

From darkness all around it, an image emerged in my memory of my brother. Most notably were his skinny, nearly bone-thin arms and legs, much thinner than I had ever remembered him to be. Thin, like Gene Kelly's leg he had shown me before his death, what had started me on this journey. Gary was in a red t-shirt and wearing glasses. He had on shorts. His eyes were closed, his face was anguished, and he was not in control of his expression.

His limbs appeared mangled, in the sense of a contortionist. I had a sense he was therefore on the ground, but the entire scene of him and he kept jumping, as if from some plateau on the ground but not on his feet. His arms and legs were bent and in jerky motions; he was jumping from his back and then back again to the ground and the arms and legs were not in natural or normal positions. I wondered briefly if the red on his shirt was a color or represented blood. His shirt was striped in wide bands of red, so I couldn't be sure. I wasn't sure how long this scene lasted for me when I was in the bathtub, but when it passed, I was able to stop crying.

I was so glad this had happened at home and that I was near my family and not in Joseph's office. I wanted to cry more while I was dressing afterward, so I sensed it might not be over, but was not completely sure of that. As the evening went on, I slept fitfully on the sofa until about 9:00 PM. A number of hours later, it occurred to me that everything I was feeling now might be a true aftermath of having seen the destruction of the person my brother was and being able to remember it, nearly fifty years after it occurred. That perhaps the door was open and the contents now released.

When I saw Joseph, I gave him a written summary of what I had remembered. I had seen these memories of my brother's seizure now, but I was not at peace with them, as much as I believed that I was. It was, however, for a time enough to have seen them.

———————

As the days went into December, I remember an evening crying like an animal for my brother. That kind of cry differed from what I had experienced the day before my birthday. The crying like an animal that I termed to myself usually was in present agony over memory of the past. The type of crying I had done on the day before my birthday was from the standpoint of a two-year-old child. I would learn to recognize different categories of crying, although each time I cried in this process it was different in and of itself.

Overall, I would cry for seven years total in this journey through time. I later learned from my own empirical knowledge that I was receiving credit for these tears. That the human mind probably pealed away layers of the past in stages, because a human being simply cannot produce enough tears at any one time. And the issue of time was key. The only way I was able to watch my eyes watch my own eyes in the mirror is if time was giving way. I was about to relive a past event as though it were happening now, and my brain was accommodating the structure it would take to accomplish this.

One night when I did cry like an animal over my brother in what was an aftermath of my sessions with Joseph similar to what happened when I resolved my trauma from the way my father died, and wept for him afterward at home, I walked upstairs to the hall in the condominium that separated the bedrooms. In it, were various pictures of Gary hanging on the wall.

I began to notice the difference in his appearance in some of the pictures, depending on when they were taken. Primarily, I noticed that when he was very young, he looked normal. I could now tie what happened to him to the trauma of what happened when he had been mistaken by the Pasadena Police in 1982 for a suspect they were looking for, and the police had roughed him up until they figured out their mistake. This incident had marked the onset of his full mental illness in adulthood. It had probably triggered as well a recollection of what the two strangers had done to him in childhood. I asked Joseph about it when next I saw him. Could that trauma account for Gary becoming mentally ill? Joseph nodded.

———————

There is a place in the human mind that is saved for the ideals we hold most dear. A place in the colors of childhood that are never brighter than we when see them there. Our children are our future. They deserve to be educated and prized and to be spared abuse. They deserve to have the chance to have their dreams take flight. To explore the universe around them where the heavier elements formed in the centers of stars.

If children are not given this chance, their minds take over for a time to make sure that it will happen anyway. I have reached the edges of the universe with my thoughts and contemplations about its origins. I saw sights on another world beyond what any human being had seen before. I can picture two doves flying from a bright scene on a beach in Canada. One is my brother. One is me. We are free.

On December 14, I watched my own hand reach for a photo album just before my final session with Joseph on this journey for some time. My hand seemed to be making the decision if I should take some photos of my brother, myself, my mother and my father to show him; it seemed right up until then a little like show-and-tell at school to be taking pictures to my session with Joseph. But, my hand decided.

I had never seen anything quite like it, except once in an Alfred Hitchcock movie *Marnie*, where it looked as if the main character's hand was reaching for money in a safe which represented her psychological problems in the plot, all on its own. This was less dramatic, but my hand did make the decision to take the photos. I watched my hand do it and reach for the albums as though it was not me doing it. Much later, I would understand this better.

In the photos I selected to take were a picture of Gary before and after what happened to him on that beach. When Joseph saw the pictures I could tell he saw everything that had been described to him, and probably more.

By the end of January 2005, Paul Kelly had left me. His explanation apart from anything else was that he did not want to be married anymore. He had been supportive of me throughout my reclaiming of my memories, but the person he appeared to be did not exist. Both Joseph Dickson and I are shocked, there was no warning, and I cannot believe this has happened. I spent the next two months dealing with what is nearly clinical shock, my returning memories, a foot injury, a serious illness, the destruction of my son's well being through a horrible surgery, and an uncertain future because of my foot, unable to work.

At home, I sit in my dressing area, and begin to remember more.

I remember myself in various stages in childhood, and then my mother's hair the way she wore it for many years in the gold swirl on top of her head, rigid and like steel. Inside that gold swirl that never moved as did the top of her head like a steel robot, it appears like a black cavern. I envision going into that cavern which was like a cave, and that I would emerge from it on a bright sandy beach, like many of the days we spent on sand in the beaches in Canada on the weekends.

I remember my mother sitting on a beach blanket in the sun, frozen there, an external shell of steel that is completely empty inside. I contrasted it to me as a child, my image, who was soft and completely without steel and completely vulnerable. My mother was empty inside at all stages of her life, even before I was alive, like in pictures that I saw of her over the years. I asked myself what that did to me.

I think of the color purple, which gives way to bright yellow and red spots. And those spots to a leopard two-piece bathing suit my mother had gotten me as a girl. I hated that suit because my body did not look like hers, and I was taught no pride in myself at any age. There was only her and her image to represent womanhood. I was shown nothing else. My memory went further and further into this fabric and deeper and deeper into the black part of it until there was only black.

I wept a type of animal cry I have never known, but I didn't know about what. I didn't know what for yet, and I was praying I would remember why. In this blackness appeared a picture of my brother as a child, making that ridiculous face he made in pictures since his life had been taken away from him when he was five years old. And my brother was empty inside like my mother, because what was inside of him had been taken away by what my parents had allowed to happen to him on that beach. And my mother had done nothing, nothing after all the years to help him, nothing to acknowledge what anybody could see. I continued that mourning cry, and I called Joseph and spoke to him, and scheduled with him for a couple of days hence.

I went out after that to the bank, and I was getting into the car to go to a fast food drive-through when I suddenly realized my mother was nowhere in my recollections of Gary on that beach at anytime recently. Where had she gone to?

More than a year-and-a-half ago when I had relived the emotions of that event in sort of a superficial way it seemed now, my mother had been in those recollections. She wasn't in the subsequent recollections. I was in the drive-through at Kentucky Fried Chicken when I called my son at home. I was crying, "Ryan, she knows the people that did this to my brother! My mother knows the people who did this to my brother! She knows them!" I managed to order food and by the time I got home, I asked Ryan's fiancé Michelle to come upstairs with me away from Ryan because he was watching Robert, Michelle's little boy, at the time play with the cats in the condominium. I wept on Michelle's shoulder. I didn't know what I meant yet, except that what my mother had always said about the event wasn't true. I was weeping and crying, "It's a lie! It's a lie! It's a lie!"

At 3:30 AM the next day, July 16, 2005, I would embark on a journey that was sadder for me than anything I have ever known, but could not touch the sorrow that was coming one month and twelve days later, when this journey through time would finally reach a destination.

Ryan and Michelle had gone to bed. I'd slept deeply on the sofa and then I sat up. I saw my left hand. It didn't look like *my* hand. The fingers were slightly closed. I looked deeply into it. It whisked past my left eye. I came upstairs and showed my hand to the mirror. My fingers continued to close. I'm not sure whose hand it was, was it my brother's? But, I'm rubbing it with my other hand and comforting it. And then, like it did downstairs, it whisked past my left eye. My fingers close and then the hand rotated by my left eye. These things were happening and I was not controlling my hand. Did my father punch my brother? Did he do that? My hand settled toward the ground. When it did, my fingers came open. Whose hand is it? What happened? Is there a hill? Are there sharp rocks that hurt my brother on a hill?

My left hand, my left eye, stroking the top of the left side of my hair. Whose hand is it? My hand wants to move in a circle by my left side. It did that before, when it was by my left eye. My hand started moving back and forth in my lap, and then swinging by my side, lower and lower, in a figure eight and then a circle, falling, falling, down, and finally just hanging there at the end of my arm.

Falling, falling. It is not moving now. It came up and then down and then up. It is weightless; it is motionless, over my heart. I knew how tired I was at that point.

The hand is doing rhythmic things. I am wondering for a second time now if it represents some kind of sexual abuse. I can't be sure. I grabbed it with my other hand at my wrist and my hand moved back and forth toward me.

I went to sleep upstairs. In the morning when I woke up, I recalled that when my fingers closed and made a fist and moved by my eye, it seemed violent. When my hand moved back and forth, however, as it did even more often, it seemed sexual, but only at moments, so I question if I am superimposing that meaning over it in some kind of adult interpretation, but it was gently rhythmic at all times and therefore perhaps not sexual. I cradled my own hand several times before sleeping. Does it represent different things at different times? Is it memories so far back that my hand can only act them out, like before I knew what language was or the acts were?

I now know I didn't know the truth, yet. When I tell myself, "It's a lie," I want to know what's there. I suspect the two people who hurt my brother are my parents, and I suspect severe abuse of my brother and me.

Help close the injured hand by stoking inside the fingers and the palm, rub the injury (the outside of the closed hand), hand opens but not fully, not moving, and then it falls.

I am asking God to help me to remember, and I am alone. It's okay. It's okay, I tell myself. I reach my hand up to God and asked Him to put what it is my hand in my head so that I will remember.

I'm rubbing my whole arm now and saying the word, Baby, Baby. My arm is my brother's body, and I am comforting him. After. Baby, Baby. I'm crying.

I say Baby in that way to my children, all of them, when they are hurt. I say Baby in that way too to my pets when I am trying to comfort them. I said it for the first time then. Ryan says it too.

Who punched my brother? The blow shattered inside of me. It exploded the flesh off my body. I am shattered. My brother destroyed. He is fallen, not just injured. He is fallen. I am destroyed. It's a lie, it's a lie, it's a lie. My mother's lie that there were two people, a man and a woman who hurt my brother. There were two people, it was them.

In short hours later, I wanted to ask Joseph if a blow to the side of my brother's head could have caused the convulsing that I remembered he did in my returned memory of November of 2004. The reason my brother looks different in pictures afterward, is because it is a brain injury.

It caused the seizure immediately after. He was never the same.

A month later, in a meeting with Celeste Peters, my lifelong friend and fellow USC graduate, I said to her, I met this little girl when she was two years old. She is beautiful. I ascertained this by the way my left hand moved, more beautifully than any ballerina's artistic motion could ever be. The little girl had pointed to her heart and to her gut when she felt the gut wrenching pain or tearing out I re-experienced fifty years later, too, when I realized my arm was my brother's fallen body. The cry in my room as my hand acted all of this out, produced the same stretching of my face that I had experienced the day before when I had cried over the memory of my mother and not known why. My hand was acting out the physical pain I experienced in my heart and my gut at what was happening to my brother as I was watching at age two. A beautiful little girl told me all of this in the only way she could. Sadly, she would not stop there.

Coincident to this timeframe, on the day my mother's sister Nora passed away in Canada, my mother decided to give me all of the family pictures. I was drawn to them over the week after I knew that perhaps my father had punched my brother. Joseph and I had talked at length about what I knew. There was a persistent theme in memory of the black and white pattern or animal patterns. I could see the belly of a new kitten we had at home stick out from the sides of its body as I thought about my brother being hit by my father. The animal print, light and dark, on the kitten; it's belly swelling as seen from the top of the kitten possibly representing swelling of my brother's head. I wondered just briefly if Gary's injuries were too severe to hide. I wondered what kind of a man could hurt my brother this much. Perhaps the war had done it to him. I knew my father had used his fists against a fellow soldier who angered him in at least one fight in the war. White and black patterns, animals prints, I always hated them in fabric. Life and death. Opposites. My mother, I was to learn, was the opposite of everything I had ever believed her to be.

In the coming week, I was drawn more and more to the family pictures she had given me. I dreamed of them Wednesday night. There was something in those pictures to do with her. I found two that actually didn't look like her or showed something that I hadn't seen before. I put them apart from the rest, thinking she's not my mom or even a wife. She is a stranger.

On Thursday, July 21 at 12:26 PM my hand put one of the pictures down and then positioned the fingers in a way that wracked one of my fingers with pain, and then acted out a stabbing motion back and forth toward my abdomen many, many times, not rhythmic, very direct, very threatening, and then my hand circled back down around to the side of me, nearly behind me.

I contrasted this mentally with the configuration of my hand during the revelation that perhaps my father had hit my brother. When, I did, "she" acted that out again for me. I felt like I should thank her, the whisking of my hand by my left eye. But, this time, when it happened, I consciously thought, "Don't look. Don't look."

I went back to the pictures of my Mom. My right hand took on the more threatening configuration now, and it hurt too when it did it. I thought, my mother is absent. Did she know I was being sexually abused? The answer is yes.

This was okay for her. As okay as all of the stories she had ever recounted about what she had witnessed as a child in Yorkton. My mother once told me tearfully that when she was 19 years old she had been raped. But, when we watched the news together, she would express no compassion for rape victims. My mother had many missing emotions, although people would probably describe her as the most compassionate emotional person they had ever met. White so close to black. Life so close to death. All of life existing, but only blackness in reality below the surface. Is it her acting that I have detected now? That everything is an act of emulation.

There was a certain appearance of my mother's face, the way she started to look in '58 or '59, but I picked it out of a picture that was taken much later when we were in the United States. I see remnants of that look in many of her earlier pictures, even though her appearance was markedly different then. Did I see that look when my mother had knowledge of abuse of me? Did I see the non-familiarity, the look that reveals everything that is not there? Was my mother present when I was being abused?

I become aware there is a scream inside from long ago of me that needs to come out.

She didn't care, I am reciting. My index finger hurts. She didn't care. I'm screaming back then. It hurts! She knew I was being hurt, but she did not care.

I long noticed that I can't see my mother on the day my brother was permanently injured. Now I sense why my mind won't let me see my mother. She links this event with my brother to the event of my sexual abuse. It became clear to me when I realized she didn't care about that either.

I spent the day in mourning; in the knowledge of what was, and with a scream that nearly surfaced from long ago.

Friday, I got my first memory. I stood by the bed and my hand filled with pain, and then nothing. So, I let it go and decided to get back into bed and read, as I had been doing that morning. My left hand filled with that stiff pain and then finally my index finger began to move violently back an forth toward my lower body with the hand not moving, and then ultimately my whole hand did that with the wrist not moving, and then after what seemed like a good deal of time it stopped, then my hand fell toward the side, toward the bed, and I could see my small body turning on its side, and so I followed my hand with my body now, and noticed that my legs came up toward my chest in a fetal position when I lay on the bed. I could see the age I was, and I believe it was the age I am in a picture my mom had taken of me about two years old.

I also realized that the unfamiliar look of my mother, which was apparently driving these memories, was on the face of a younger woman, before she actually evolved into the appearance in pictures in '58, so these things happened much before then.

As I bathed, I got another near image, comforting myself, calling myself "Little one" from the pain. I took the dog to get him groomed in Pasadena. As I was driving, I was realizing what my parents had done with their two children, and wondering how anyone on Earth could have done such a thing to innocents, trying to deal with my suffering, and recognizing that the image of a part of my father's body from a certain perspective was not just a thought I was having, but a memory. By the end of the weekend, Sunday night I came up into my room when I was alone in the house just to scream from anguish.

I saw Joseph at 11:00 AM Monday morning. He urged me not to try to remember anything more because I was under too much stress. I had been forced to ask my son if he had been sexually abused by his grandparents, which he had not and I later learned was not a possibility; there was too much sorrow all around now with everything that was happening to me. Against Joseph's better judgment I told him that I was going to be well and nothing on this Earth was going to stop me. He agreed to conduct the session.

I see my mother, the face I had seen when I was a teenage girl, the unfamiliar, stone face, when she looked "different" than she had at anytime in her life. She had gold earrings on, and she began to speak in her most elegant tone and mannerisms, as she would to people she was trying to impress. She appeared so refined, so elegant, perfect speech. She was wearing a black and white zebra print dress that was not fitted and flowed, as if from her shoulders; she had such a dress. Then, she began to spin. The zebra pattern of her dress began to meld together from spinning so very, very fast. She formed what was like a pencil and it was sharp at the end. And spinning, spinning becoming ever thinner, until it became nearly not there and out of where she was a dark room with walls very far away appeared. My mother's gone!!!! Where's my mother?????

Now, I can't see anything further. I tell Joseph I am hiding. He says to me, "Think about hiding." So, now, I am a little girl about eight years old and I am in pink shorts and a top and tennis shoes that I had forgotten that I had, and I think about a day I was playing hide and seek. But, that image, which feels harmless, begins to modify and I shrink to the size that I was when I saw my body falling sideways "afterward," when I was a little girl, two years old or younger.

I am hiding then. It was so hard, so dark, to see the room that it was a room, but it was. It contained a very large bed. It occurred to me that this might be like a vacation cottage, like the beach where my brother was hurt during a vacation. I saw my father, he was in his swimming trunks, standing there, much different than I had anticipated him to be. He looked like he had in one picture I had selected for Joseph to see in the past when I was determining that my brother looked different in pictures before and after his injury. I am remembering Joseph's comment that my father looked completely egotistical, and how I had told Joseph that wasn't the case, he wasn't like that. I am remembering now that image only, an image of my father that wasn't recognizable as anything I actually remembered until now.

I am now remembering my father's word for penis in this dark, unfamiliar room that is becoming clearer that it is a room. I see red, blood. I see drawers, a chest of drawers with rounded edges. This is something of a much more "real" quality, more familiar. This is my parent's bedroom at home.

Joseph stops me. He says, "Linda, are you prepared to remember what you might remember now?" He is worried about me. I tell him yes, that I am ready, and that I insist that he continue the session as I had insisted he conduct it when I came in. He says what if the images are difficult? I tell him I have already considered over the weekend what it means for two adults to have two children and do THIS to them. I have already considered, and I need to get well. He reminds me knowledge is power and it means to me that I will be well, and I say, yes, yes, I want to be over this and well. I have no other goal, but to get to the end of this nightmare.

Now I see me. My little body naked in their bed, uncovered. My head is near the pillows, but beneath it. The covers don't reach me, there is small place in the bed that has been carved out for me in terms of the covers and I am naked there. I am in a fetal position, but my legs are not tightly against me, as I had re-enacted it at home. I probably hurt too much to bring them up any higher. There now, there I am.

So small, like an approximation of a straight line at any point along a circle. I am too small for this bed. I am wounded in this bed. I am crying from deep in my soul. I am thanking Joseph out loud; I am thanking him for being able to see. I have never in all my life endured the intensity of pain over the last two years, when my mind wouldn't let me see. I am sobbing and thanking him over and over again.

And now, I see my brother. I keep saying how cute he is, he is so cute, so unbelievably cute, the way he looked before. It's before, the way he looked before. My father is on top of him and I think my brother has on a t-shirt, but may be naked from the waist down. My father is pummeling his head. He is a brute. We are being brutalized.

The image of my brother is in the room that is more unfamiliar, during the vacation. My images to do with me are in my parents' bed at home. I have only one recollection of that room until now, but never being in it. But, when my brother and I were little, in the "world" that I could remember before, we looked through the keyhole once and saw my parents having sex. Until now, I had no recollection of ever being in my parents' bedroom.

I am still crying and Joseph tells me to breathe. He tells me that breathing will let out the intensity better, and it does. I am crying out the agony in my soul and it is working.

I say that my mother could not have been too far away.

I thank Joseph for having the faith in me. He says, "Linda, you are a trouper."

At my next appointment, I tell Joseph there is a scar on my soul from the violence that I have witnessed and I know I will have to address that. I had evidence of this from some thoughts that I had when Ryan was being mistreated at the hospital during his surgery, I felt broken by what was happening to him. My soul is damaged, and I know I will have to face this. I will face it sooner than I ever dreamed.

On August 22, 2005, I was driving near my mother's apartment on my way to physical therapy for my foot. I had passed the general location of her apartment twice a week on this route, and since I was no longer seeing her, I often anticipated what it might be like to catch a glimpse of her after all that had happened. But, this time, unlike any other, I was stopped at a red light. I had a sudden reaction of terror at the prospect of seeing her face. The "face" that I was afraid of seeing and "see" before me to this day, is the same one that I had woken up from nightmares envisioning; even as recently as days before, her skin drawn taught across her face, her hair out of the way. It was a similar manifestation of her face that I was drawn to in pictures during a phase of her life when she was in her prime, and which led me to the reclaim the memories I have.

With the level of terror that I experienced that I would see her and be unable to move, unable to get away, not passing her rapidly driving as I had been every other time, there was something very specific and very real here. By August 23, I had to let it happen. I was walking my dog and told myself I had to allow myself what I couldn't allow the weekend of my revelations of sexual abuse. I allowed myself to know that my mother had participated in my abuse. That the image of her in my mind wasn't symbolic of anything; it was a real memory as had been my father's part of his body. I suspected her molestation of me. As it did for moments as I remembered now, when I first learned of my abuse, everything got quiet in my heart.

It's knowing the reason for the fear that seemed to help. I had the benefit of no longer having that image of her face, specifically, evoking strong emotion. By late evening though, I could sense something that I hadn't sensed since the week prior to that weekend of realization about the sexual abuse, that there was a scream deep inside of me that wanted to come out. After the session about the revelations about my father, I didn't feel the need for that scream anymore. But, now again, seemingly with these new "possibilities" about my mother, I wanted to scream, a scream that originated 50 years ago. It felt like another memory unfortunately somewhere still left inside me.

I had an appointment scheduled with Joseph for Monday, August 29, 2005 at 3:00 PM. I was crawling along during the week, though, trying to muster the strength again to ask God's help in remembering, but I wasn't strong enough. By Friday, I had seen a TV ad of some ladies in old-fashioned bathing suits like my mother had doing odd calisthenics on the beach that evoked some kind of a flashback in me. I weakly asked God's help in remembering something about my mother's image early Friday morning during half sleep. My mind focused on a specific part of the lower half of her body wearing such a suit.

I went into the weekend in bad shape. Saturday, I didn't do anything. Sunday, I was suffering as badly as I ever had with the possibility of emerging memories. At 10:30 PM Sunday night the recollection was just below my breastbone; it was coming up. I want to remember. I am asking for God's help. It's here; I can feel it. I need to remember. God, what do you want me to remember now?

I closed my eyes. It came up. I see my brother in the darkness. He is in the red t-shirt that I saw he had on during the seizure. There might be something in his hand. His eyes have flames in them. He fought back. He tried to fight back. I'm screaming! I am screaming! The loudest scream I have ever screamed. And it's coming out silent now. I am screaming. I am crying. He tried to fight back. He looks grotesque somehow. There is fire in his eyes, like the devil. I see his skull. All heaven and Earth have come together to make me see the horror that I saw back then. He tried to fight back.

I am breathless, but I am calmer, I think. I am crying still, wailing. Help me, Joseph, is all I can think, and I will know what we should concentrate on to get through this. I'm rocking more quietly in my chair now. I had to see this. There was no choice. I had to see the horror that I saw. Calmer. Not since November of last year. Very similar process. God, I am praying not too many more times like this. The way my brother looked suggested something too horrible for a baby like I was to comprehend. It was the worst waking vision of my life now. The red in his eyes like a skull with molten fire in the place of its eyes. It could have been a reflection, but the scene was surrealistic as a child might see the kind of violence being done to him was unimaginable. Something about his lower body was crumpled. I cry and wail.

At 5:00 AM, I ask, was this blood in the whites of Gary's eyes? Yes!!! Skull fracture, possibly. Brain and eye damage! Definite discovery as abusers!!! Blood in his eyes!!!!!!!

At 6:00 AM Monday morning, I reread what I had written about this for Joseph. The line about blood in his eyes. My eyes focused on those lines, blood in his eyes. Then, the weirdest thing happened. I closed my eyes and could feel my eyes doing rapid eye movement beneath my closed lids. I placed my fingers of my right hand, one finger on each closed eyelid. My eyes moved rapidly under the closed lids and did this for about 15 seconds. It tapered off like popcorn popping out in the microwave until it stopped.

Midday, I was getting dressed for my appointment. I walked away from the mirror and into the bathroom. Somewhere in my footsteps upon my return I suddenly realized this was a life and death struggle for my brother and there was nothing symbolic about him dying. He was supposed to die. And the reason was, he was trying to protect me. It was a weapon in his hand that I had seen the night before. At age five he had given me his life.

I couldn't catch my breath. I began to hyperventilate, as the first time I had gone to see Joseph Dickson with my first anxiety about the way my father died. I knew I couldn't function and would have a hard time doing anything but getting to Joseph's office.

I sat in his waiting room. Sometimes I could control the hyperventilation and sometimes it would just start up again. I waited. Joseph showed up himself and walked through the waiting room. I watched him go by. He said, "It will be just a minute, Linda." I sat there completely unable to simply breathe.

When I got in his office, I handed him the summary, which did not include what I was telling him now. I couldn't breathe. How will I ever repay him? How could I ever repay my brother? His injuries were so severe that he succeeded. My abuse ended that day he gave his life for me.

In my session that day, I saw the full picture of what I had begun to know as time progressed. The picture of my brother is what emerged. A picture not in childhood, but in young adulthood, when he had come as close to normalcy, as he would ever be able to achieve. If you look closely in those handsome images of his from high school, you can see the damage still from his injuries. The damage is still there and so is the potential for a normal life, which my parents took from him. He could not achieve it. He would succumb to the damage of his brain.

I screamed that they killed him. I folded my body in half as I sat there. I saw the bright colors of a childhood image of that terrain where my brother took his stand against my further abuse, and only those idealized images of childhood could shrink my mother's image in her bathing suit, in which she did whatever it was with her body parts and everything else that belonged to her that she pleased. And I told Joseph that I saw two doves fly away in the bright colors of childhood, free. And I am reminded we are nothing without love.

I will never forget when I first saw him. I came to interview for a job teaching Astronomy at Victor Valley College in Victorville, California, in December of 2006. He was to interview me, in fact, I was to be his replacement. He was leaving to live in Colorado closer to his elderly parents. His name was David Meyer. Whenever I was around him, I felt happy, and talked freely. In fact, I told him very early in our relationship, particularly about my mother and my abuse. One thing about David Meyer was that he was particularly religious. His family was long rooted in the Lutheran faith. I believe a little girl drew me to him in the hopes of bringing me back to God.

I pace in my bedroom in this state of stunned disbelief, stare in the mirror of my dressing area with a sick feeling returning. My journey is not over, as I had hoped and believed in August of 2005, when I had last remembered the past.

On January 17, 2006, I am forced to acknowledge there is something I had experienced, but not understood in August. Only nine days before, I had a remembered that somehow I knew my brother was going to die that day.

Over the interim time, since August, I had seen images of my mother hitting, swinging something long that were fleeting, but a regular occurrence since my final session with Joseph on August 29, 2005. I attempt to deny that this is happening and fight the necessity to call Joseph Dickson. I deny this feeling of more memories of abuse from my past trying to surface, until I can't do it anymore.

By late in the day, January 17, 2006, I write in a fax to Joseph, "I [am now forced to] suspect my mother was an equal partner with my father in the physical violence against my brother and it is possible that she administered the final blow against him when he armed himself as a five-year-old to protect me... I'm not certain that this violence of hers in conjunction with my father's was the ultimate, catastrophic act... [yet], in my heart, I believe that two-year-old little girl [I was] saved the things that were least possible for my mind to handle until last."

It is unimaginable to add to what I already know what my mother did in terms of participation in the sexual abuse of her children, the equal amounts of violence that my father displayed. It is simply not something the mind associates with a woman, a mother, and is perhaps the hardest of burdens for a mind to deal with.

I had attributed the mortal blow to my brother's head that my hand acted out during returned memories of abuse, the year before, to my father to this point. I had consciously hoped I would not have to deal with the fleeting image of my mother swinging a long, stick-like weapon.

But, by the morning of my scheduled session with Joseph, two days later, I decide whatever will be revealed in my session with him is not something I will ever be ready for as long as I shall live, this time.

Because, this time, after I called him and put the phone down, I see my mother swing the object, a strange brown and white image, and I literally jump, bring my hand to my mouth and gasp; this time, when I walk away from the phone, I hear the crack, perhaps of my brother's skull breaking.

I wake up every hour the night before my appointment on January 20, 2006.

I don't know what I mean, but I tell Ryan and Michelle, I will never be ready for this as long as I shall live, before I leave for the appointment.

With Joseph, I remember a picture of my brother at his best before the injury to his brain takes over in young adulthood, but my mind will not let that stand.

Then, I see him as he is in actuality, rising like a stone monolith in the grip of the pills he takes on a weekly basis, to fight his mental illness and keep him from becoming catatonic. This is who he is; this is what his life is like in the institution where he lives. I collapse weeping in my chair.

But, there is only silence inside of me for what my parents did to their children. I tell Joseph that I have trouble remembering the extent of my parents' atrocities, as if my mind is still disassociating me from them. He asks me if I have silent rage. I tell him, at best, I can only envision a transparent wall that I am beating against, and my mother, a Narcissist with one thousand percent of her considerable efforts in life dedicated to deflecting any blame or suggestion of wrongdoing is safely on the other side.

I disintegrate in tears and beg, "Help me! Help me!"

Joseph asks how he can help me.

"Help to know who I am. I am that little girl in my parent's bed, or do I really know it yet?"

Joseph suggests we can begin again next time by asking who I am.

I don't realize what is happening.

I have seen some of the things that she has. It does not even register now that I have already heard something she actually heard, for the first time: the crack of the weapon. It does not register with me yet, that I have heard her voice.

It was her in that session asking for help.

———————

When I get home, I turn on the TV and hear the folk singer Judy Collins' song *Albatross*.

I walk toward the television and listen to the song featured in the extensive promo for an old movie, *The Subject was Roses*, which marked a famed actress's return to the screen, Patricia Neal.

Suddenly, standing before the large screen TV, listening to this song, I remembered being the young woman that I was when I first heard, learned, and loved that song. And then for the first time, ever, I see her there with me thirty years in the past. The little girl was standing there beside me when I was twenty years old.

Suddenly, I realize that the two-year-old child had existed back then, in parallel with me, even when I could not sense her then. She had been there. In a parallel universe.

Chapter II

In The Presence of God
Given a Choice

My experience at the computer lab at USC in which the computer operator had scoffed at my chances of getting a job at JPL was not unique. I had a similar experience when one of the dearest teachers I ever had looked at our statewide test results in the sixth grade at McKinley Elementary in Pasadena some years after my family had come to the United States. My family was still living in the run-down duplex. Upstairs was a lady whose husband Henry was always getting drunk and winding up in jail. When she had her baby boy, John Henry, she ultimately left Henry and took her baby to her mother's place in Texas. Henry could never stay out of jail.

My mother had taken work as a saleslady, since one income in Pasadena could not pay all the bills. My father began work at his shoe sales profession in what was to be a temporary structure for the Bullocks Department Store in downtown Pasadena. That structure still stands today, forty years later.

Mr. Smith, my sixth grade teacher, told my class after seeing my math test results, "Linda didn't do too well, but she skipped a grade and will always be a little behind." I knew then too that he was wrong and if he believed that, I knew more than him. I didn't test well in math at that stage in my life; I knew that was the reason. I loved this teacher.

Mr. Smith got an idea for our class one day to create a game show presentation put on by the students for their parents. He constructed a framework out of wood that would sit on a table, and he ran sets of wires connected to switches and light bulbs around the framework. Each student was to memorize important quotations, historical references, and excerpts from literature, and then we would compete in a game show format. If you recognized the quotation that Mr. Smith began to read, then you flipped the switch in front of you at the table and your light bulb would go on, and whoever was first would have to recite what they had memorized correctly.

I memorized several of the possible quotations that might be used. However, during rehearsal and practice for the evening event, listening to the other students recite what they knew, I memorized all the rest of the quotations I hadn't already. When the evening of the game show came, one child's light went on first the entire evening long. It was mine. No one including Mr. Smith seemed to hold it against me. People were just laughing and marveling, maybe like the feeling people had watching winning contestant Ken Jennings long run on the TV show Jeopardy, long after this event at my elementary school.

Mr. Smith seemed to love not only me, but Gary too. He was my brother's teacher two years before, and took a great interest in our family. He owned some new apartment buildings, some just under construction, and when my brother and I were still at McKinley Elementary at the same time, would drive us around in his car as he ate cookies and called them his lunch or dinner, since half of his stomach had been removed from ulcers. He offered our family a chance to move into a new building that he owned. My father refused, and my brother and I cried from disappointment.

Miss Drake had just married and she had a new name. She was the first teacher I had at McKinley Elementary in a third/fourth grade combination class. She asked me how much of my times tables I knew and I told her I knew them all. My brother had taught them to me when he had come home from school in Canada. She told me I was to be sent directly to the fourth grade, but could remain in her combination class. The school district had done testing on me and determined that I was gifted. The school was very interested in the minds of its young people, and being located right next to the Board of Education made us a testbed for opportunity. For the first time in my life, I had adults as friends. These teachers were my friends, and cared about my mind and about me. I was thriving.

Word reached the school principal and she adamantly refused to skip me to fourth grade. I had started school in Canada at the age of four and I was exceptionally small for my age as it was. The principal said I looked so young that I would be out of place for the rest of my academic life and wouldn't even resemble the same age group as my peers. Miss Drake aptly pointed out to her that my best friend was Becky Wiseman, the tallest girl in the school. Hearing that, the Principal changed her mind and dropped any objection to my being placed ahead.

Becky and I were inseparable. My best friend, Becky, who once wrote in a report of hers that I read that stars twinkled because they moved back and forth in place (Becky was actually not very intellectual, but an amazingly beautiful girl), was responsible for my future just by being my friend. I was skipped to the fourth grade and joined Becky there. I had literally begun to accelerate through school.

––––––––––

Summers were filled with dreamy days of the visions young girls have of the future. Becky and I tried everything fun together, from getting our pictures taken in a photo booth that could only seat one person on a stool, but we managed to fit ourselves into the view to looking into acting school so that we could become famous actresses. I certainly didn't want to become a famous actress and never knew what Becky really wanted out her young life. Mainly, we wanted fun.

At an acting school run by the formerly well-known actor Jock Mahoney, Becky's mother agreed to pay large sums of money for her instruction. It was out of the question for me to join her in this endeavor, but my mother and I later learned that Jock Mahoney had taken the liberty of kissing Becky, who was very mature for her age, on the lips, often. Jock and his female business companion also sold Becky's mother large quantities of silverware for Becky's future trousseau.

When my mother heard such stories she would comment about things she had seen take place as a child. Apparently, she had seen a priest molest a girlfriend of hers. There was a sect of people in her small, Saskatchewan town who practiced incest. My mother would recount this with the adventuresome intonation of a whale watcher who had just spotted whales. She would always say she saw everyone sleeping with everyone, which when pressed she would divulge fathers were sleeping with their daughters, and ultimately went so far to say one day that children were born as a result.

There was something about the way in which my mother conveyed this information, which would ultimately result in her saying something to the effect of that nobody seemed to mind. As the years went by, and my mother would re-share these visions of her childhood, it always struck me that she never mentioned the psychological damage it does to young people who are molested. Her conveyance was victimless. After years of recounting these particular stories, it was what she never said that became far more obvious than the story itself.

I had other friends growing up as a young girl in Pasadena, too, many of them. My years growing up in Pasadena included urban adventures with an "Adventurer's Club," named by a few of us, who explored apartment buildings as children in the country would explore fields. All my friends were my brother's friends too. I believe Gary may have had only one friend of his own making through school.

At some point when Gary and I were growing up, my parents became friends with a couple they would know for years and spend their Saturday nights with. My mother met her friend Roberta in a neighboring retail store to where my mother worked where Roberta was managing a lingerie department. The friendship allowed Gary and I to spend time with their son Bobby, a shy boy who was our age. We held card games, Monopoly games, Scrabble and Twister games that would go on long into the night when our parents were together. This was a very wonderful time for us during junior high school years.

My friendship with Marcia Corbett, a young girl whose family ate only Campbell's Soup for dinner every night, and who attended McKinley Elementary for a time, marked the time my love of science, exploration, and particularly astronomy was moving into the mainstream of my life. During sleepovers, when I would spend the night at Marcia's house, we would set up a tent that was just a sheet on top of her bed and with flashlights would explore the pitch-dark unknown world just outside our enclosure, which included a black and white TV set to the latest science fiction being featured, such as *Invaders from Mars*.

I loved science fiction, then, now, always, everything from these very old movies to the *Lost in Space* TV series to current science fictions as they are released onto the big screen. It was the only tie I had to the world that interested me most. There were no role models readily available for a young girl who loved science. My parents once bought a book for my brother's birthday for him called *The Boy Scientist*. I knew I wanted to grow up to be the boy scientist in that book. There was no other way I could reach out to this world of science, no one else I could talk to about it, except my brother, and except through the world of science fiction movies. The female protagonists in these movies always had a romantic role, but that didn't deter my serious expectations of myself in their adventures in exploring some unknown world in space or on Earth when an alien would invade. I wanted to be just like them and the movies told me I could be. Nowhere else could or would anyone enforce my dreams. And I was quiet and naturally shy. My worlds came out in my imagination and it was profound.

Sometimes the real world would intervene. If Jet Propulsion Laboratory had a planetary mission that was successful, coverage of rooms filled with men in white shirts and black ties, the engineers who had made the missions happen, would make the evening news. I saw this coverage on TV on a couple of occasions growing up. I thought, one day I will be one of those men.

I watched the astronauts of Apollo 11 land on the moon in the summer of 1969 and cried from joy along with Walter Cronkite, who reported it, and prayed with the rest of the world for the safe return of the astronauts of the crippled Apollo 13 spacecraft in the spring of 1970.

———

David Curkendall hired me for the temporary summer position at JPL in 1973, based on my interview. On July 9, 1973, I went to work for Tom Duxbury, who was one of fifteen engineers in David's

Outer Planet Navigation Development Group. It was a perfect fit. Tom was a handsome and brilliant man, with an ironic sense of humor and an IQ for the work that he specialized in that was humbling. I was tasked for the next two months to familiarize myself with that Group and the large mainframe computer at JPL, which was a UNIVAC 1108. I had the right approach to this work. I was exact, precise, and perfectly suited to it.

The work involved predictions for earth-based astronomical observations of the moons of Jupiter to improve our knowledge of their positions and orbits. The Outer Planet Navigation Development Group was not working on the site of the Laboratory proper, but in a building the Laboratory leased along Angeles Crest Highway in La Canada, called the Crest Building. It made David Curkendall's Group seem very special indeed. Parking problems were nonexistent instead of abounding, as they were in a facility as large as JPL, which employed thousands of people, on Oak Grove Drive in Pasadena. Our parking was located simply at the rear of the Crest Building.

When Tom Duxbury and I in later years worked on the Viking Flight Team, and became co-Guest Investigators on the Viking Extended Mission to Mars, once again, we achieved a very helpful status as guests at the very place that employed us, JPL. We were permitted to park in the visitor parking lot at JPL, because our usual place of business was off the Laboratory at the Crest Building. Visitor Parking was just a short walk from Building 264 on Lab, where we had a lovely, open office space up against large windows and positioned right next to the Viking Science Orbiter Imaging Team, which made many discoveries on the Viking mission to Mars in 1976. In that case, it was just Tom and I who reaped the benefits of this special status.

Charles Acton was an engineer in the Interplanetary Orbit Determination Group in Section 391, one of six other groups in the Section. He and Tom were best of buddies, and it was apparent. Chuck would come into Tom's office at the Crest Building several times a day to shoot the breeze about technical issues or any manner of subjects, and had a propensity to sit on top of upright trashcans that were found in every office, when he did. This put Chuck oddly considerably lower to the floor than if he were sitting on any of the available chairs. There were plenty of those, but Chuck preferred to sit on trashcans.

Chuck would sometimes touch on a recurrent theme that I noticed he mentioned. He wondered what it would be like to take a summer off and in essence play, as we had all done in childhood, but to do it as an adult. Chuck had very blond hair that was exceptionally straight and as Tom, was extremely handsome. In retrospect, Chuck could have reminded any woman of Robert Redford as Tom could easily have reminded them of Paul Newman. They were very much as I think of them now, in resemblance of Butch Cassidy and the Sundance Kid. I had no way of knowing how greatly Chuck's curiosity about taking summers off would ultimately affect my future at JPL.

The separation between church and state wasn't as definite as it is in today's world. The school at McKinley Elementary, a fully public school, had a program of religious education during school hours. For whatever reason, my mother, who considered herself Jewish, told the school that I could participate in the Baptist religious program as long as the religion was, in her words, mild.

One day a week, an ancient and sweet old lady would drive her small Volkswagen car to the school, pick me and a couple of other children up and we'd sputter along in the Volkswagen until we reached the courtyard of a nearby church. There I heard religious stories that are taught in Bible school to young children. The stories did not have that much meaning to me, but the impression that old lady left on me in her caricature car and the outdoor beauty of that courtyard was indelible.

At a later time in my life, in High School, when I was sad and depressed and needing guidance, I adopted a stage in my spiritual development that was purely Christian, but that stage transitioned to more philosophical stance and completely away from organized religion. I could never have known what was coming in my life that would lead me back to a place I had already been.

When questioned about her Jewish beliefs, my mother would divulge that her grandfather had been a rabbi, and that he would spend long periods of time talking to her about Christ. My mother would then go into an extolment of Jesus Christ that even as a child sounded more to me like Christian precept than anything else. My mother was clearly confused about her own definitions of religion that concerned herself, or so I was fortunate enough to believe for the vast, overwhelming majority of my life. What I came to know and understand later was not a revelation I would wish on any human being on Earth.

Ultimately, in old age, my mother's best friends were Christians and she would attend church regularly as I did semi-regularly leading up to my adoption of Christian principles that was not lasting, then, but very real for me at the time. When my mother found out that I had accepted this doctrine in early High School, she became irrational and literally went berserk. She began to scream that I was Jewish and could not accept Christ or attend church as she later did in life.

The impact was so profound on me that I developed a retinal hemorrhage in my left eye, which was discovered on a routine eye check I had at Sears department store for glasses, by an optometrist. He told my father it was very serious and had it been located in a different place, I could have lost my vision. He said it was probably due to emotional trauma and questioned what had been taking place in my life. My father said nothing, told me to follow him and we left the appointment and never spoke of it again.

My father didn't speak much at any time when I was growing up. To him, I attributed qualities of high ethical standards, complete lack of prejudice, honesty and integrity. At the time that I attributed those qualities to him, I believe they were indeed his. But, my father was one of only a few human beings I have ever known who would hold their head in their hands and rub their head as though they were suffering some admonition or pain at the very moment you witnessed this. He did it often and consistently, as if he had some overwhelming burden to atone for.

In January of 2006, I am fully in the grip of the unknown. Rather than discrete episodes of returning memories that had happened over the last two years, I am now both lost and submerged in the past. I do not know nor cannot even guess what my mind is trying to reveal to me. But, I keep returning to the case of premeditation on the part of my parents in my brother's destruction. I am on the brink of knowing fear in progression that will grow exponentially; and rapidly accelerate. I am experiencing a type of fear lost in time because my memories are of fear. I am ultimately terrified looking back, and I look back at terror. It is beginning to compound in me.

On January 20, 2006, after my session with Joseph Dickson, I write a letter to my son Ryan, which I do not intend for him to see anytime soon. I write, "There has always been a disconnect between the images that I have seen about Gary's and my abuse indoors in bedrooms, on vacation and at home, when we were so little, and the out-of-doors scene where he has fallen, had the seizure with his eyes filled with blood and his skull cracked as he tried to fight back for him and for me. From what I believe…my parents probably made the decision to kill him. It was a decision I was aware of…"

The most comfort I am to receive in the coming days is when I tell Ryan, IF there is evidence of premeditation in Gary's attack, I will try to have charges brought against my mother. It is at this time, I am suddenly struck by what the little girl's life was really like. Her need to be safe was never met. She had no refuge in which to live, no home that provided an enclosure of security. Her home trapped and enclosed her in desperate pain. I know this for an instant, with riveting, stunning clarity.

In a fax to Joseph that I do not send, I write, "Joseph, I think we need to treat the two-year-old. We need to help her get the help she didn't get back then. She very much still exists, a complete entity. She is frozen in time and her suffering will not stop until she gets help… Maybe I can't get well until she gets some help…Is it possible that we can try to help her?… The adult weeps often…, but the child still does not get help…Can we put ourselves in her place, what she knew and what she saw? Can we please, please help her?… She is crying out for help…[and] has gone to great lengths to let me know she [still] exists… acting out the sorrows with her hands and any means she could… I will try to help her over the coming week in any way that I can think of." I am good with children. I am going to help her. I am going to reach out to her, and take her in my arms.

Since I had skipped a grade at McKinley Elementary in Miss Drake's class, from third to fourth, Gary was only a year ahead of me in school now. I knew my brother was highly intelligent, had a powerful memory, and a passion for knowledge and learning, in these regards we were alike, but I heard at all times of his difficulties.

His sixth grade teacher at McKinley, Mr. Williams could not get Gary to clean out his desk in class. The problem became so acute that Mr. Williams was sent into retirement a complete nervous wreck made so by the situation.

My mother always told me that Gary was never right, never completely in good shape as a child, from the moment of his birth. The doctors had used forceps to deliver him, which misshaped his head and had caused fluid to develop there. Over time it normalized. My mother would repeatedly tell the story of how my Dad's brother Lou noticed that Gary was not a handsome baby and how he had pushed his hand into Gary's face as a baby, declaring him ugly. She told me that my father had sprung to Gary's defense and sent Lou packing after such horrible behavior.

Much later in life, my mother would change that story to admissions that my father wondered why, when he and his wife were so comely in appearance, they could have a baby who was not. In pictures of my brother as a baby, I have noticed he was a fine looking child.

There were eight siblings in my father's family, although I had believed at one point there were nine. Two of the sisters lived an extremely secluded life and when one passed away, the other did too. It was suggested or hinted at by my mother that perhaps a suicide had been involved.

My father had a twin who had died at birth, or so my mother told me. I learned decades later, however, when my mother came into possession of this sister's will and I read the date of her birth, my father's twin Sarah had not died at birth and had lived into old age, although no one in the family spoke of her. That accounted for the ninth person I believed to be in the family. Her identify had been conveyed to me at some point by my mother, but not as my father's twin. It was hinted at, as well, but much more strongly, that my father's parents committed suicide. I knew this even as a young school-aged child in Pasadena, California. There were only one or two occasions when my father ever spoke about his family in all the years of his life that I knew him, and he lived to the age of 84. I believed my father had emerged somehow from his background as the one sterling person who had not been scathed by it.

My mother made it clear to me as well that Gary was an accident, that she and my father had not wanted a baby then. At some point in my early adulthood, she indicated that my father had insisted she have an abortion. The procedure administered illegally by a pharmacist in Vancouver in the form of a pill, made her violently ill and failed to abort him. It wasn't until my father became terminally ill that my mother happened to mention to me that I had been an accident too. In retrospect, it seemed like a disclaimer.

I wondered when I was growing up what was wrong with Gary since birth. I questioned my mother often about this. She finally put it into context one day. She said, when Gary was very young, he had looked up at the enclosed cases in a restaurant that were mirrored, which showcased desserts that could be ordered, pointed, and said he saw a cat.

I thought about this for a long time after she told me. Apparently he needed glasses. Was my brother not right since birth because he was nearsighted? I thought about this in the context of his difficult delivery with forceps and believed there must be more to it. Without more, it hardly made any sense.

I walked downstairs to the 9300 computer Remote Site, which was on the main floor of Jet Propulsion Laboratory's Angeles Crest Building. In the summer of 1973, our offices were upstairs. If I had to make a change to a computer program, I had to do this by punching cards, and replacing or adding lines of codes on punch cards. I had certainly done this before I had arrived at JPL, but remember the very first time I typed and replaced cards in the large predict program that generated geometry of observations. I handed the large tray worth of cards to an operator to load them and see what the changes to the code had done. That is the only time I had any conscious recollection of that process. From then on, making changes to those programs, and ultimately writing new ones of my own I had wholly researched and developed, and running data through them was as much a part of me as breathing.

There were characters among us. Jay Lieske was involved in the improvement of the orbits of the Galilean Satellites of Jupiter and even his warmest goodbye at the end of a week as he was leaving his office, sounded like all the rest he had ever said. It was curt and to the point and never hinted that he might be having any different kind of a day than he had always had.

Engineers often seemed impenetrable to reach through to their personal demeanors, but at this new stage of exposure to these established engineers, I still had hope they were knowable. Everything was engineered, it sometimes seemed to me at the time, including them.

Jay drove a fabulous motorcycle to the Crest Building everyday that had a sidecar, which immediately took one to thoughts of Germany during WWII or *The Great Escape* when you saw it. That seemed to be the manifestation of his individual expression. Many others, nice and respectable hardworking and talented family men did not own such a motorcycle to distinguish themselves. They were quiet, reserved people, whom you immediately felt at ease around.

Then, there was Pencil Man, whose name I never learned. He was known to everyone that I knew as Pencil Man, and only seemed to converse with another engineer, whom like himself didn't have a known name to me either. Each wore an identifying pencil protector over his shirt pocket brimming with pencils too. Every day, rain or shine, the pencils of these two engineers were worn and ready for action. These men would stand out in a crowd. They did not look like people you see everywhere. They were on a fringe.

While working in Building 264 on Lab five years later, someone once recounted to me through an article that was circulating around from an external publication outside of JPL, that only a few percent of the general population in the United States was working in technical fields. I wasn't sure I could trust the written source, but I have profoundly good instincts on what a good number percentage might be on any such subject, once the initial gist of the information is conveyed to me. I realized that percentage probably wasn't too far off, but I was shocked at how low the figure was. I had never considered this world of seeking scientific knowledge through investigation to be on a fringe. But, that is exactly where this world was.

On the table in our sixth grade class at McKinley, were two boxes that came especially for our school and our class from the Board of Education. They contained special, advanced and experimental reading and mathematics programs for us. What it meant to me to have those boxes in our classroom cannot be described. I wanted to dive into them at all times, not just when we were told to walk over to them and lift a section out for our teacher, Mr. Smith.

Once, Mr. Smith sent me into adjacent hallways and past the location where student were allowed, to get him soda in a vending machine. These hallways were a restricted area and under the auspices of the Board. I bungled the attempt to get Mr. Smith his soda and managed to empty even the additional amounts of change he had given me for extra measure into the machine without reaping even one soda.

Yet, walking through these halls in an area that was otherwise not open to young people, tapped a great pleasure in me I would enjoy when working seven years for The Planetary Society in Pasadena, California, in a much later stage of life. I loved interfacing with celebrities and going places behind the scenes, not because it imbued me with some special power or prestige to do so. That power and prestige were within me already by the time I came to work at The Planetary Society, the largest space interest group in the world. I had all the confidence in the world, because in the matters of space and moving forward through the field, there were few things I hadn't already accomplished by then.

The love of the United States of America came to my brother and me from my parents, undoubtedly, but was within us. McKinley Elementary, the teachers and the friends that we had found there had brought light into a world that was for us in Vancouver, primarily dark. On November 22, 1963, as I sat in Mr. Smith's class and watched television for a special broadcast that was called *Escuchen y Repitan, Listen and Repeat*, designed to introduce us to the Spanish language, the show was interrupted by the news that President John F. Kennedy had been shot. Mr. Smith turned off the television. My brother and I cried over the assassination of John Kennedy, as we would have a family member.

We were already living the American Dream and the President of the United States embodied that for us. Our tears were followed by more for the assassinations of Martin Luther King Jr. and Bobby Kennedy that happened in the coming years.

One of the highlights of my parents' lives, I'm sure, is when they became citizens of the United States. They took classes in American History and Government to obtain their citizenship. In my heart, as a child, I honestly couldn't picture my parents being able to pass a test like their naturalization required. My fifth grade classroom cheered when my father had finally passed his California Driver's License test and could buy a car for the first time in his life, although he had driven in the army. He had made multiple attempts at passing.

My mother told me that during the naturalization test, some of the proctors had helped them. If that was so, it was a measure of how badly my parents wanted this and how hard they tried. On December 16, 1966, my parents became naturalized citizens of the United States.

Although they were told they could pick up certificates for my brother and me of our own, if they did so immediately, they never did and it was not clear if that offer was as simple as it appeared. Gary and I technically became citizens on the day my parents did as well. More than thirty-five years later, it came to the attention of the agency that issues U.S. passports that my mother had written over her birth date on her certificate to alter her age, when I tried to get a passport for a business trip to Vienna, Austria. I was using my mother's naturalization certificate to establish my own proof of U.S. citizenship. My mother's altering of a government document angered the passport officer and this officer confiscated my mother's naturalization certificate. My mother was forced to reapply for her certificate.

After that difficult process, which I oversaw for her, I felt it was best to obtain my own citizenship papers, instead of relying on hers and my father's for my proof of citizenship. Thirty-seven years after I became a United States citizen, I applied for and received my certificate of naturalization.

McKinley Junior High School was right across the street from McKinley Elementary. Junior high represented an even better time for my brother despite an episode where a student held a pencil straight up in my brother's desk seat. When he went to sit down, he was badly injured. The red blood on his clothing evokes vivid images with me even now. People were often cruel to Gary and he was picked on and assigned cruel nicknames in school. Fortunately, these things seemed to lessen over time, as Gary got older.

The Junior High offered a treasure trove of riches not only in mathematics for me, but in the arts. One teacher, Mr. Coday, was so incredibly gifted, it was as if a New York Broadway producer had sat idly around one day and decided he would give up his Tony Award winning productions and go teach at a Junior High somewhere instead. McKinley Junior High School got that teacher. Mr. Coday was Gary's art teacher and brought out the best in Gary's talent. My only interface with him was in a ballet production for a usual type of Christmas production, in which he asked me to dance as Thumbelina. I was the perfect choice and it worked.

But, there was nothing usual about the production that Mr. Coday put on once a year, called *Broadway in Review*. He put junior high school girls into gowns that made them look like gifted adults who were as talented in voice as they were beautiful. The young men in the production hardly seemed that, and you would forget you were looking at anything that had to do with a Junior High. The production elements were astonishingly professional. The music filled my brother's and my lives from one year to the next, in a couple of hours. We also enjoyed concerts put on there, and I developed a love of my favorite composers, first Mahler and then eventually Holtz, from attending them.

My strategy was to let the education that was being offered to me in Pasadena fill my life and meet my goals. I wasn't a science groupie. My goal became to meet each challenge that came to me, whether it was in a science class, a math class, or an English class, and have it take me that much closer to what I needed to know. As a consequence, I got a lot of high grades in Junior High.

This philosophy allowed me to also experience diversions. Song girl competitions were coming up, for the girls who would perform on the sidelines at the football games. This was a popularity contest, and although I aspired to hang around the popular kids, I certainly wasn't one of them. I was known as the little girl who was very smart. It didn't bother me a bit, but at this age, my physical development was far removed from my classmates. Yet, I could dance.

At the gymnasium, before the judges and before the students who showed up for the illustrious competition in the balcony bleachers, I danced. After years and years of ballet that I had continued on with in the United States, even sharing instructors with Darlene Gillespie, the former Disney Mouseketeer, who would eventually succumb to a life of crime, no one could dance better than I could.

A hush fell over the entire McKinley gymnasium when the competition ended. In a popularity contest, the judges weren't going to be able to exclude me on the basis of popularity, and everyone in that gymnasium who saw me dance knew it. I was a scale above anyone who had performed. It was just that simple. I was named a song girl that day and no one in the history of school at anytime anywhere has probably been selected on that basis. I was basically a very cute little girl who was a nerd; and now, along with the most popular girls in the school, also a song girl.

This infuriated my adult cousin, Angela, who saw me with the other song girls in the Rose Bowl about to perform before a football game. She chastised my mother as to why she had allowed me to skip that grade in elementary school, and to enter into a world where, by what she was seeing, I clearly did not belong. Then, Angela saw me dance the first time with the other girls. She said nothing after that. She could see it was okay. But, she wasn't entirely wrong. I will never forget my embarrassment at the fitting for our song girl uniforms. All the other girls were wearing bras and fortunately left the room, knowing I either didn't need one or hadn't been given one by my mother yet, when it came time for my fitting. My uniform looked like a doll's dress, compared to the other girl's. I would eventually tell my mother that she was going to buy me a bra, when my development definitely needed it. In this same way, I told her that she was going to give me a party when I turned thirteen the same as I had seen others of my friends get. I insisted, and my parents followed through. On April 14, 1967, for my ninth grade Social Science report, I wrote a report for which I received an A grade, which projected my future, entitled "My Job in the World, Astronomer."

I finished off two remarkable months in the summer of 1973 at JPL, and was asked to continue on by Tom Duxbury and David Curkendall as an academic-part-time employee during my senior year at USC, but I had already agreed to a Teaching Assistant position for the Department of Astronomy at USC. Over the summer I had gotten married to a young engineering student David Morabito who I had met at USC in the preceding year. David and I, who briefly stayed in an apartment rented in the same building as my parents' apartment, where I had so few recollections of being during

High School, moved into the Married Students Housing complex at USC, and began our senior year at USC.

There is a Board meeting of the condominium association, for which I am treasurer on the morning of January 21, 2006. As I sit through the meeting with the other Board members, I know what I am going to do when I get home. I have been picturing myself reaching out to this little girl repeatedly now. Reaching out to her fifty years in the past, my hand extended. I picture myself down on one knee. If I can get her hand, if I can get her in my arms, perhaps I can give her the help she did not receive so long ago.

The meeting is over. I go to the place in my room, well behind my computer chair. I try to get down on one knee, take her in my arms, at various levels of my kneeling to the ground, but am not successful. I don't sense her at all and do not succeed.

But, then, I imagine wanting to take her hand. I walk forward and reach out with mine. Along my slightly bent hand, I am reaching back through the decades. I do not know what I expect to have happen. I reach to find what's there.

In screams loud enough to knock me back into my chair, my mouth is screaming silently, three horrendous times, stretched open as hard as any human being's mouth could be. I am knocked back flat into the chair. I am stunned, beyond belief. I see no images, but this scream is as loud as when I saw my brother's injuries last August in that returned memory. I screamed once then with the most horrific vision of my waking life. I have done this three times now in a row.

The level of terror concealed inside of me in unimaginable to me now. That there could be something at this level locked inside my body. I have lived an entire lifetime with it there. It seems inconceivable and impossible it remained there and does so now, undetected. It cannot be.

I walk around for a while upstairs; go downstairs for a while as well, trying to put all of this in some perspective. I decide I will write about what has happened to Joseph Dickson, and I begin to. As I reread what I have written, and sit at my computer desk, she screams again an hour later. She cries, "Help me!" in a contorted voice that would take voice processing equipment to decipher her words. I know the words, because my mouth is trying to form them with my face stretched upward, in as high a pitched wail as I have ever cried.

Now, I am concerned. It is not even 2:30 PM on Saturday, and twice now, I have already experienced a succession of terror from her at the level of the most disturbing terror she had revealed to me in my remembering my brother's injuries that had lasted only seconds. I cannot imagine what will happen next.

I call for some reassurance from Joseph Dickson, knowing he will not get the message on a Saturday, which I do not denote as urgent. I suggest to him it would be best if he contacted me Monday afternoon, after a doctor's appointment for my foot, to see how I was doing. I put the phone back down and decide to leave the bedroom, water plants on the patios downstairs and try to put this out of my mind. I reach for the doorknob to leave the room. When I reach toward it, I begin to cry, not just crying, but wailing.

I am wailing so hard that my body moves backwards away from the door. I am so stricken I am moving backwards and by the time I reach my dressing area, I am on the floor, literally, with my face headed toward the ground. The tears are so strong that I imagine that I will injure my eyes with the contact lenses inside of them being compressed against my lids. My mouth is stretched sideways as I wail.

But when I am flat against the floor, it has stopped, completely. I have no emotion at all, not anything in the aftermath of having cried so hard.

The thought of demonic possession through the ages occurs to me; how would that be interpreted if somebody had seen me? How am I interpreting it? I have no emotion. It's like I watched someone else cry.

I stand up and sort of brush myself off.

I am in too much shock to know the significance of what has happened.

Her tears, her voice, her senses are opening up to me.

I'm terrified this is more than I can endure. I leave an urgent message for Joseph.

I move around the house in fear desperately waiting for Joseph's call.

I am repeating to myself, She is coming to the surface, and hell on Earth is coming with her.

I know now, I cannot help her. I realize the foolishness of believing that I could change the past in that way. There is a long time of terror, in which Joseph does not get the message from me. The way I placed the call was transferred to his cell phone and it was in another room of his home, he explains later. He had been watching a movie with his family, and hadn't seen the message on his phone.

I walk my home in terror; the only thing I can do is wait for her arrival. I am most afraid that this is more than I can handle. I remind myself of an impression I have from Joseph that this process must take its course and that perhaps that I am safe. The only thing he has ever warned me about is not trying to duplicate the way he conducts sessions in the office on my own, and that is not what is happening here. But, nothing that I had ever experienced was anything like this to date. It was far too extreme to deal with on my own. Unlike any other time, any other time, I am shaking physically. Trembling from the cold. It feels very cold. Hell is coming with her.

I go back upstairs. I make no breakthroughs to relieve the agony of this state I am in. I want to get warm. I get into bed sitting up; I take off a ring of my right hand, because it is uncomfortable and place it in my left hand. My left hand falls to the side of me, as it first had months and months before, when I came to understand I was sexually abused. The falling off of my hand to the left of me had come to mean, in my understanding, the way in which I would go into a fetal position, after the sexual abuse.

This puts me on more familiar ground. It begins to feel more like a memory is trying to return, the way it had felt on previous days when I had seen my brother's seizure for the first time in returned memory, and then the true extent of his injuries. Those two memories actually returned a year apart; they had happened one second apart fifty years before I remembered them, and in reverse order. Instead of dying, my brother's seizure had probably saved his life. After that, as he lay destroyed on the ground, he had not been hit again.

I go downstairs. I watch a movie to get distracted. The returned memory is rising within me.

Robert, whom I consider my grandson, is home now, with his parents, Ryan and Michelle. He is sitting beside me; he decides he loves the movie I am watching on TV, and as I sit there waiting until the end of the movie, the memory moves from the area central to my breast, up higher into my chest. When the movie finally ends, I tell my kids I must go upstairs.

I try reaching toward her upstairs, but nothing happens, and I get into a semi-fetal position on the ground for a while. I get up and wait and sit at my computer chair.

I feel the memory rise up when I do, move into my throat and from there it's simply gone. It vanished. It should have been released at this moment, but I do not see anything. I'm cold again. I get into bed, sitting up, my lower body covered by the covers. I feel the need to reach out to her again, with one hand. I reach out high ahead of me and slightly to the side, as if high and away from the bed, and then I suddenly realize, she can't take my hand.

Is that why I can't reach her?

Is it that her hands are clenched in fists?

No, it's because her hands are busy.

And then an image forms there surrounded by darkness. I see an image beyond anything I have ever seen before.

Her arms and hands are flailing in bed, about the area of her chest, like a rag doll being beaten as she is being raped. Her size is so small that she cannot possibly resist the violence that tosses her arms like a fabric doll's with no possible resistance in the fabric of the arms against the onslaught. She is like a rag doll with a rag doll's arms, at the end of a violently shaking stick.

Tears stream down my face.

I taste the salt in my mouth.

As she did, I imagine, many times.

There is a sound that lingers long after the image. I hear two beats of my own heart sitting there in bed, two higher pitched thumps, followed by a lower "finishing" beat, an exhale, but it does not vary in frequency by the violence I have seen, or the violence itself. It is my perception of a noise she was hearing under those circumstances; I am mimicking it with my concentration on my heartbeat and my own breathing. I am hearing once again what she did.

I imagine it is a house sound; the sound of a clock or a furnace she heard, at times when she was being raped.

Fifty years does not seem so long ago anymore as I am going back through time.

There is less distance between her and me than ever before.

———

Joseph calls six hours after I left him a message I had tried to mark as urgent, when he notices the message. I begin to shiver when I tell him what has already taken place. By the next day, I realize it is because she is cold. She is often cold. Joseph is most concerned if I am sleeping at night. I tell him that I am.

He asks me, "Who was raping you? Was it your father?"

I tell him in this memory, I could not tell.

I have removed the remaining pictures of my parents off the walls of my home before the end of the evening. The transparent wall I had once described to Joseph as protecting my mother from blame or responsibility is gone. My blows against it fell my mother in my mind now.

I weep, God help this child.

I feel shell-shocked. I wonder, Where was God?

I wonder, Is God with me now?

For some reason, I think so, but I cannot imagine why.

———

On January 25, 2006, I am suffering, and know there are more memories trying to surface. I summarize these feelings and fears in a fax to Joseph. I review the senses of the little girl's that are being shared with me now. I have heard the crack of the weapon, the sounds that I mimicked with two thumps of my heart and the short exhale, those three sounds in repetition, when she was being raped, experienced her crying when I wasn't, screaming out of more terror than I could ever envision in any lifetime I am harboring within my body now, and then screaming for help. And, my shaking from cold, I write, is not me, it's her. She's cold.

And then I continue, "Of course, I wonder why I see her during these scenes in bed and why I am not her; in a complete guess I'd say that it would be too painful to be her. I need to give her permission to tell me more. My suffering isn't going to stop until that terror is to the surface. I wonder if she and I will ever cry at the same time."

I finish my fax and explore the issue of premeditation with Joseph within it. I tell him I have no proof or actual memories of it, but that I seem to know about it.

I put for the first time in writing on January 25, 2006, "I am certain of some things, and one is that my brother was attacked because he was trying to protect me. It is possible, Joseph, that he was old enough to threaten to tell about the sexual abuse."

The transparent wall between my anger against my parents for their actions against my brother and against me is gone. I have no trouble expressing the actual anger that their actions warrant. I finish the fax mentioning to Joseph that I am nearly as damaged as my brother given the level of what I must have endured.

The hardest thing I have ever had to accept is that my parents did this act to my brother to stop him from exposing the sexual abuse of his little sister, decided to kill him, and had probably threatened to do so when he decided he would tell. My mind has suffered nothing more difficult, and I have fought to deny it with every ounce of my strength. The returned memories of sexual abuse when they first occurred, were like a sickness of my heart that I cannot ever put into words, and I would wish this on no one on Earth, but my need to deny that my parents planned to end my brother's life because he was disturbing their sexual perversion, and followed through, is beyond what my mind was willing to accept. This need develops in this one afternoon.

Each time I try to deny it, in any form, my mind began a chant, "Why are you trying to deny this?" until I put my denial aside. I am far from lacking sanity. As a scientist, astronomer, and engineer, simply as a human being, it makes no sense to deny this again, and learn that I cannot deny it for as long as I shall live again.

I write to Joseph in an addendum I add to the fax of January 25, 2006. "Denying this is like denying that I am that little girl! I cannot do it. It's wrong. It's starting to come out. I'll see it in my next session with you. Maybe sooner."

By the time I reach Joseph's office on January 27, 2006, it is not clear to me that I will survive. I need help desperately, but have held on out of too much fear of the memories unfolding at home. I do not believe I can withstand what will happen at home when I am alone anymore. Joseph questions me quickly about my state of mind, because the hour can go so quickly and the healing processing of memories is accomplished gently over a session, and there is only one hour.

I hand the words of the song *Albatross* to Joseph that I have printed out from the computer, because the song will not leave my mind, and he recites them. He wants to know the significance of the song in connection with my inability to deny the premeditation on the part of my parents now. They are the same issue as is often the case with these prongs of issues that arise in returning memory. My mind knows the connection before I do. The song is the abuse. The denial of premeditation is denial imbedded in the abuse. I can't do it anymore.

Joseph queries rapidly, sometimes reading aloud from the lyrics to save every precious minute of time to try to alleviate my pain in one hour.

Joseph says "...looking North to the sea she finds the weather fine... "

I respond "The beach where all this happened."

"She watches seagulls fly silver on the ocean..."

I had never told him of the time last year after a session with him when I had seen birds fly overhead outside of my home and for a single instance my heart stopped. I had seen birds fly above that beach.

"Many people wander up the hills from all around you..."

I remind him of an incident at a car wash in which I had been in a crowd looking into people's faces, because I had accidentally ended up in the same location as my ex-husband Paul, and did not want to see him. I had discussed this with Joseph, and this incident had re-jogged the memories that I knew my brother was going to die that day, but had been too young at the age of two to tell anybody what I knew. Looking from face to face evoked the memory of desperation.

"Imprisoned in your bones beneath the isinglass windows of your eyes."

" I am a prisoner of my past."

"...the colors of the day that lie along your arms..."

"Something about my brother, a prince, if only we had escaped before he was attacked."

"And in the dark the hard bells ringing with pain."

"I have only pain."

The song has become the placeholder for the returning pain that I have not faced yet. This had been true in my early sessions, when I had been unable to remove the songs from my mind that were torturing me by playing over and over again. Those in the past had only peripherally had significance to the central issues that were uncovered as the layers of my memories returned, but they held the suffering I was enduring at a place, until, with Joseph's help, it could be uncovered and released.

"There's something else too. There is something about my hand being flat," I tell Joseph. "I showed my flat hand to the mirror in my dressing area yesterday." In fact, my hand being completely open had first gotten my attention that my sentence to time exploration might not be over, when I had first re-contacted Joseph about new memories. I tell him, "I decided to reach out to her again with the flat hand, when I showed it to the mirror, but my middle finger began to ache, which is her signal for the sexual abuse. I couldn't face this at home, alone.

I ask Joseph, "Am I going to survive this?"

He says, "That is our hope, Linda."

———————

As the session begins, my mind sings the lyrics of the song, the entire song, until I find some peace. I find the first bridge between us. I am on the brink of tears. I am fearful I will not survive. So was she fifty years ago. I tell Joseph. This is the bridge. In science investigation, the truth of new discovery is always singularly marked in my mind by a surprising element that could not be predicted; one thing that the person, the discoverer, did not expect.

"She, back then, and I now, both want to survive." It's not that we will cry at the same time. We both have the desperate desire to survive, and neither of us, her back then, or me now is sure we will.

Just barely, I begin to remember the faint edges of the cottage where we stayed on vacation that summer of 1956, from the vantage of the bed. It is the same wall I had remembered last year when I realized my brother and I were being brutalized by my father, and I tell Joseph this.

"Help me! My mind is forcing me to see images of her that are like from pictures of when I was that age. But, I am seeing the edges of the room come faintly into view. But, they are fading! And in return come more pictures in my mind from old snapshots of me! I cannot give in anymore to just seeing her from the outside! I want to be her, and see what she sees, the edges of this room! I do not want to see her anymore from outside of her!"

Joseph says, in an action that helps me more than anything I could ever have accomplished on my own, "Picture getting into bed."

I have some trouble doing that, there are no actual memories of that, but that is the missing element. I know it now. The missing element is to feel what she has felt. There have been only a handful of times that I have felt her feelings from inside of her, not from some remote place returned to me. I have wept from a place inside of her, last year, just before I got the returned memory of my brother's seizure.

I have, once, seen her own chubby little feet wearing white sandals on that vacation. Once, I experienced the emotion she had when my mind first allowed me to superficially see the anxiety of the day my brother was attacked, the year before last. I had seen the attackers arm in a fleeting moment, and hadn't understood why it didn't look like a man's arm. It was smooth and in one instant had reminded me of a woman's arm.

I had once comforted myself and called myself Little Once when taking a bath, after the thoughts of being sexually abused became real, and she had acted out the abuse with her hand. I remember now my terror just days ago, when I realized it was her asking for help, not asking for help for my brother, which had been the basis of all the returned memories until this year. I remember realizing that, realizing I could not help her, and then out of complete terror in real time, wondering, "What do I do now?" But, that is the missing ingredient; to feel what she has felt.

I look to the left and I see my little arm and hand against the sheets come into view. I am seeing this from her own eyes. I am not outside of her anymore!!!

"This is huge! This is huge!" I am crying, about the breakthrough.

"Is your hand flat against something?"

My left hand now is against the chair in Joseph's office and it is like hers, hand and fingers curved slightly feeling the material beneath it. I am looking at my hand on the chair, as my fingers feel the fabric beneath it, watching my own fingers move this way.

"No, no, my hand is not flat! But, this is huge! I am seeing what she is seeing from her, not outside of her!"

My fingers touch the material beneath them on that hand, the sheet back then, the chair fabric now.

My shoulders come down.

I am saying, "I will know soon. It's okay. I will know soon."

This is the type of returned memory process that had usually taken place at home, but it is so much more seamless now here, that I don't even notice the similarity of my words until later to what had happened at home with significant return of a memory, when I say, "It's okay."

I look down my body and I see my little chubby legs apart from the vantage point of lying on my little back, and that something too large for me is forced between them.

I see his face, my father's face as he looked back then, every detail exact. The slant of his hair back then. The perfect rendition of his eyes. A determined look is infested in his eyes. A look no child should ever see.

And the image of his face will not fade!

It is there too long, getting closer and closer, too long and I cannot escape from it then, or now.

I scream when the image won't stop!

This time I can hear my scream. It does not come out silent.

We, at long last, scream together.

I run from the chair to the corner of the room, demolished by weeping. I get into the sofa, and hug the sofa corner for any comfort that I can.

I realize that Joseph has left the room for Kleenex and returned, but I cannot look at him away from what has happened. I take some Kleenex when he returns.

Eventually, I am able to say, "Daddy" to identify the picture of his face seared into my consciousness as he raped me.

I am able to look at Joseph when I say it, and I repeat the word with the spitefulness and irony that the word suggests.

The protective figure as the word Daddy suggests is my father, who raped me

Joseph asks, "Was your hand flat against him, pushing him away?"

I wonder about this and sit quietly there.

I look at my hands.

In this dead moment of my soul of empty reflection, I say, "Maybe, when you reach out to someone to hold them in your arms, your arms curve to embrace them. When you reach out your hand to take someone's hand in yours, your hand curves to cradle theirs. It was my mistake to reach out to her with curved hands. She isn't a separate person. She is me. My hand, flat, is hers."

Joseph says, "You are the same person."

I stand up from the sofa when I am able to collect myself.

I leave the place where I was raped by my father, again, fifty years after he did.

I have endured the rape twice.

I traveled back in time to it.

I survived twice, but it was doubtful both times that I would.

I have a feeling of emptiness and sorrow that follows me everywhere in the days afterward. I quietly tell no one about this.

By late night, I know the reason for all the things that I am, the decency and the honesty.

I did spend fifty years making sure I was not anything like my parents.

A week and one day would pass. It was one thing to be experience the terror of my father's face, the nightmarish image that would not relent or go away. What would happen to me next, was quite another. It happened very much without warning, Sunday, February 5, 2006, in a day that can never be forgotten.

———————

One night after being raped by my father, fifty years after he did, I remember being very afraid before falling asleep, but the feeling was so subtle at the time, I hardly noticed it. I did wonder where infinitesimal moments of nearly sheer terror were coming from, but they passed so quickly. They seemed almost childlike, like a child who is afraid of the dark. I had not consistently been able to sleep with the lights out since my husband left a year before.

On Sunday, February 5, 2006, Ryan and Michelle and little Robert left the house in the early afternoon.

As they were closing the door behind them, I had the distinct thought that I didn't want them to go. I didn't want to be left alone.

I was nearly willing to run to the door, throw it back open, and beg them not to leave. I wondered what that was all about, where these feelings were coming from. I never thought about them again, until I decided I was being much too lazy that day, and it was time to go upstairs and dress. When I went up there, just by the side of my bed, near the pillow as I approached it in the area where I would get in bed, should I have done that, I felt the need to scream.

It came upon me suddenly, and without any other warning.

I nervously remembered I needed to take something downstairs, and went downstairs again. As I reached the middle of the living room to go back upstairs, I began to scream, one scream, which I continued all the way up the stairs. I did not know a human being could do that.

The dog, which always follows me wherever I go until he reaches the baby gate upstairs, watched this with disbelief in his eyes. I pet him as I went rapidly by screaming, so that he would not be too afraid. There was nothing I could do to prevent this from happening.

I have tried hard to reconstruct since then how one scream can continue from a human being's voice box, that could be sustained that long. I know I must have breathed, but the scream went on to my hearing in uniform intensity without breaking until I was back at my bed.

I lay flat against the bed on my face. I had a compulsion to make the room or what my eyes were seeing darker and darker and darker. I found if I pushed my face into the shadow of my nightgown folds that draped from my arm against the bed, I could find darkness there in the small shadow it created. I got up periodically, turned off the lights, and closed the door to make it as dark as possible. As I became more successful, it got darker in that shadow where I literally pushed my eyes into. With near complete darkness I learned how to create, I pushed my eyes there again and suddenly I was startled with fear.

I kept thinking, "Go into the dark place."

There was a cadence to any thought that I had.

Eventually, in the darkness I saw the snow white back of a hand and some cheap jewelry, like large beads on an elastic sting, tight around its wrist.

The fist-like hand was in the air and may have been clutching a knife, but the image of the knife was elusive and I consciously debated if it was there.

That hand was my mother's hand and it was gyrating like her entire naked body, and I told myself from the standpoint of a little child, "She is riding a bucking horse." There was enormous violence to this rape. I could not feel myself being raped, but the image of her face and her gyrating body riding this horse brought so much terror that I began sobbing into the bed.

There were more of my tears produced faster than at anytime in my life, so much more than the sheets could absorb there quickly enough. My lower mouth was engulfed in a pool of liquid as my sobbing continued. I will always remember this sobbing as the lowest point of my life.

And I learned the truth in those most horrific moments of my life that the violence being perpetrated against me is so intense that the cadence that I heard being raped by my mother and I had mistaken for an external noise when being raped by my father is the cadence of my weeping and screaming combined at the time back then. It does not vary with the violence. It cannot.

I can see my mother's face. It is the image that I had recovered long before, but much more real. What's in her hand, even if it is just the hand, is representing some enormous kind of violence and I am the victim of that violence.

When the imagery stops, I am able to get as far as the entry to my dressing area. I am on the ground there. I lay down and my mind is cavernous. I do not believe that I can move. I cannot anchor on anything. There are no boundaries to my thoughts and nothing of substance within them. Out of necessity, because I have never experienced this vacuous state before, I force myself to get to the phone. I call Joseph and try to leave an urgent message, but I am not successful at marking it urgent.

When I lay back down on the ground, there is no improvement in my mind. I clutch the phone in desperation and hold it to me as if it is a doll in my arms. I cannot concentrate, but I believe within the ether of my mind, the possibility that I clutched a doll like that fifty years ago, if I had been permitted to be near one, or had imagined one for help, after the rape by my mother. That, and the soft hair on my head that falls at extreme angles against my face is all that is keeping me alive right now, I believe. I feel it fall from the crown of my head and that is a positive sensation, when no others are possible.

I am alone in the universe, clutching the handset of the phone, laying there, and I know I cannot move, I know that I am but a speck of sand on a cold, parched desert with the vast universe around me and there is nothing to help me here.

Perhaps an hour goes by.

I am uncertain of what I will be able to do when I stand up. Each motion is accomplished with doubt that it can be and quiet vacuous surprise when it is. I gather up my things and bathe. Once dressed, I know I am too afraid in the way that I have been, with a two-year-old child's fear, to be completely alone.

Sadly, because I cannot reach Joseph, I turn eventually to my son, once he has returned home. I ask to please sit beside my son. But, this is too much to ask of him to see me like this. He didn't know what I had endured just over a week before, with the returned memory of my father, and what I have endured now. The night becomes the lowest day of my life rapidly.

In an attempt to deal with his pain and my own, I find myself ultimately in my car parked in the dark along some street, where I had stopped to weep. I weep out-of-doors and question the universe and whether or not I want to live.

I cannot understand what innocents, children, could ever do to be given so much suffering at the onset of their lives.

Ryan calls me on my cell phone with his love. He says, "Mom, we support you."

I later write to Joseph Dickson, "God help me, Joseph. I questioned today if there is a God."

I am hanging on only loosely,

Before the end of the day, February 6, 2006, I hear the love theme from the Franco Zephirelli movie, *Romeo and Juliet*, in an old television performance of Peggy Fleming's ice-skating, in a documentary about her life. I would write to Joseph in faxes that I do not send to him, that she was a ballerina on ice, and that I had studied ballet for about ten years. I would hear that theme play in my head many times over the next two days, a favorite movie and song of mine from young adulthood. When I first do, I begin to move my arms with tragic sorrow, in ways that I knew with the training of all those years. I cannot stop my arms from doing this; it is the outward manifestation of my pain.

My hands move as beautifully as the little girl's who showed me my abuse last year through the motions of her hands, that were when she acted out the blow to my brother's head and his fallen body, as revealing of her nature, by the way she moved her hand more elegantly than any ballerina, as anything else she did. That beauty was me, before what my parents did to me. It was my left hand that had almost exclusively acted out what she saw. Now, I cry and mourn for what was done to that beauty.

By the next day, as I allow my right hand to move in ballet motions as the left once did, telling me of the abuse from the standpoint of the beautiful little child, my left hand begins to ache with abuse as it often has as well. My right hand begins to encircle the abuse, the left hand, but cannot at first touch it. It feels too powerful to be reached.

But, then, significantly, after nearly a day, I can pull the left hand toward my heart and encase it with the right, comfort it, and weep for me. I have a well of this weeping from the abuse I endured that feels infinite.

I weep at long last for me
I know I must find out why I believed I would die.
What is in my mother's hand as she commits this rape?
I know with certainty I believed I would die.

––––––––––

February 8, 2006:

I just manage to make it to the appointment with Joseph Dickson, to hold within me an infinite well of sorrow for what I saw myself endure in my last returned memory of Sunday, February 5, 2006.

I tell Joseph that I am at the lowest point of the onslaught over the years of this journey; there are no moments of reprieve. I tell him that I have another song in my mind and it is a tragic song, and later let him know it is the theme from *Romeo and Juliet*. I tell him that I am not certain if my mind needs shelter or to continue forward, which is why I haven't faxed him since speaking with him two days ago, or let him now know what my progress is now. I do not know what my progress is. I know I cannot stay where I am.

I state, but am asking him, "I do not believe my mind will destroy me."

He nods. He says, "We will respect the process." We will find out together if I need comfort or progress or both.

I search for comfort from what happened last Sunday in the recollection of the violence against me, and I do receive it, but then the feeling of foreboding returns within moments. I gather strength each moment that I can, and extract every drop of comfort from the mental onslaught that has literally reached the point of no more breaks. And then, I reach the bottom of the well of mental pain that I had that reflected the knowledge that I had now, that my life was treated with such inconsequentiality, as to be a prop my parents so abused when they pleased. I can literally see the edges of the well when I reach the bottom, as I had described it to Joseph when he queried me. I said, "It is a parabolic well of pain."

And now I am at the bottom of the well, and much stronger now.

I begin to say, "I believed I would die." I say it again and again, after I reached the bottom of my sorrow. I felt my eye twitch, one time, and I am reminded of the rapid eye movement I had experienced twice succinctly over the last year, but at different intensities.

If I had verbalized this to Joseph, he would have also known that since the beginning of the year, my rapid eye movement on a very subtle level had been going on in waking moments, often. Sleep was shallow overall, superficial, and suggestive of some kind of processing rather than rest. My brain was processing information from fifty years ago often, much more than I would ever consciously know, I realized now.

I tell myself, out loud to Joseph now, "My eyes know what I must learn. My eyes know." And then I felt it lift.

Whatever I was reclaiming, was no longer buried.

"It's not buried anymore."

"Where is it?"

"It is in my chest. It feels like a knifepoint there, and weighs a million tons."

"Is it pain that you haven't felt for a long time?"

"It does not seem symbolic."

"Put your hand on it."

When I do, I began weeping into the knifepoint in the center of my chest and this type of weeping into the injury begins. It lasts at least twenty minutes to one half-an-hour.

During this time, if Joseph had not instructed me to breathe, I would not have been able to. I screamed and wept so intensely that I breathed only at Joseph's suggestion. I would hear his instructions to breathe, as if they were an oxygen supply that otherwise was not available to me. He would say, breathe, and I would inhale in a huge gasp for air, that otherwise would not or could not have come, repeatedly.

As I did this with my right hand on the injury in the center of my chest, my left hand, which was holding Kleenex began to tingle.

I dropped the Kleenex from it, and told Joseph what was happening

My hand locked and I could not move my hand.

I began screaming, "What is it? What is it?"

Intense pain began in some of my fingers, so intense that at least one finger went white cold with pain, in a sensation I have never experienced before.

"Weep into the pain."

I do

"Touch the left [frozen and injured] hand with the other hand."

I couldn't.

"This is what had been going on since yesterday!" I tell him. I had been trying with ballet motions of my right hand to reach to the injured left hand, with a central finger hurting, nothing this intense as now.

"What is stopping you? Is it you stopping you?"

As I tried as hard as I could to reach from my right hand to my left, the pain went into my right hand. It went into a finger that I can point with. I can point at the people who did this to me. I can point to my mother. It went from a helpless finger to a finger with which I can point. The white cold pain froze my finger, and then I wept into that pain.

Joseph tells me, "Take the right hand with the left."

I can't. But, I want the pain to stop.

I cry to my hands, "Don't hurt this much ever again! Don't hurt this much ever again!" As I did, I am able to encase and enfold the left one gently within the right. The pain stops.

I am exhausted and have been screaming and crying most of the hour altogether.

I looked up and say to Joseph, "Was that the physical pain?"

He says, "The body remembers. Are you disoriented?"

I say, "No, absolutely not."

"Can you drive?"

"Probably not, I will sit in my car for a while."

I never made it past the bench down the stairs from his office, where I had to sit and gather strength to make it to the car.

Before I left, I turned to Joseph. I say, "I would never have survived what I just did without you," and then I remembered where I was fifty years ago, "but, fifty years ago, there was no one there to help me."

Joseph comments, "There was no safe place to go."

David Meyer is the type of person I have never known before. His gentleness and courage as a retired Air Force pilot of 22 years, who became an instructor of Astronomy at Victor Valley College in Victorville, California, in retirement, make for a person who is up to the challenges that I would face with him. Very few people on this Earth could withstand what David has experienced at my side and at the side of my son, because of Ryan's declining health from his devastating injuries from the surgery he had five years before in 2004. When David came to me as a stranger whom I first met in a job interview in 2006, I knew I could talk to him, even then. I told him of the process I had already been through, not knowing at that time, that the process was so far from over.

I had no idea the way parallel universes work. I had no idea that sometimes we see leakages from them, as perhaps the force of gravity that some scientists surmise is perhaps leaking into our own universe from a parallel one. Whether the force comes from another universe or another scale that fits an extra dimension we are not aware of in our universe, the way the mind works, first there are fragments, and then there is the full reality. My mind hadn't yet gathered all of the pieces, but it was about to.

By November 30, 2007, I have been working for the Lewis Center of Educational Research as their Global Curriculum Developer for 7 months. The Lewis Center is in Apple Valley, California, only a few miles from my home in Victorville that I purchased for Ryan, his now wife Michelle, and my two grandchildren, Robert and Nathan, who was but a pregnancy at the time of our move.

My work at the Lewis Center takes me back often to Jet Propulsion Laboratory. I will help design the curriculum for the JPL Juno mission back to Jupiter, the Ames Research Center mission LCROSS, to the Moon, and NASA's Spitzer Space Telescope in regards to Active Galactic Nuclei research.

I am sent to Texas to speak at a conference about the 34 meter radio telescope the Lewis Center commands for students around the world, which is part of NASA's Deep Space Network at Goldstone, California. When on the drive home from the Ontario airport on November 30, I scream for two or three miles. And then, my heart stopped and skipped a beat. Not only was I screaming for what was done to me, during the attack on me by my mother, but something had caused my heart to stop in sheer terror. I tried to tell myself this couldn't possibly be, but I knew with certainty I had seen something back then that couldn't possibly be; that it was the single most fearful moment of my life.

Dave Meyer drives me to see Joseph afterward. It is an hour's drive down the hill that separates Arcadia from the High Desert, where we are in Victorville. I told Joseph I had seen something that made my heart stop as a two-and-a-half year old child. I told him it was difficult to feel God's love in the presence of such horrors in memory. I would become baptized at Faith Lutheran Church on February 8, 2008.

Joseph told me that the writings of Mother Teresa had recently been released. He indicated that her one request of God for her entire life was to feel and experience everything that Jesus had. She confessed in the hell hole of Calcutta, India, she had gone years and not been able to feel God's love. This is an amazing revelation to the world. Then, she realized what had happened in her life. Jesus' greatest suffering was when he was on the cross and asked, My God, My God, why have you forsaken me? She had been granted her wish by God.

Dave and I visit his family in Nebraska a month later, in December of 2007. We drive there, and during the drive, I re-experience my mother's attach on me like a video from end to end, the screaming and the rhythmic horror of her assault with the weapon in her hand with which she rapes me.

When we pull into a gas station in Texas and the shadow of a truck occults the sun and prevents the light from reaching me as I sit in our parked car and wait for Dave, I re-experience the presence of the single most fearful entity that could possibly exist in this universe, present in the room at the onset of my mother's attack. It is there for a fleeting moment of horror beyond what any entity upon this Earth could ever produce. My mother is but a buffoon in the presence of such evil.

––––––––––

I understand dissociation and how the human mind protects us emotionally when the pain we are experiencing is too great for our minds to handle. We break off and dissociate. I have experienced that. In a sense this is a trick of our mind to survive. In March of 2008, I begin screaming to Dave that what I experienced the day of my mother's attack was not a trick of my mind. I scream and cry to him in disbelief, when my mind lets me know, "It's not a trick! It's not a trick! It's not a trick!"

My mother is attacking me. I see the attack from behind her back, not because I have dissociated, as I have in many of my memories; gone outside my body, but because I am dying.

I am pulled back like a small child wearing a harness. It folds my body forwards, as I am pulled backwards in this way, and I am now in a body behind my mother's. My screams in the body that is left behind lessen. I experience the greatest single sorrow I have ever known on this Earth. I do not want to leave. It is the strongest emotion I have known in my entire life. God wants us to love life that much.

I regret that I have to leave, but I am forced to accept it, and do. I say goodbye to life.

I know now why I was always so overdramatic and feared the worst when my son Ryan was ever infirmed as a child, and I would rush him so quickly to a doctor. When you are sick or injured, you are close to death, as I am now, dying. This I learned at the age of two, and coupled Ryan as a child to my experience.

I think of the Angel of God. My arms ache from being overwhelmed in the presence of God. I am in God's presence.

I watch the pain that my body left behind is experiencing from my mother's blows. The screaming that is left is the end of my life of physical pain in the body I have left behind, and is going on even in the presence of this; as I am in the presence of God.

It was glorious. God parts the substance of the sky and I see the gold Angels of God, full grown adult women in gold with gold wings, three of them passing in different directions through the skies of Heaven in a color of sky that exceeds anything that can be found on Earth in its blueness, amid the pure white clouds. Who am I that I am experiencing this? I am but a small child, and God is giving me a choice, as my screams from my dying body get fainter in the background and stop.

I am looking around on my tiny feet, turning from side to side. Now, spinning, rising up; flying back rejoining my old body and its screams begin again; rejoining more slowly than I left. Back on my back on the bed.

I chose to go back. I believe, for my brother. God Himself gave me the choice.

Baby Angel

By the time my brother and I reached Blair High School in Pasadena, we had reached paradise. There was no senior class yet, when my brother entered the school as a freshman, Blair was that new. There was something in the spirit of the school, something about the excellence of the leadership and teaching there, and in the camaraderie that knew no racial boundaries (that centered around a dynamic and illustrious football team) that approximated the dream of a vision held by Gene Roddenberry when he created the *Star Trek* original series which aired while I was a student at Blair. I aspired to that dream. There was finally a tangible representation in *Star Trek* of the life I hoped to lead. I would go on to college, I decided, to become a Star Ship Captain.

Something about my years at Blair took on the character of an enlivening dream. There was nothing I could not do or accomplish. Physically, I jumped over more girls lined up side-by-side with heads and bodies tucked against a gymnastics mat, than it made any sense to do in some fearless "astronaut preparation" as if I were the daredevil Evil Knievel on a motorcycle jumping cars.

I climbed faster to the tops of ropes than any other girl, bringing an awed look to the gym teacher's face once again.

I became co-chairman of the California Scholarship Federation chapter at Blair, played fairly good chess on the chess team, which my brother insisted I do, and took all the math and science I could get my hands on.

I wrote reports in Social Studies and History classes that captured the attention of my teachers. I remember a particular night when researching the causes and effects of the Hundred Years War late into the night at the library, when I became aware of the industrial lights around the area of the High School. The lights were like stars in the heavens. In my mind, I began to compare the physical beauty of the natural world and the beauty of the world that could be created by the human mind through technology.

Mankind had a manifest destiny to reach out into space to discovery his origins; to merge technology into the natural beauty of the universe in that process. The major clue was in the fact that stars had lifetimes and that our Sun, like every other star, would live and die. If we were not off the Earth when this happened, humankind would not survive. The Earth was not our home as much as the universe in that regard. Our survival depended on reaching other worlds; we needed to go home to space. I intended to be part of that.

I did a report on poverty in America. My Social Studies teacher, Mr. Guzman announced to the class that in all of his years of teaching, he had never seen a report as good as one of the students in the class he read. I had a small hope it might be my report, into which I had put my heart, and then he said my name. I was a humanist and an activist, and hated the war in Vietnam because I didn't think the young people fighting whose lives were on the line were being allowed to win the war. High school included coming home everyday to the news of how many American youth died that day in Vietnam and moratoriums at school to absorb the protests brimming in many of the students' souls.

I worked on the report on poverty for hours and hours in a new apartment we had finally moved to. We had moved several times since the very humble apartment that was the duplex. We had found a much nicer one on Madison Street in Pasadena, and ultimately moved to El Molino Avenue to a one bedroom, where my mother remained nearly 40 years.

The bedroom, divided by a screen into separate sides, was for my brother and for me. My parents held the living room with a sofa that converted to a bed. I really didn't live there. I lived in my studies and my dreams, and I was never home.

I began working as a saleslady selling women's dresses in the spring of 1969 when I was 15 years old, while in High School, before I was legally old enough to work. I didn't want my parents to have to support me anymore. From the day I began, they never paid for another article of my clothing or for my shoes. I paid for everything.

This trend began much earlier when my brother and I were old enough to venture out onto Colorado Blvd. in Pasadena, which was the main and old shopping district. We bought my parents a small organ that was one step above a toy, and had it delivered by the store with money we had saved on our own. We bought a stool to go with it from a Singer Sewing Repair Center, and carried it home ourselves. We bought other small gifts for Christmas. My brother and I made our first official Christmas celebration, all ourselves. We asked for nothing, but only wanted the satisfaction of seeing our parents happy.

Gary and I had also set a remarkable standard in the family. There were hugs and kisses goodbye for our parents, even if they were just leaving to go to the market. I remember this warmth within our lives stand-alone. I did not remember its origins coming from Gary and me, however, until decades later.

At the Civic Center in Pasadena one day, after researching in the large city library, I watched huge cumulous clouds gather in a crystal blue sky. I began to understand that this vista was exclusive to our blue world. I began to sense the other countless worlds that undoubtedly existed in our galaxy alone, and how many beyond that there were in other galaxies. I had no idea I was approximating something I had seen, in death, as a two-year-old child. I knew at that point the size of the universe. I sensed its grandeur and my place in it as a tiny explorer on a tiny, albeit breathtakingly beautiful world. The sky overwhelmed me. My destiny was set.

———————

Blair High School spawned a remarkable graduating class in 1970. Among our ranks, were a molecular biology professor, a U.S. Federal Attorney, a doctor interning in Pediatric Nephrology at UCLA, and an Astronomer. Our High School reunions for the next thirty-five years were filled with warmth, camaraderie, and unique set of memories that could only come from a level of teaching that we received that was profound. In retrospect, I had two teachers at Blair High School who were college-level. One was Robert Salley, Advanced Placement American History, one of the best lecturers I have ever had in school, and the other was Stanley Sheinkopf, Advanced Placement English Literature.

Stanley Sheinkopf loved to get on top of his desk and jump around when he was expressing an interesting and invigorating motif in literature to his students. I would receive college credit for both these courses after passing the Advanced Placement exams at the end of my senior year in High School in each. I received Blair High School's Department Award in English for my writing.

As a future scientist, this astonished me, but Stanley Sheinkopf always said I had fabulous ideas. I had taken actually two high level courses in my senior year on English Literature from Stanley Sheinkopf, who also taught at Pasadena City College. I will never forget how much I enjoyed those courses, reading everything from Dante's *Inferno* to James Joyce's *A Portrait of the Artist as a Young Man*, and everything in between.

Stanley Sheinkopf was a sensitive teacher at the time and was much attuned to one of my classmate's psychological problems. As I only loosely understood, my classmate had some conflict to do with her feelings about her parents, which prevented her from doing her homework, but in class she participated to the fullest extent. Stanley Sheinkopf permitted this. He was astute and aware.

One day, he came to me and asked me if I was okay. I said that I was. I vaguely knew and understood this had something to do with my brother, who was a former student of Sheinkopf's and still at Blair. When he asked again if I was okay, even after I answered, I insisted that I was. It cast a shadow on my brother's perception by other people. I remember being clearly aware that my brother was not right as my mother had indicated, but I never understood exactly how. In his pictures, he always looked like he was squinting or somehow suffering in a very sad way, no matter how handsome he was, and he was indeed very handsome. Stanley Sheinkopf's question to me suggested that he didn't think my brother was okay, and therefore wondered if I was okay too. Whatever I sensed about my brother, Stanley Sheinkopf knew it too.

In a twelve hour period, my mother had nearly killed both her children. When? Where? Why?

Up until March 5, 2006, it was only a matter of inference. I had only known the date by my mother's admission that I was two-and-a-half years old at the time when "two people" as she put it for fifty years "took" my brother "for a walk," when asked how old I was, once I knew I had been present at this incident, if nothing else. That put the incident, likely in July of 1956. It was through that, and no other way, that I knew the date.

My parents were apparently creatures of habit. They took no photographs of their children other than in the spring of each year when the weather was not terribly cold, although in warmer climates, our attire would hardly evoke thoughts of spring, since it was still quite brisk in Canada at that time, and again in June and/or July of each year, once or twice, rarely in August or September, but still summer, and at no other time. If we were vacationing, which we were when this attack on Gary occurred, then it was either in June, more likely July of 1956. That is what date patterns in family pictures suggest.

Family pictures suggest a whole lot more than that. In the summer of 1958, my mother did something she had, with one or two minor exceptions, never done before. She wrote on the back of pictures from that summer vacation. She never put dates on pictures, and never wrote locations where they were taken, with the exception of pictures taken during the summer of 1958. And, it seems to me that she may have added this annotation at least several years after the pictures were taken.

The annotations themselves were odd, as though she was trying to cleanse her record, jesting at Gary's mood in a picture of him. I believe my mother rarely cared what anyone's mood was, only as it pertained to her. It seemed these annotations were made after we came to the United States, and she had imagined wiping the slate of her crimes clean in moments of self-adoration.

Accompanying each annotation that she did write, she added the word "Canada" on the bottom. Perhaps my parents, as adults, were discussing a move to the United States in 1958. But, since my mother had already spent 37 years in the same country by then, since birth, it is unlikely that she wrote Canada on the pictures in 1958. Why write the name of your country on a location where you had lived all of your life to identify the picture?

My mother must surely have added these annotations later, and in further support of that premise, I notice she misidentified a couple of the locations in the same batch of pictures, obviously taken at the same place. My mother wasn't that good on details, with the possible exception of her children's ages. [1]

---

[1] Because of my inability to look even closer at these annotations at this stage of my remembering, in retrospect, I have since noted that my mother's unusual display of annotating pictures was prompted by me as a child around the age of seven, indeed directly after our move to the United States. My mother never used

Up until then, I had simply guessed the location of Vancouver Island as the scene of the tragedy that occurred in 1956. I questioned that consciously now. Until May 4, 2006, I had never done that. I had assumed that a ferry ride was associated with all my summer vacation memories in Canada, and ferries take people to and from Vancouver Island or one of the other Gulf Islands off the coast of the Mainland of Vancouver, British Columbia. I remembered a ferry ride, with automobiles onboard the ferry. In the back of my mind, however, I probably always knew that my parents level of sophistication in Canada was not in keeping with such a, albeit minor (approximately one hours sailing time) voyage.

Believing that omitted any other more exotic, smaller island from any consideration at all. My parents did not own an automobile until coming to the United States in 1961. Furthermore, their lives were simple and not complex financially in any way. They did not own their own home at anytime in their lives, they owned no land or housing. It never seemed likely to me that they could manage the planning for a cottage stay, which included even a somewhat admittedly "simple" voyage, so it does not actually seem in keeping with them that these events took place on Vancouver Island. However, I always believed that they did, for the reason of my definite certainty of a ferry ride at vacation time.

I never examined photographs of my childhood in an analytical way with two very notable exceptions. First, the evidence was in photographs that after the age of five, Gary does not appear normal, or appears brain-injured, and before he does not. I had also scoured photographs for a look on my mother's face; the way her face appeared during my sexual abuse.

On May 4, 2006, that changed. I realized I had not, or perhaps could not have made myself look closely at the family vacation photographs before. What I learned from examining the pictures analytically was astounding.

---

printing and only wrote in cursive, and I did not recognize my own printing at that age. I had specifically interviewed my mother about each of the pictures with annotation on them, those many decades ago, and wrote her responses. Her effort "to wipe the slate clean of her crimes in moments of self-adoration" was synergistic with my amnesia at that age. Also of great interest is her response about two pictures taken in 1960 whose misidentification by her is blatant, and consistent with what I have remembered since that time.

There were no pictures at all from the summer of 1956. Visually identifying picture dates by our ages, prior to 1957 before pictures came with dates on them through the popular development process then, there are no pictures of us during the summer of 1956. Furthermore, my parents did not begin taking pictures of us summers or otherwise again, as they had prior to 1956, until the summer of 1958. For two years they took no pictures; they did not want reminders apparently or evidence of my brother's altered appearance. In the summer of 1957, my Aunt Nora did take pictures of Gary and me and apparently gave them to my mother, because they also include some pictures of my parents taken at her home. My brother looks brain damaged in these pictures.

On the back of one photograph from the summer of 1958, when my parents resumed taking pictures, I found the words, "Beach Grove."

Over more than sixteen hours, on May 4, 2006, I would travel to Beach Grove via the Internet and find the visual references of my returned memories. The first find was Beach Grove Motel.

Beach Grove is the name given to basically an area, not a distinct community. It is situated on the edge of Boundary Bay, located on the east side of 56th Street, between 12th Street and 17A Avenue, in the suburban, mostly residential community of Tsawwassen, which lies in the southwestern part of the Corporation of Delta, British Columbia, Canada, according to Wikipedia. In 1960, exactly one year before my family left for the United States, BC Ferries inaugurated service from a humungous landing they built at Tsawwassen for transport from Vancouver to Victoria on Vancouver Island. I likely took my ride on the ferry in the summer of 1960. My mind had linked the ferry with the horrific acts of my brother's and my abuse, because they occurred in the same place, less than one hour's bus drive from Vancouver where we lived.

The Beach Grove Motel is the only named place of lodging that I could find on the Internet that includes the words "Beach Grove." It boasts a three-minute walk from the motel to a trail along the seaside of the Boundary Bay. At the end of the trail is Centennial Beach Park. Not only does this park match my photos of the vacation in the summer of 1958, but also in the summer of 1955, and more to the point it matches my returned memories of the beach where my brother was destroyed.

The gulf waters don't look like Pacific Ocean waters along the coast. There is land on the other side of one's vista. The waters are more still, perhaps even cleaner. A vista opens up like one that I keep housed in my returned memories of Gary's attack, unlike what I have ever seen on a coastal beach either in Vancouver or California Beaches. What I have seen in my returned memories is the vista adjacent to the Beach Grove Motel.

Beyond that, I immediately noticed on the website where I found only one limited view of the motel, the motel itself, with minor remodel to the exterior siding, even before I had visited the motel's website, matched the cottages where my brother and I and my mother are pictured standing in 1958. In more photographs that I discovered on yet another website, and enlarged, the exact one-story building where we stayed is photographed. I would later learn from the notable historian in the area, whom I hired and who helped me so much with my quest to learn about what had happened there, the Beach Grove Motel may have been at that time on the opposite side of the street it is on, and the buildings were later moved to where they now stand. In its earlier manifestation the motel was called the Beach Grove Auto Court. Beach Grove is one of the best kept secrets for its beauty in Canada, and hasn't changed much in 50 years.

In an aspect that is so disturbing it is difficult to think about, but also on the website of the Beach Grove Motel is the bedroom inside one of the cabins. It is the only photograph of a hotel room I have ever seen that reminds me of a "graphic," a drawn rendition of the room, because it is so fiercely angular; the bed, the simple table beside it; and so fiercely stark; the room just like a box with no pictures on the walls. It looks like a crude graphic drawing of a room. That is exactly the room I had described to Joseph during my father's rape of me. I had told Joseph, "The room looks like a graphic drawing," when I remembered the images of my abuse and my brother's abuse in bed during the summer of 1956.

Since the outside structures of the rooms had not changed in fifty years, it was indeed possible that the insides of the rooms had also not changed in ambience as well. The room that I see on that website for Beach Grove Motel until the website is changed is the place that I saw in memory where I was attacked. It is like the appearance of no motel room I have ever seen otherwise, even those pictured on other websites at the Beach Grove Motel that appear more remodeled than this room.

Yet, when that vista of the beach unfolded for me in late 2004, I had specifically stated out loud to Joseph Dickson, "There is a dock! I hadn't seen a dock before [in my returned memories of the place my brother was attacked]!" I had in fact used the word dock. To the best of my recollection what I remembered was more like a pier, very high over the water, very wide, massive, and in a sense "thick," and then I had seen my white sandals of my little feet against wood, which I assumed to be on the dock. It wasn't until I had seen a commercial on TV that depicted a little girl running down a wooden pier, actually, probably not specifically a dock where boats dock, because it was too high off the water as had been in my returned memory, that I was startled into reclaiming the memories later that day, nearly two years ago, of witnessing my brother's seizure.

I searched until exhausted for such a dock on the Internet anywhere on Centennial Beach. There appear to be none notable, neither presently or formerly standing. The massive landing at Tsawwassen for the BC Ferries was not even considered by me in the determination of what this dock memory represented. It has a two-mile causeway, made of 2.5 million cubic yards of boulder, rock, and gravel fill.

It wasn't until I saw a tourist picture on the Internet of the car ramp leading to a ferry in "dock two" of the ferry terminal at Tsawwassen, that the image a person would see standing on the car ramp, accessible by bus, reminded me of the closest thing I have been able to find of the thickness, shortness, and wideness of this dock that appeared in my memory in the middle of the beach landscape where my brother was hurt.

Without this, there was no concrete memory that would link the beach to Tsawwassen at all. All such piers that I would see in later life were made of wood. And, it is clear that the rails along this car ramp leading to the ferry have the appearance of those of wooden piers. I have this exact image of the shortness and stockiness of this high-over-water section of the car ramp imbedded in my memory.

But, the wood beneath my feet that I remembered might have been the boardwalks of the trails that lead among wild flowers and plants and many, many birds to the Centennial Beach. Once, after a session with Joseph Dickson I had looked up and seen birds flying to the coast as I returned home. My heart had stopped in one instant in my chest. I had seen many birds at Centennial Beach. It is a stopover place for thousands of birds along a significant migratory route, and as such famous for bird watching and replete with sanctuary. In one instant, in that same way, my heart had stopped with recognition, only once, in seeing a historic picture from the fifties of a Delta police car in my Internet search on May 4, 2006.

Most notably, Centennial Beach is littered everywhere with wood sticks, drift wood that falls from the trees above the beach, like the kind I saw my mother swinging, and the object my brother was holding in my final returned memories of his injuries more than a year ago, as he fought hopelessly for his life. Although I have no pictures, of course, from the summer of 1956, I am most certainly aware that we were there in the summer of 1955, 1958, 1960, and the summer of 1956.

On May 8, 2006, I found an on-line photograph from Canadian website digital gallery, of Centennial Beach, Boundary Bay Regional Park, using a search under "Centennial Beach" using Google Images.

I first observed that the terrain was exactly as I envisioned in my return memories years ago, when only my hand had acted out the blow to Gary's head, even though I had concentrated more on what my hand was doing at the time. It wasn't beach terrain, it wasn't park terrain, it was somewhere in between the two, with elements of both.

And most importantly, it was elevated above the water. Like a hill, which I hadn't fully thought about since my first returned memories of Gary's fallen body; elevated terrain. The hill in the Judy Collins song *Albatross*, which I had always included among the things that made the song so poignant, was relevant.

Soon, viewing the photograph on May 8, 2006, I was rocking in my chair; soon, I was clutching a hard copy of it I printed out to my heart, in a fetal position, in bed, weeping.

———

As the years went by, my parents had acclimated to life in Pasadena, California as a fish would to a tank of water. Seamlessly, they became Californians enjoying a sunny, sophisticated and happy life that developed into a rhythm of both attending work. My parents dressed well, always had a nice, large automobile, their apartment on

El Molino gave the feel of spaciousness although there were basically only four separate rooms. They furnished it nicely, but their decorating didn't have as much to do with appearance as it did functionality.

They frequented art shows in communities near the Southern California beaches, collected art they loved, and covered the walls of their apartment with it. They still went out on the weekend evenings as they had in Canada, but also added the practice of going out nearly every night somewhere, if only for a late night snack at a restaurant, by the time I was in high school.

Celebrities such as Telly Savalas would see them regularly at Lounge areas in places like The Century Plaza, in Century City, nearby Pasadena, and Savalas would repeatedly ask them to join him at his table. The piano player would begin a special song for them when they arrived at the table where they usually sat. The parking attendants knew them respectfully by name.

My parents would not join celebrities, who always assumed they were celebrities somehow themselves. No one could have known how hard they both worked in jobs that were exhausting and of course underpaid them.

My mother was indeed a people magnet, and no matter where she went, people would walk up to her and begin conversations. My mother had stories about these people that were usually interesting, but the facts were not so much about the people as their interaction with her. My parents were invited many places and unless the event had to do with family or very close friends of my Aunt Clare and the husband she had married after coming to the United States, Gerry Gruber, my father refused nearly all invitations. My mother was at the center of his world and he wanted to keep it that way exclusively, for himself and for her.

My parents went to Las Vegas twice a year to play the slot machines, if not more often. They did visit the homes of a couple of very wealthy cliental of my mother's at Magnin's department store. Whether my mother was talking about meeting Elvis Presley and getting his autograph for me, or the personalities of her wealthy cliental, once it happened it would take on a life of its own, forever after.

I was awarded Honors at Entrance by the University of Southern California and the University of California at Los Angeles in the summer of 1970, the two universities to which I had applied. I selected the University of Southern California, because the atmosphere at UCLA seemed less personal to me. I was awarded full scholarship to the University of Southern California to study Astronomy.

I received word of my California State Scholarship, Lifetime Membership in the California Scholarship Federation, and an American Legion School Award, on the awards day assembly at Blair in June of 1970. I had met my goals and was going to make my dreams come true. With student loans for the dorms, my parents were not going to have to pay for anything, although my father co-signed the loans for my first year, which otherwise I could not have attained.

I had already received one proposal of marriage, although I was only 16 years old. It came from a young man who worked with my father at Prober's Shoes in Alhambra, and who my father had recruited to take me to my Grad Night celebration. A young man at high school, Brian Bailey, I was most interested in, attended the Grad Night precursor with me on the organizing committee for the event; he and I are pictured in the yearbook in a spinning tea cup at Disneyland, but he was not able to go to the actual event. He told me this with at least a look of explanation. Hence this young man my father worked with stepped in.

My father had unfortunately run across some form of embezzlement at Bullocks where he worked, in which he refused to participate and it blacklisted him in a sense from getting other work, because he could not get a good recommendation from the place he had worked all those years when he had to leave. He ultimately worked in Beverly Hills for a while then settled into managing Prober's Shoes in Alhambra. He made the owners wealthy with his management skills.

Going to work with my father in the early years of my life probably had a very good effect on me. He was thoroughly competent, nearly feared by the employees as a manager, but obviously the people around my father respected him. It was important for me to witness that level of competence.

Mother continued to work in dress sales, and her personality, which attracted people to her like magnets, and which caused my father to ultimately spend fifty years of their marriage pushing such people away, served her very well on the high-end selling field of I.

Magnin's. She was probably no different than she had been as a little girl when hoisted on the shoulders of the towns' people.

She waited on the wealthy of Pasadena and observed celebrities like Elizabeth Taylor whisk through the store, and sold more than any person in the history of their sales. Both of my parents worked long and endless hours on their feet and my continuing in such work, even on weekends to supplement my income during college, spurred me on to wanting a professional degree even more.

This young man who worked with my father was not a serious suitor in my eyes. Yet, I had experienced desperate crushes on at least one young man in high school, and of course, before. I was madly in love with Greg Tomioni in elementary school and the handsome little boy gave me a St. Christopher, which was breathtakingly beautiful. I threw it over a building once because another little boy suggested I should when he gave me a Hawaiian Tiki necklace to wear in its place.

I had a crush on a hall monitor, a young man who wore a sash like a uniform to monitor that no children run in the halls of the elementary school when the bell rang. But, later in life, perhaps always, I became enormously shy. In far more recent years, my mother asked me why I didn't use my personality more. I held this in tragic juxtaposition with what she had done to deny me of the status of a human being in the beginnings of my life, and the loss of personal development that had caused.

One boy in junior high fell madly in love with me and managed to get a photograph of us together at a dance, which he prized like gold.

I saw a young man walking near Caltech one day; a very handsome young student and I winked at him. But, the time I was in college, my shyness forced an older student who worked part-time in the dormitory cafeteria to go out of his way to bend to meet my eyes and smile at me.

I had very deep feelings about love and how wonderful some young men seemed to me. Growing up I had very high expectations of where love would take me in my life. I believed in love and was romantic to an extreme probably. Mixed in with all the adventures in space depicted in television and the movies, romance that usually ended well, was ever-present in my thoughts.

I met the mentor of my lifetime, when I met Gibson Reaves. He was Department Chairman of Astronomy at the University of Southern California when I began there. I had talked to him on the phone about my coming to USC only once before I met him. Something clicked even then to tell me I had arrived at the place I had always sought to be, under the guidance that would take me forward.

Gibson Reaves had the highest IQ of any person I have ever known, or expect to know in my lifetime, not just about science, but about life. He became a father figure to me, and to others of the majors in the department. When Gibson spoke, I listened. I always learned something. Gibson put me immediately to work the first moment I arrived at USC registration. Here I was registering myself, the first member of my family to attend a four-year college, and within minutes of that, I was registering other people for the Department of Astronomy at USC.

I remember wearing a sundress that day that made me feel clearly as bright and vivid in the summer sun as this world of potential around me. I don't think my appearance or lack of tutorial-looking appearance was lost on many people. I loved feeling and looking good.

When I wore a blue hot pants outfit that was modest, but fit perfectly, with a very short skirt, I heard students in the classes when I became a Teaching Assistant (TA), convey they had never had a TA who looked like me before. The outfit had been given to me by a beautiful Hawaiian security guard at the dress shop where I continued to work even after my mother left there to go to I. Magnin's. I believe that security guard was a tinier person than even myself.

There were two days at the University of Southern California that I remember most poignantly; the day I arrived and met Gibson Reaves and the day I graduated with my degree in Astronomy. Both days, I could not believe the good fortune that was happening to me.

In between was spent the weeks and months of wish fulfillment when you are working too hard or playing too hard to notice exactly how the time goes by. I was living a dream of intellectual curiosity and soaking up knowledge like a sponge. Before I knew it, four years of heaven had gone by.

By evening of my Internet search, May 8, 2006, I re-experienced the transfer of intense tingling and stiffness in my left hand to my right, my left index finger playing more a role than it had in the past, my hands wanting to become buoyant and nearly trying to levitate while I did.

And, now within minutes, May 9, 2006, because I have been concentrating on my mother swinging the object, the full color panorama of the picture opened up in my memory.

I see Gary as I have seen him only twice in two returned memories of his attack, and he is running through the terrain of the picture that I found like a tiny ant, dressed as he was when I saw the returned memory of his seizure and I saw the returned memory of his blood-filled eyes.

And, I am terrified and crying and alone and I call Joseph Dickson immediately and his recorded message says that he is out of town for a week and cannot be reached. I cannot put Ryan through this final day of agony with me, he doesn't deserve this although now he believes, now he has seen the photographs and knows there were no pictures taken for two years of my brother and he has seen the before and after pictures of Gary. Now, I sit here having blasted through to the past to the full color vista of this place of horror, and I see my mother's angry face a look that is devastating in full color and the outfit she was wearing as she swung the object has come alive. I am terrified, and I am crying, "Momma, Momma, Momma, no!"

I cannot reach Joseph and I long for his voice as a child longs for her mother. And I want his help and he is not here and I am alone like I was fifty years ago. And, I weep and ask God to let me see, because I know that I am going to. And, it's okay. It's okay. I know I am going to.

I lay on my back and reach out to God beneath that huge sky fifty years ago, now at home in a different country in my dressing area of a condominium I own; I reach out to God and I understand why I once thought God was with me when I first saw an image of my rape. Because, if not for God, there is no one else; there is no one else in the universe with me then or now.

He is running like an ant, his tiny form in the red t-shirt that he would be destroyed in and the light colored shorts. These are his last minutes of normal motion in this world.

I had touched my tingling and frozen (not cold, immobilized) hands to my face and head area last night as they levitated up. My pain is perhaps the pain of my soul. Gary runs like an ant. What is he saying, what is he doing before he dies? I want to reach up to the sky. I do so now. Keep my arms up. Am I asking for God's help? The index finger aches now. Reach up, reach up, reach up. Is it because I am very small? I am only two. What I am reaching to? To God? I don't know! I'm saying, Momma. Repeating it in some hollow tone. Reach up? Pick me up?

I stand up now! I reach upward and cry, "Momma, pick me up! Pick me up!" Now I fall onto the ground in a fetal position. I am rocking in a fetal position. My hand are circling one another in the air like gears locked in some rotation. They end up not moving in that configuration like a washed surgeon's hands in front of me. My index finger on my left hand aches. I am in shock. Was I hit too? What is happening? Joseph, I'm so scared.

I'm standing. Something is telling me to look to my left. I do; I sit in my computer chair, and I am twirling in my computer chair, and the room is spinning, with my left hand straight out, looking to my left. That stops things for a while. Things get quiet. God, I am asking you to let me see. I'm not afraid anymore.

"There, now."

I am walking aimlessly now in tiny little steps. At the ends of my hands hung at my sides is the knowledge of what I have seen. Joseph once told me the body remembers. God put the information into my hands and tried to take it out of my brain. Perhaps last night I was trying to put it back.

My chest is tight on and off, and I contemplate now if a memory is surfacing there. If so, I am ready for it. My body has relived what I did on that day. God help the little girl who is me. I am two. I have lived in this world only two years. I rocked on the ground in a fetal position with my curved hand trying to reach out for my brother to hold him, my mother to stop her, to be lifted from the ground to comfort, there was none to be found anywhere. There is an intense pain in my chest now, a weight like a thousand tons. It's rising. I will know soon.

My heart beats heavily with trepidation and foreboding to know. I am ready to see. Show me God. It's at the lowest point of my upper chest, so it has risen. I want to weep. I suspect I will soon. It's coming up. I look in my right hand. My heart is pounding. My arms weigh so much, with the knowledge they carry at the end of each, in my hands. My heart is pounding. In these moments in time, I am between two universes, locked in the past and the present at the same time. If I am released, I will go home again, perhaps for the final time. I'm so tired and I hope my heart will stand this strain.

The word, "Baby" pops out of my consciousness. "Baby, Baby," I'm calling my brother. "Baby," I lament. I had done this once before in returned memories, but this is sustained now, after my brother is fallen. I do not see anything yet. But, I know that I will. He is on the ground. I reach out to him with my fingers and hands and arms that have the knowledge and lower my head to his body, and my soft hair is all that I can feel. "Baby." I lay against the ground. I want to sleep forever.

I do for fifty years.

The pounding of my heart is just below my throat. One or two pounds to tell me that it's there; my heart doesn't belong there. It has been moved.

I lay down on the ground.

It's what I will see when I look up. It's what I will see when I am begging to be picked up.

I lay on my back and try to put my arms up and see the ceiling.

It's what I will see when I am begging to be picked up. What do I see? I have chills. What do I see? I whimper like an animal that has lost their young and it is already known that they are dead. What do I see? Everything else has already happened. What do I see? I am not two. I am fifty-two. My mind could not take it then. Can my heart take it now? What choice do I have? I have none.

I have an intense, definite desire to bathe, and actually do.

After the bath, I am resting for a while. I crawl into bed and sleep for a while

When I wake up, I realize the possibility that I acted out what I witnessed, but only fragments, fragments that would run like a video once again, in about a year. I realize it is quite possible that I cannot face the images or the full sounds even now at age 52, I think my mind is sparring me what I can never view. I was given a bath fifty years ago, and would later learn where, and took one again today so that I would never again see what was seen on that day. I think I never can again.

I called my mother with some good news. Although she had stood by me with Paul Kelly's astonishing abandonment of me, her needs made that support wane sometimes, she always came first, and everything was always about her. But, there was a predominance of her support for which I was grateful and which I had experienced over a large period of my life on and off, particularly when my father was alive. I felt that she deserved one phone call for goodness sake when I didn't sound like I was dying of grief and stress. I called her up to say that I was actually going to go out on a date. It had been seven months since Paul left in January of 2005.

I picked my mother up for a Friday night visit just after. I had tried as best I could to maintain Paul's decision to see her weekly for myself now. Many times, like when she went into an unexpected rage now and then, I would find a way to excuse from seeing her for a long time. I did have a couple of dates with someone I did not intend to see again, but I had a nice time.

My mother then began volunteering things about her own love life, some were especially absurd because she had been stringing along a man for sometime to make a boyfriend of hers jealous and now she professed to love this gullible man. I smiled thinking that was fine; this was girl talk anyway.

Then, my mother went on to describe in graphic detail an encounter she had had with her lover. In all the years she and I had ever spoken this was far more graphic than anything people normally share. I remained speechless for the rest of her visit. I knew at that moment that she had devised this encounter with her lover based on the fact that she knew I was dating again. She had to have the attention. I knew then that my mother had no respect for me at all. I knew it was far more than that. I got a glimpse of her and I wasn't sure it was human. The situation she described was complex in its betrayal to the people in her life.

After I took my mother home, I sat down at my computer. I was alone in the condo that weekend. I brought up the word Narcissistic and I began to read about the personality disorder. It took all my strength not to collapse in my chair. All the things about my mother that I had been dealing with over years, particularly after my father passed away were in front of me now like a manual; the Narcissist rages when anybody would challenge her, imbuing the people in her world with special qualities because she associated with them, lying whenever it would suit her. I could understand now that it had worsened when her primary supplier of attention, my father, had died. The abuse to the suppliers of attention was synonymous with breathing for the Narcissistic. Her needs from them and others would ultimately amount to betrayal.

She sentenced my father to hell without hospice care to deny that he would stop supplying her needs in death. I had taken my father's place. I began to count instances of her betrayal of me in important things over time. There was a constant theme of the attention from men, which would grow over time into a worsening picture of every man she associated with having some kind of plan with her to take her away from my father. Those were her secrets that had come out little by little in a changing picture.

She had learned over time what it was appropriate to divulge. I would later equate that the truth would bubble up eventually from her like torn pieces of human flesh.

By June 8, 2006, I do not see my mother anymore. On that day, she calls our condominium, because the day before she sent a letter to Gary for an unknown reason to my address, with her decision to first modify and then withdraw an element of Gary's support in the institution in which he is housed, the original initiation of which and modification of which are all of her own doing and volition. It is not that much money, but it is crucial to his survival at the present time and which only she can provide, since I am completely out of work with an injured foot. She does this for arbitrary reasons related to her Narcissism.

Ryan picks up the phone when she calls, having read her letter and knowing her intent and what this will do to his Uncle Gary, and reasons logically with her from every possible basis on behalf of the well-being and survival of Gary. When it is hopeless and she is already well into a Narcissist rage, Ryan is forced to speak over her.

In his brilliance, he changes from the specifics of this current situation with his uncle and the continuing propagation of lies from her on this subject, as is customary to the Narcissism.

For his uncle and for me, who did not yet have the emotional strength to face this reliving of her potential for harm, he interrupts her yelling with three words and a date. He had only alluded in the past to her that I had remembered things from the past, but as was her characteristic she had always been impervious to any suggestion of blame. But, this time, for his uncle, for me, he says only:

"Marline, Marline, Beach Grove Motel. 1956."

When she understands what he has said, she screams at the top of her lungs that she cannot stand to hear what she has just heard. She hangs up immediately.

The most resounding silence I have ever experienced follows from that phone from her.

The next day when she leaves a voice message at our home on the subject of resuming Gary's crucial support, which she has decided to do as Ryan knew it would accomplish to keep Gary well, in her voice is the full knowledge and realization that what she has done and what she is are somehow known. At that time, we could never have imagined what that truly was.

On May 16, 2006, Joseph Dickson calls in response to a fax I sent him, after his return from being away. By this time, I have already contacted a historian in Tsawwassen to check archives of the local papers housed in a museum in Delta, for a report of a young boy being severely injured on Centennial Beach, although it was not so named then, during the summer of 1956. I realize that my decision to not visually see what I have acted out, including the notable omission of the impact of my mother's weapon against my brother, is my reliving of the onset of amnesia fifty years ago. I tell Joseph that the details from the mind of a two-year-old child were exact to the pictures that I have found on the Internet. I know by the sadness that I feel since remembering and the bath, that now I cannot think of a reason to live; but it is not that I am thinking this now, I am reliving that a two-year-old little girl feels she has no reason to live after what she saw. I will correct her amnesia with Joseph in a week.

On May 19, 2006, he conducts a session with me to explain the rapid eye movement I am experiencing since the phone call to him, when I view the picture of the ferry dock at Tsawwassen. It makes no sense that this dock should in any way be part of my returned memories of my brother's attack, and it confuses me and makes me cry, albeit that the ferry dock was in the same place as these events, but didn't exist for four years after his attack.

With Joseph's help I learn about my intense reaction to the ferry dock photo, that it represents my father to me, and what he did when my brother was attacked.

On May 19, 2006, at 11:00 AM, I emerge from Joseph's office in Arcadia, California with the memory of my brother as he was hit, the image of my mother swinging the weapon, the true amount of power and thrust like swinging a baseball bat to hit the ball far into center field, and the image of my father just standing by, just abiding.

The car ramp leading to the ferry that I had witnessed four years after my brother's attack was the gateway to my memories of my father's role in Gary's attack.

Instead of the image of a dock or pier opening up in my memories of the beach where Gary was attacked, this ferry ramp became my father, standing motionlessly watching, with the same beach opening up on both sides of him in the imagery. My father had replaced the dock my mind had transported from the ferry to one standing at Centennial Beach, as a place-holder for what was too painful for me to see before.

Joseph indicates that the car ramp at the ferries with its powerful steel mechanisms represented the masculine to me, on that later trip, where we had first seen the ferries in 1960 and then returned to the place of Gary's attack. The massive dock unlike anything I believed I had ever seen before, abides by its size over everything else. My father had just stood there, allowing my mother to perform the attack.

At the moment I recover the image of my brother, the moment of impact, that I reserved for exclusion when I had relived the onset of amnesia at home, I am sitting in Joseph Dickson's office in a white suit, with my head against my knees, and I am screaming, "Don't hit him! Don't hit him! Don't hit him! …" and then only "I love you, Gary. I love you, Gary." after it is too late, as many times.

I ask Joseph please, "What will I do with this image of my brother [at the moment of impact of the weapon]?" because I cannot make it fade once I see it, and holds the horror that I have seen. Gary's mouth is opened round, his fingers spread, arms up in horror. It is a look of frozen horror on his face. It reminds me of a cat we euthanized because she had cancer and was emaciated. When my son realized she was a skeleton beneath her fur, although having been under treatment, this was her expression at the moment she realized that she had been injected for death, instead of for treatment; the instant she died. Gary's face has a level of shock and realization that is frozen into my consciousness forever.

It is easy for Joseph or at least necessary for Joseph to say that I must retain the image, while I still cannot make it fade from horror. But, finally, it does, into an image of my brother's childish face, with an expression much more babyish than his five years of age, which he retained at times throughout his life until succumbing to complete mental breakdown, and which most importantly I have learned began immediately after the attack. That, is why I have always known the mental illness began with the impact to his head.

The fragments are beginning to come together. I tell a wonderful man about them, David Meyer, when I believe they are a complete picture and once again that I am living only in our known universe. By August 26, 2007, when David takes me to a barbeque at his pastor's house in Hesperia in the High Desert, I already sense once again the universe that is parallel to my own.

My first year at USC was filled with the challenges of the weed-out courses. In particular, Fundamentals of Physics I, Mechanics, Heat and Sound. The professor was German and his job was basically to let students know if they were in the wrong area of career aspiration by even dreaming of a career in physics. He would stand at the front of the large lecture hall, and slam the pointer he used to highlight which equation he was displaying behind him on the board, and when that pointer slammed on the podium, he would scream, "You will (pronounced vill) learn!" If anybody had any idea of doing anything else, it was quickly dispelled.

This class as all of my many physics classes at USC, placed me in direct competition with the Physics majors, who were the only other people besides Astronomy majors who had any reason to take the classes. These students were exceptionally good at Physics and I really hadn't spent any time working on cars as a young woman or doing much in the way of mechanical pursuits, which I felt would come to haunt me during the hours of laboratories associated with all of the upper division physics classes.

Fun Physics I, as it was abbreviated was the first of the progression of these challenging courses. During the final in this first year class, for whatever reason I will never know, the German professor decided to stand by my desk and watch me of all people take his final exam. I admit to being not entirely quick on the uptake for these demanding classes. He watched me struggle with the most difficult of problems on the test, and maybe because he was standing there, a light bulb that had been trying to go off in my head for the entire semester finally did. When it did after a great length of time, he screamed, "You got it!" and jumped into the air.

I wasn't sure what was more astonishing at that point, knowing that I got it, or watching him cheerlead my efforts when several hundred other students, nearly one hundred percent of them men, were there taking his test too. Sadly, for some who had studied at the very last minute and just couldn't get it right and had given up, he woke them up.

By the end of my first year I had achieved A's in every class, a 4.0 Grade Point Average, including an A on the dreaded weed-out course of Fun Physics I, I had earned right in front of the professor.

Things weren't all work and no play, although I slept only a few hours on the weeknights. My roommate, Anne Schnee, who was short and petite, like me, on several occasions made sure I didn't spend all my time hitting the books, and had fun too. One evening she simply put on everything in one drawer of her chest of drawers in the dorm room, several shirts at once, ski gloves, a few of pairs of socks, a nightgown, and sunglasses. I was sure to take a picture of her once she was done.

She once walked determinedly into the downstairs lounge at the dorms with a ladder and in front of everyone including dorm officials removed a very large sign that said WOMEN ONLY. When she got it back to our room unhindered, because no one who watched her deliberateness could even dream she had no authority whatsoever to remove this sign, she covered up the W and the O so that the impressive sign in our room would read MEN ONLY.

There were panty raids conducted by immature men from the men's dorms across the way that nearly resulted in me and countless other women getting trampled, as men too afraid to stop and collect any panties ran like herds of crazed elephants through the narrow halls.

There were bomb scares that "bombed out" the dorms and often sent us in our nightgowns into the neighboring prestigious classroom halls, in sleeping attire to wait it out until the threat cleared. An arrest made by the FBI, of a football player eventually and none too soon put a stop to those sometimes genuinely frightening exercises when police woke you up by pounding on your door in the middle of the night.

There was a surprise party for my birthday one year, which I ran to at top speed down the very long halls to where it was being held, because someone wisely told me they could see a UFO through the window at the end of that hall. And, there was an earthquake that woke me up to the screams of terrified young women, as sections of the dorms, at least from the inside appeared to crack off from other sections from floor to ceiling from the damage.

Anne and I had been chased across the campus one night by two horrible men from a USC movie being shown on campus; it was one of those things where you can tell something is not right just by the comments and demeanor of some people even before there is a problem.

Another night, Anne wrote a nineteen-page research paper for an important class of hers without ever visiting a library and there was no Internet to use back then. She was simply creative about the information and the sources she quoted. When I fell asleep the night before she had put off this massive project until it was due, she was in the same position at her typewriter as when I woke up. Her professor knew the paper may not have been thoroughly researched, but she did receive a passing grade.

One time, she had gone through all of my precious astronomy hand-written note compilations and annotated them with the cartoon characters that she drew in ink that looked a lot like the Microsoft Word paperclip "help" character. Anne meant it as a happy gesture. To this day, my valuable astronomy notes include the artwork. Over the years Anne and I have stayed in touch.

There were long lunches my friend and fellow USC student Celeste Myers (who later became Celeste Peters) and I had outside at the Student Union Building, eating salads bathed with delicious dressing before our Optics Lab. We shared the position of Astronomy Department Secretary in our junior year. We divided the work between one another and our individual schedules and everything ran smoothly.

Celeste would later leave USC and finish her astronomy degree elsewhere to marry Bill Peters, who graduated from USC Astronomy the year before I did. Celeste went off to a different life, which included authorship of many books. Bill became President and CEO of the Telus World of Science - Calgary. Celeste's and my life cross still at many points in deep friendship.

There were football games that spoiled USC students with enough victories to make it to the Rose Bowl Game on New Year's Day 3 out of 4 years that I was there. I attended some of these games with my brother and a girlfriend he had briefly. He had valuably invested his time in getting an Associates Degree at Pasadena City College and then transferred to USC, which he attended another year after I graduated to get his Bachelor's Degree in Political Science. He lived off campus at USC in an apartment. His living conditions by his own doing were deplorable. Yet Gary was ever-brilliant and his grades at USC were good.

No matter what was going on for me at USC, the influence of Gibson Reaves began to build in my life like a presence that answered my questions about science and about life. Gibson and his wife Mary and their young son Ben were staples of existence for many of the undergraduates. Gibson and Mary welcomed us into their family. Gibson was a magical force in my life that could only come from a person of complete honesty, integrity, and brilliance. Gibson made sure that I knew I was a spectacular student, I don't know, but maybe the best he ever had.

In 2007, the memories begin to return because of the safety I feel in Dave Meyer's presence. Some begin in his home, others in my home, intensified by the weekend, when whole days are lost in the turmoil of the leakage from a parallel universe. Some begin to happen at work, and many on the drive to work. These experiences are protracted and agonizing, and no longer with year-long breaks between them. I go from one to the next, minute to minute, day to day, and sometimes their effect spills over into the actions in the universe we all live in, that I perform, not even knowing what horror I am reliving, until it is upon me.

Dave and I are headed for Staples to pick up some office supplies, when I ask him, "What do I believe?" He of course cannot answer. He has held me in his arms, as I have wept the horrors from the soul of a child who has endured enough to have wished multiple times for her own death. He is patient, understanding, and astounding, as he has been his entire life, I am certain, long before I ever met him.

He goes in to Staples and I must stay in the car, in fact, I do so even in his house garage, when he goes inside. Memories come to the surface often there.

"What do I believe?" Finally, I tell myself, I don't believe anything, because it is too painful, I think. And then, "I believe they will kill Gary."

I turn to my side, beside me during the attack, was Gary being pummeled by Father, one of the first images of our abuse that had returned to me long ago. I saw my brother's picture in my mind, and my father, they were both there during the attack on me. I believed they would kill Gary, that is what I believed.

It was the next morning, when another memory came full circle to the first symbolic images I had ever experienced years ago. During the recollection of Gary being present during the attack yesterday, I pictured my mother's jewelry she had on during the attack on me. I had not seen this jewelry since the very first moments I had known I was raped by my mother years ago.

The jewelry reminded me of jewelry she had years after that.

I had years before pictured that my mother was wearing a zebra striped dress in later years after we came to the U.S. and that she was speaking in her most eloquent speech, and then began to spin into a sharp object. I knew now in her most eloquent voice, my mother had threatened to kill my brother after my attack. Calmly. As if she had done such a thing before, enough to be practiced. In her most eloquent speech my mother had told Gary she would kill him. Gary had seen everything they had done to me in that motel. My father had pummeled him to subdue him. It became clear to them what they had to do. My mother followed through.

———

The next weekend, I went from room to room in my house, as Dave napped, looking for a quiet place so that our dog would not bark to wake Dave to relive what my parents did next.

My mother and father set out walking with their children to the place they had selected, along the path from the Beach Grove Motel toward Centennial Beach, first thing in the morning. Gary is trying to convince them of something; he stays away as any child would in disbelief of what he knows my mother is going to do. He runs a far distance from her, away from the rest of us. I am being carried by my father. She screams at him to get him closer to her, when they arrive at the place I have Gwen Szychter take pictures of decades later; which Gwen says is completely isolated. My mother's rage and anger brings the sad boy toward her, like a helpless insect hooked to fly paper. He comes forward when he does not want to, he comes forward to a destiny he could not have envisioned for his young life; he comes forward to her.

He is on his knees, begging for his life. I scream and scream and scream in the only thing I can do to try to forestall what I know is coming. I know now the reason why images of his attack have always reminded me of old black and white or brown and white movies I have seen on television, the first ever made, that jerk along and seem to fade in and out; because my father was serving as a lookout, and I am in his arms, and he keeps turning!!!!!!!! I keep compensating for his turning body, twisting around which ever way works best so that I can see, as in the swivel chair I sat in when I acted this out in Arcadia, once finding Beach Grove on the Internet.

I have to see, I don't want to look. I scream!!!!! I am held by my father above the ground, I realize, as a person would be on a dock above the ground. My mother had only divulged one injury that she said Gary had over the many years of my life, and that his feet were badly cut when he was taken for a walk by two people; taken; the word has so much more meaning for me now.

I see my mother swing the weapon and his seizure, as it truly appeared from my vantage point, seamless, put together, like a video playing. I am in a closet in my master bedroom in Victorville, hoping to keep the dog quiet. I experience pain in both my hands.

I look down on my hands, after I had stood up and walked into a different room to get away from the dog's barking downstairs. I walked to a different room at the moment I escaped my father, fifty years before. I realized, as I look down on my hands that they were my feet back then, and I was experiencing searing pain in them. My feet are cut to shreds by the rocky terrain as I run to Gary; it wasn't just Gary whose feet had been sliced by the rocks. My mother had omitted me from the story all these years. Gwen said the terrain she saw would cut feet without shoes.

I see Gary's face two or three times clearly, he was unconscious. My world ended as I lay my body on his; I am destroyed, as my hair falls softly forward as I lay my body upon his body, it is the only comfort and sensation that I can feel, and hold my little arms under him.

In the bright, searing sunlight above me, my mother looks down on him, to see if he is dead.

Early in 1983, I did something I could never have envisioned. I stopped working outside my home to raise my children. Although I had clues about the importance I placed on parental responsibility to stay home with children, I had never applied that principle to myself, and had never believed my identity as an engineer and an astronomer could give way to that of being a mother. I would spend twelve years out of a formal workplace, although much of that time was spent in productive research and writing.

In the course of that time, I returned to JPL on more than one occasion, once to interview formally with my former Section Manager Frank Jordan about returning to the Laboratory, when my youngest child was still quite young. Circumstances changed at home and I no longer sought to return just then, and let Frank know.

In a vague sense, however, I began to visualize some scenes at the Laboratory from my many years there. They had to do with how things looked out-of-doors when I was aware of the how large and vast the Laboratory was around me, even when I was indoors there. My years at JPL exceeded even the exhilaration that I felt from the glorious four years I had spent at USC. What, I wondered, in some ethereal way, was I being haunted by at JPL? What did I not want to go back to that had played some part in my turning down the potential opportunity to return after not too many years?

The question like the one I had asked myself about USC after having graduated there had no answer. I was at home with my children and the importance of being a parent had made that decision.

Had I been keeping tally in a book whose pages I had never opened yet, though, I might have tallied another mark. I had not achieved my advanced degree, because I didn't want to go back to school, because of some haunting feeling that school gave me. JPL was a workplace I loved completely, yet in some way I did not want to go back there either. The second mark I tallied might have been for giving my career and my place in the life and times of my peers completely away as well.

———————

On February 2, 2008, I begin to tell myself it had something to do with my eyes. I take a picture of me as a baby, when I was about two off a nightstand I keep in my bedroom. I tell myself, "Her eyes have to become my eyes." I pull the picture of her eyes toward my eyes. It was then, I heard my mother say, "If you tell, I will kill you."

Later in the day, as I remembered more, my mother had pulled me off Gary's unconscious body, shook me by my arms until my neck nearly had muscle damage, and said this.

I realized in the morning immediately after I remembered her words that at that young age, because I was only two, I mistook them to mean that she would bring me back to the large place under the sky where the killing was done.

I realized now that is why I could not return to any of the large scale places that had played a key part in my life; the institutions which covered a lot of ground in their many buildings under the sky, like where my parents had taken my brother and me that day in 1956, once I had left them.

I didn't want return to JPL after having Ryan, I didn't want to return to college after leaving either, I wasn't sure I could return to teaching Astronomy at Victor Valley College after winter break now.

I didn't want to die.

———————

Later that night, in February of 2008, Dave and I went to a meeting of the High Desert Astronomical Society held at the Luz Observatory in Apple Valley. Before, we got inside, while in the car, I realized that the onset of amnesia was coincident with my mother's threat.

I stood under that sky in my mind and realized that I had stopped all emotion with my mother's threat, that I had stopped all remembering. I had stopped the anguish of a million screams, but now as myself as the person who I am neither two nor fifty-four, I screamed under that sky for the first time in over fifty years. It was my scream. It was me.

These things had not happened to a two-and-a-half year old child, who was separate from me. They had happened to me.

I was reciting to myself, this is who I am. This is who I am. This is what happened to me.

———————

On March 16, 2005, I have jury duty. My primary physician, overseeing the care of my foot, doesn't understand the injury in the same way the podiatrist does. She protests my high heels that I continue to wear, and I cannot express to her satisfaction the comfort that shoes like this always afford me, especially now that I was injured. Shoes like this that I have worn my entire adult life, have thick rigid platforms under the ball of my foot and prevent to a large extent the pressured bending at my toes where too much force was applied holding the heavy equipment I used for Mt. Sierra College for long periods of time, hunting teachers to cooperate with the college-recruiting presentations on high school campuses. What I will experience with this injury is but a small fraction of what my son Ryan will undergo over years of injury from his disastrous surgery. Had I never experienced nerve pain, I would never have been able to imagine the world in which he has lived, what he has endured, and how he has stayed alive only for his two children.

Dr. Gomez insists that I wear low heel shoes, in fact, athletic shoes. I hear her and the specialist Dr. Ferrante repeat this insight so many times, I eventually give in. And beyond that, Dr. Gomez insists that I can attend jury duty, despite the fact that three hours on my feet is the maximum I can stand at this point in my treatment, probably only because there is enough swelling still left in the foot to mask pain, and I have been reduced to tears from pain and postponed the jury duty as many times as I possibly could until March 16, 2005, when postponement was no longer an option.

At this point, I hadn't learned to stop doing activity, period, prior to the onset of pain caused by the activity. I would eventually learn to do very little, when no treatment was successful enough to prevent what would always happen from normal activity. I hadn't even learned to lock my heel when I walked, as I at some point trained my mind to do to encase my own injury in some protection from pain. Once I was given an MRI and the injury better understood by myself and the physicians, I would never have been granted leave to attend jury duty in Los Angeles, parking at the very top of a parking structure and a series of at least six flights of stairs with no elevator, four long city blocks from the courthouse and a days worth of on and off walking within the long corridors inside, let alone in athletic shoes, which proved detrimental to the injury because they did not provide enough rigid support as I walked.

But, I was granted no such disposition from the duty. It actually made no sense; this was as much activity as a person would do in a workday. If I could do this type of jury duty, I could simply go to work; forget I had ever been injured. It was a mistake.

I sat amidst the large numbers of people also called to the superior court in Los Angeles that day, wearing a blazer and blue jeans to go with my athletic shoes. That alone made this day different, because I seldom wore jeans anywhere. I had never served on a jury. I had at one time brought Ryan as an infant to jury duty in Riverside County, California, which prided itself on no one ever getting out of jury duty, including women with their children in tow. Sure enough my baby came with me just as in the news coverage newspaper clippings on the walls of that smaller potential juror's waiting room, which showed women with their children waiting to serve. But, I had been dismissed on that day before being selected for a jury, and never even obligated to come to the courthouses through telephone pre-selection other times I had been notified to serve on other courts.

I thought about what kind of case I might be selected to serve on today, if selected; Jerry Hyder, my former husband, had often served on cases and seemed to enjoy this service. He had after the conclusion of one trial where he served, mentioned that his case had been a robbery case. As a young man, Jerry had been a prison guard.

I imagined what type of case I might get, as I sat and waited with the other prospective jurors; a newspaper with open employment opportunities in the classifieds, kept me occupied. Having never been injured in my life before beyond anything that kept me from accomplishing life's tasks, I psychologically, as well as the doctors it seemed, hadn't adjusted to the severity of the injury. I envisioned that if I was able to get a new job that didn't require constant lifting, that I could just go upon my way, not having been exposed to enough examples over time of what this injury did to my ability to function. If one's foot is aching so much as to reduce one to tears, a person is shut down, completely.

My name is called. I think perhaps I will get a case of business fraud or like Jerry of robbery. These are the only two types of cases that occur to me. It doesn't occur to me it is possible that the case will be for violent crime. A young man sits accused as the lawyers begin to question the prospective jurors selected for this case, in the courtroom, of violent attack against two other men. I am already upset when I realize this is the crime that I am being interviewed to serve for. I am trying to sort out what is bothering me most. For one thing, this is too soon after Paul having deserted me. I am still experiencing shock. I don't belong in the courthouse at all, let alone the ability to show up here everyday with my foot as it is. One day will prove too much.

The attorneys for the defense and prosecution prepare to question the prospective jurors about our service. The judge is lecturing us on the importance of our service. I am afraid of being around the young man who is accused of committing the violence. I don't want to be here. We, the prospective members, with only several additional of us beyond the twelve that must be selected and the necessary alternates, sit where the jurors will sit during the trial in this courthouse. There is not that much distance to the young man accused of the violence.

The judge is skilled at lecturing people of diverse backgrounds and education. Some of us are professionals, others laborers and he is able to rationalize the complaints against service in these various "languages" and perspectives that are being expressed. He is highly skilled, very good at this.

I decide what I will do and on the basis that I will do it. I will ask to speak privately to the judge. I cannot dismiss from my mind that this young man in this courtroom is automatically guilty, because he is accused. I am capable of intellectualizing any situation and know intuitively that I could successfully fight the automatic urge that I am feeling about the violence of which he is accused, since his well-being would be at stake, but I know my compulsion is to not be able to see things clearly because of the violence I have been exposed to in my life, because of my brother. Also, I cannot stand to be around the discussion of violence, I have a terrible feeling about it as I have in shadow all my life.

It is hard to imagine now, but on this date of March 16, 2005, all that I have yet remembered in returned memories is that my brother was indeed taken and hurt by two people, and I had been present when this happened. My mind has not allowed me to remember that it was my parents who "took" him. My mind has not allowed me to remember our sexual abuse. My mind has allowed me to witness Gary's seizure when these two people hurt him, but in what way I didn't know, except my mother's claims that his feet were cut by sharp rocks when she and my father agreed to let these strangers take him for a walk, an unlikely story as it is.

As I wait for my turn to talk about my background and whether or not I have any circumstance to prevent this service, I am overcome by a feeling of familiarity that I do not understand. I am familiar with some aspect of my being here in the courtroom. I do not know if the feeling is specifically being familiar with the violence or the system's response in the law to such violence, but I know something about this. It is familiar.

The judge allows me to approach, with the attorneys at my side. Everyone else goes away in my consciousness. I ignore the fact that the judge's microphone is left on and people in the courtroom are protesting they can still hear me when I begin to speak, as this conference of this type is suppose to be protected by privacy, but I don't care. I tell the judge, two people committed a violent act against my brother and I am just recalling it at this age that I am in flashbacks. The judge sees something in my eyes, because then I see something in his. There is a connection here.

I do not tell the judge that the people are never brought to justice. Then, I envision them as two faceless strangers who got away with their crime in my parents bad judgment and confusion in allowing their five year old to accompany two strangers. I cannot tell the judge, what I do not know then, that these two people were my parents.

I sit and wait as others are interviewed. One other woman asks to come to the judge and speak in the same way that I have.

The attorney for the defense asks please if I could not still make a sound judgment in this case, since my background in science has been made clear to her, and I concede that intellectually that I believe that I could, but frankly that I am upset to be here.

At the end of all the proceedings that day, the judge calls two numbers. One is my juror number. He says I am excused to go home. I feel and am genuinely shocked. He sees that in my face. He has helped me. I look toward him in gratitude.

But, from the standpoint of a two-year-old child, I will never forget his old and comely face. Intellectually, I know he was not that much older than I, perhaps fifteen years. Intellectually, I recognize that in that room, as did he probably, that our backgrounds of education and accomplishment might not have been too different than one another. Yet, I cannot help but see him from the standpoint of a child.

This wonderful man helped me on that day, and understood.

My foot was damaged so badly from my one day of jury service that it took me two weeks to recover from the setback and reduce the pain to a level I could deal with.

In January of 2008, as I drove with Dave along the main street in Victorville, I got a glimpse of a memory of the sheets of a hospital bed and a nurse. I knew then that I had been taken to the hospital after Gary's attack. Because of my recognition of the vintage police car circa 1950s on the Internet during my initial search of Beach Grove, I surmise I was taken by police there.

On February 3, 2008, I got into a bath to wash my hair. When I lifted my left hand from the water, it stung in a million places. There was pain when the nurse bathed me. My flesh was torn in many places. I had died from that attack and God had given me the choice to return. My skin on my feet was shredded as well. The pain during the bath was nearly unbearable.

I remembered the nurses moving around very officially and the red marks on their white caps. I believe they had blue aprons on, perhaps stripes in the dresses or aprons they wore.

I stayed in agony in the bath with Dave holding my other hand to comfort me. My left hand froze in pain for about 20 minutes to half an hour. I would later learn how to manage such a return of pain much better at home. It is the most pain I have ever experienced, back then. It had no end. They hadn't given me anything for the pain.

Later, a doctor the age of the judge who had dismissed me from jury duty in adulthood after Paul had left me, came into my hospital room. I saw the look in his eyes. There was no inkling of pity, or sympathy, there was only understanding. Understanding that went deep enough that I could sense the reflection of what he had seen in my brother's condition, perhaps in a neighboring room in that hospital, in his eyes. He understood. He must have given me something for pain, and I began to sleep.

In an analysis of what happened to me and to my brother via the help of historian, Gwen Szychter, I have deduced this doctor was responsible for the end of our abuse.

I am weeping on the bed in Victorville, California, inconsolably. Dave and I had already learned that I had seen God as a child and been given a choice to live, and in our religious perspective, the beauty of this experience was the fulfillment of our prayers to God everyday of our lives, and signaled the end of my memories.

Joseph Dickson had listened in complete silence via telephone to my report of what God had done for a small child; a tiny being who mattered to the Almighty Being of our existence. It was a religious affirmation that meant that all of what I had endured, all of what all people on this Earth endure is fulfilled in what God has promised us.

Earlier in the day, Dave had been interested in downloading some music via computer. He asked about a song, I later remembered was called *White Rabbit*. I explained to him what I had heard about that song decades ago, its symbolic meaning to the drug culture. Eventually, I began to hear in my mind, the sick cadence of a drum beat that grew from that song in my head. I was weeping in complete desolation, inexplicably telling Dave, "I think I know something about a sub-culture!"

Joseph Dickson had warned me over and over again to get a therapist in my local area, since my move to the High Desert. He had kindly agreed to continue seeing me via telephone sessions, and Dave had driven me "down the hill" to see him a couple of times. Now, I realized why. I had answered where and when my mother had attacked me and my brother, but never why. I was so busy staying alive from the onslaught of memories and the excruciating way the horror would emerge from the parallel universe, that I could not see the obvious. I was two and a half when these things occurred. What made them occur had to have happened before.

I contacted the office of Connie McDonald in Victorville. It was my incredible good fortune to have attended a department meeting for the physical sciences at Victor Valley College only weeks before, and met the other faculty members, beyond the Astronomy instructors, who of course, I knew. One instructor was the husband of Connie McDonald. Although Connie was not accepting any new patients, her husband David picked up the phone when I telephoned the office of the counselor I had found on the Internet, during a business trip I was making for the Lewis Center for Educational Research, which was my other job. I would work the two jobs, one at the college and the other for the Lewis Center for more than two years, and nearly exhaust myself beyond reason; this I did gladly in the support of my son and his family. This instructor at Victor Valley College, after listening to why I was looking for a new therapist, realized that his wife was the best person I could possibly get, and appealed to her on my behalf. Connie McDonald agreed to take me as a patient.

Joseph was kind enough to see my one last time in the transition between him and Connie. I asked please if I could descend the cavern with no bottom that I had symbolically envisioned, that was a caricature of a demon moving downward on a ladder of stairs into perhaps hell, moving its hips with horrendous iconoclastic blaspheme as it went, in the safety of Joseph's office. I saw small thumbnail visions in that session, which would forecast the next two years of memories.

At some point in those two years, I would learn that the object my mother attacked me with at Beach Grove, was a cross.

———

In the first of these ceremonies, the person at the front of the altar, clothed in a long robe, used an apparatus to shake a baby. Apparently, the knowledge that shaking an infant can kill is not new. It leaves no marks. I fragmented into three people the day I was shaken in that ceremony near the altar of this dark place.

I rose up and saw myself watch myself in like a snow globe that children shake until the objects inside scatter into a snowy storm. Inside this object, as I watched myself look around as a baby, I rose above the steel and harness apparatus that encased me as the leader of the ceremony shook the baby.

I did not die.

My mother was so angry that I did not die, that when she took me home, she placed me in her pedestal sink in the bathroom of our apartment, and filled the sink with water and pushed me under. She knew she would be caught and that there would be evidence of drowning. But, she was angry, very, very angry.

I told Dave as he sat near to me, more than half a century later, don't become frightened no matter what happens next. I could feel the fear that was about to come on me. I remembered my mother swinging the knife she brought, and stabbing me as I lay in the water. I was lecturing students at Victor Valley College when I remembered the knife got me in the abdomen. In Connie's office before I remembered what my mother had done, I remembered the color rendition of a dress she is wearing that day, found in black and white family pictures taken on my first birthday. The water filled with my blood.

She contacted her sister Nora and brother-in-law, who understood what had happened. I was taken to the hospital and operated on. They used no anesthetic on a child as young as I was.

I felt a kind of pain that is indescribable and I screamed with my face held upward as I remembered it later in the evening with Dave, as I rose above into the light of the operating room.

God's voice said to me, "You are not done with life yet, Baby Angel." I was told to live. I was named Baby Angel.

I play among the objects that the operating room light scattered into as I rose, like stars. God knows I am there. This is His place. He barely takes any notice of me as I play among the stars, and perhaps with other baby angels.

Trade the pain and earthly concerns for what you are doing, I realize. There is only worship and the objects in the universe. Objects in the universe, of God's creation. I became an astronomer at the age of much less than one year.

You don't sing to God in a chant like I would come to remember so clearly, in this realm, you instead worship. That is why the universe is so big, we can view the objects for eternity.

To span the depth of consciousness, the universe must be that large and that intricate. I am doing now, what I will be doing later. My mother is Earthly, put her aside. Spend your time in worship of the objects in the universe, made by God's creation.

Then, I hear, "Those who die as babies…Send your soul to God…Say goodbye." I was given last rights at the hospital with my parents and my Aunt and Uncle present. I think, "You are dead for now, Baby Angel. Fly Away." The blue of heaven turned into the post-op, and the deep red colors of my wound.

I would spend a lot of time in that wound, remembering the fat belly of a kitten Ryan and Michelle had, and why I could see the layers of the kitten's belly in my mind's eye, as I had seen the layers of my own flesh. I spent a lot of time in that wound of mine as a baby, it represented death, and I didn't want to die, and it would feel like it was tearing when my father would rape me.

Save Me

Gibson Reaves had invited me into his office at USC in the basement of the old Science Center Building, stacked nearly to the ceiling with books, in some fabulous dusty image of everything a person would ever expect a sagely professor's office to be.

He told me the University had done some work for Jet Propulsion Laboratory and had taken some plates that JPL was using for ephemeris, orbit refinement, work for the satellites of Jupiter. He had spoken to an engineer there named Fred Peters and asked about employment opportunities over the summer. Gibson had a name for me to call.

This incredible opportunity was done quietly as Gibson did all else for the betterment of every student. Much later, he would tell me such news as this when he suggested to a man named Ted Bowell that a minor planet he had discovered should be named for me for my discovery of active volcanism on Jupiter's moon Io.

My accomplishments in college were not all in my science and astronomy classes. Professor Wesley Robb was a dynamic man, whom I had the good fortune to have for a class in Human Values in the Department of Religion. Out of the hundreds of students in this class, I was one of only two who were asked to help write the final exam. In our discussion section, which broke down the lecture into smaller groups held by a Teaching Assistant, we were asked to write an essay on our human values. I wrote a one-page essay.

The Teaching Assistant was a young, nearly albino man, whose sharp features on his face were eye-catching. I had written, of course, about the desire that was fundamental to my love of Astronomy, my desire to help and improve the human condition. When I got the essay back, he had written across it, "Interesting!

Altruism. Where does it come from?" Even then, I knew this written comment would stay with me.

Then, I hadn't realized that altruism was unusual at all. It's a quality I had attributed to all people in the absence of any other information. Now, I think that I had never wondered where any of my points of view came from or anybody else's if the thought was not something positive. Primarily, I didn't question. That characteristic was equally as ingrained as the altruism.

I was perhaps the first Teaching Assistant in the Department of Astronomy at USC (there may have been one other time the department may have gone this direction) and because the department had no graduate division, I was an undergraduate. Such an accomplishment, which could be viewed that the opportunity was created because of me, only occurs to me now. I just took to the work and did it.

I held two discussion sections per week going over the main material of the introductory astronomy course, "Astronomy 100," given by Professor Reaves. Subject material included everything from the history of astronomy, to stellar evolution, description of celestial objects and their motions, basic equations such as relating stellar apparent magnitudes (brightness of stars) to distances, and exposure to extragalactic astronomy and cosmology (the study of the how the universe was formed).

I graded homework and laboratory type assignments for my students by the hundreds on a nearly weekly basis. I kept records of the student's homework grades and of their attendance. I attended regular weekly meetings with Professor Reaves and second semester Professor Russell, for the discussion of grades, problems as they arose concerning the progress of the class, and planning for the next week to come.

I proctored during all major exams, gave quizzes which I graded and recorded, to my individual discussion sections, gave planetarium shows, held office hours (which were so well attended that I would be forced to move from my office to an adjacent classroom to go into a lecture format), and produced a set of lecture notes by attending the main lecture of Professor Reaves three times a week, which were displayed without being recopied, and proved valuable to the students.

I gave one main lecture to three hundred students in the class, a presentation on the Hetzsprung-Russell Diagram as a stellar age indicator. I was so exceptionally shy that talking in front of such a large group of people was terribly hard for me to do. It would be years before I would be able to accomplish this equally as well without memorizing every word I would say.

The teaching skills proved valuable long before they would play a primary role in my life. The clashing of brainpower against a type of teaching I consider raw equation teaching in the upper division physics classes went on for me. My Quantum Mechanics Professor whispered his lectures and refused to use a microphone. The physics majors struggled and the lectures were useless. But, I tried very hard to extract anything from them that I could when others had given up long ago.

I sat as close to the front of the classroom as was possible to hear the whispers. One day, the professor whispered, "If you do all the homework in this class you will pass." Half the class failed because the exams were impossible. I did all the homework, and passed.

My study methods were done alone, I couldn't study with a group. A wonderful young astronomy major Mark Giampapa probably studied with me to make sure I wouldn't do any better than he did during for one of Gibson's challenging Extragalactic Astronomy tests.

I played along with Mark and then hit the books the only way I knew how. I had been doing it all my life. Nothing was left undone. I got a higher grade than Mark and Mark was genuinely surprised. But, this had its disadvantages. My Physical Optics class final was open-book. I studied much differently than I would have for a closed book exam. In the first minutes of the test, Professor Ogawa said close your books. It cost me a top grade in that class.

But, the teaching sent me to the top of upper division Electricity and Magnetism. As a final project of a course that was literally a year long, two semesters, the students were told to teach the class any concept of their choosing.

The physics majors in large quantity overextended themselves with devilishly sophisticated concepts far beyond their reach. Furthermore they couldn't teach, and had no experience on presenting their material to their fellow students. Most bungled it. I took a simple concept that a form of a laser is replicated in nature in interstellar dust and gas clouds. I re-presented the material our course had offered us over the last semester in that context, and I did it well, with the experience I had gleaned from the Department of Astronomy Teaching Assistantship.

I learned from this that I was equally as effective if not more so than many of the students whose IQ's were higher than mine, although mine has been measured at the genius level. Too, my sensitivity to how a course is taught is reflected in my desire to be an excellent teacher. My grades in college are blueprint for the quality of the teaching I received.

The way that my mind works is not typical for engineers, I do not believe. One engineer in particular who I locked heads with during my discovery and who caused me the most grief probably cannot to this day understand the type of value of my brainpower, which combines quantitative and qualitative strengths. It implies weakness to him that there is a qualitative element. It should not. It is the very reason I made my discovery and he dismissed it.

I am not dismissive either of the differences between the way people's minds work, there is absolute necessity for both kinds of brainpower, those exclusively quantitative, and those not exclusively so. I can never aspire to the ideal of what I found in Gibson Reaves' division of the two. Yet, I can approximate it.

I find that the people whom I most admire can recognize this value in the way my brainpower is applied. In working with the programmer who worked for me on The Optical Navigation Image Processing System, which performed the optical navigation image extraction for Voyager, Joe Donegan, we could see that one of our computer programs was not functioning as it should. Joe looked at the image of the ellipse the program had done on the computer screen. "What is it doing?" he said out loud as we attempted to pinpoint the error. "It's erasing itself each time," I told him, instead of building on the image. He looked at what was happening and at the code.

"How did you know that?" he asked.

———————

On a beautiful California sunlit day, June 6, 1974, I was awarded my Bachelor of Science Degree in Astronomy from the University of Southern California, Cum Laude. The young man I was married to at the time David Morabito, received his Bachelor's Degree in Electrical Engineering. Gibson Reaves was present with all of the Astronomy graduates.

After the ceremony, someone walked up to Gibson whom I did not know.

Gibson said to them, "I would like to introduce Linda Morabito. Astronomer."

———————

On June 16, 1977, I submitted my application for Mission Specialist Astronaut Candidate for the Space Shuttle program to the Lyndon B. Johnson Space Center in Houston, Texas. Finally, civilians, not just military personnel and not just pilots, would be given the chance to fly in space. This would be the first of three interfaces I was to have with the Space Shuttle.

The most recent was nearly twenty-six years later on January 16, 2003. I attended the launch of the Space Shuttle Columbia (Flight STS-107) with Dr. Neil deGrasse Tyson, Astrophysicist, Director of the Hayden Planetarium in New York, and then member of the Board of Directors of The Planetary Society.

The Planetary Society was founded in 1980 by Dr. Carl Sagan, Dr. Bruce Murray, former director of Jet Propulsion Laboratory, and Dr. Louis Friedman. The organization's mission statement is to inspire the people of the world about the exploration of space. I was at the launch of Columbia as the Society's Manager of Program Development.

We had an astrobiology experiment on the mission. Neil deGrasse Tyson, a brilliant man, had arranged for the two of us to receive VIP treatment on the day of the launch. We traveled in one of the NASA Administrator's busses from the space center to the viewing area, which was as close as anyone could get, passing a few Florida alligators on the good-size trek via bus along the way. Sean O'Keefe, the former NASA Administrator gave a special presentation for our group just prior to the launch.

The night before, as our entire team was assembled, we dined at one of the nicest restaurants in the area. Neil was filling our minds with the reasons space exploration or any form of exploration had been supported by political leaders historically and his fascinating thoughts were not lost on another diner there. The wife of Illan Ramon, Israel's first astronaut, had been listening.

It was only hours before her husband's shuttle mission would blast off into space. When she finished her dinner, and before she left the restaurant, she came over to our table and said hello and passed out shuttle pins made specifically for her husband's mission, which were precious keepsakes. Her calmness infected me.

Members of our team were at the Cape awaiting Columbia's return on February 1st, sixteen days later. I had returned home to Pasadena right after the launch. It had been a difficult, but rewarding trip for me. Ryan had not been feeling well when I left, in fact, he had been losing quite a bit of weight. He was my only child still at home, his older half-brothers, Brett and Jason, all sons of Jerry Hyder, mathematician and former JPL contractor, had left their father's home some time ago for careers of their own. I had been there sixteen years, raising all three children.

Ryan's health issue was about to launch him on a serious adventure of his own; it was a flair up of his appendix that was never diagnosed as such until after his appendix surgery, which both saved his life and sentenced him to a life of pain from surgical errors. I was so nervous about Ryan being so ill when I left to attend the shuttle launch, that waiting in the line for my return flight at the airport in Florida for security check I was singled out for special observation by my anxious behavior.

At 5:59 AM, Saturday morning, February 1st, Ryan was still working on his computer in our home and watching CNN, when they reported NASA had lost communication with Columbia.

Ryan rushed into my bedroom and woke me up immediately. He told me communication had been lost with Columbia. NASA does not lose communication with a shuttle during re-entry. It meant only one thing.

Ryan was just over three years old when he saw the Challenger Space Shuttle explode at launch on TV in January of 1986. On board was Mission Specialist Astronaut Judith Resnik, who had submitted her application to become a Shuttle astronaut at the same time I had in 1977.

I scrambled downstairs and called the director of The Planetary Society, Louis Friedman at his home. His wife Connie answered and I am afraid I was crying and quite breathless. I kept repeating, "Tell Lou to turn on the TV!"

The seven astronauts of Space Shuttle Columbia were already dead.

———

In the spring of 1974, Jet Propulsion Laboratory and The Aerospace Corporation, whom I only briefly remember speaking with me when they came to USC, offered me full-time, salaried Engineering positions. This was as a degreed Engineer, not as a non-degreed Technical Assistant as I had spent the summer before at JPL. I accepted JPL's offer and declined the Aerospace Corporation's. Dave Morabito, whom I had married just before my senior year at USC and I moved to an apartment in La Canada right by JPL. I began work immediately. This would be the real thing.

On my way to work at The Lewis Center for Educational Research in 2008, I began to remember a sound of chanting. It was amazingly beautiful, and disturbing.

Sadly, I once had a fairly reasonable singing voice. A college roommate of Dave Morabito's in the apartment in which he lived at USC, once told me I sounded like Joan Baez, when I was singing along with a group of their friends in their apartment. But, my years of screaming, wailing, and crying from the horrors of my returned memories over many years, destroyed any portion of the acceptability of my voice when singing.

When it first began to happen, I sang this chant in a most powerfully even and resonant voice, without words, only the melody. It would rise in the reconstruction of it from my memory in voice, to where the once solid voice that I had was once again resounding, sending the foreboding chant around the inner walls of my car, as I drove to work in Apple Valley at the Lewis Center. I would think about my mother.

I would wonder if my mother had a record player and a record of this uncannily frightening eerie and melodic chant. I remember asking Connie McDonald in one of my first sessions with her, if my mother might have had a long playing record of this chant.

But, by the time I would arrive very near the kiosk entrance to the Lewis Center, the chant had changed to the most unholy sounds that my mouth had ever emitted. It became the deepest type of sound that one would expect from Linda Blair in *The Exorcist* during the time she was taken over by a demon.

I had never made or imagined such guttural sounds in my life. And, then when I pulled into the parking lot there, everything, all recollection would stop.

It took me nearly a year to consciously draw the connection of my trek to work each day, to what I had seen as a child on visits I had made to Hell. (This comparison stems *only* from the following;) Coincidentally, there were double railroad tracks in a journey to a place of atrocity, and a similarity *in appearance only* to where I had ended up, passing a Mormon Church, which is only moments from the Lewis Center.

Right away, when I had first seen her, Connie McDonald understood what had happened to me as a child. Like Joseph Dickson, I give Connie my heartfelt and unending gratitude as I would to any people who had saved my life. They both did so many, many times, helping me to raise up the memories of unimaginable abuse, and then to live through them, again. I could not have been more fortunate than to have found Joseph Dickson, and then beyond any imaginable good fortune, to have then found Connie. Connie hoped it would only take a year to get through the remainder of my journey through time. She underestimated that by not too much, fortunately.

She warned me, "Linda, you might never know where and why, exactly." Ever so fortunately, she wasn't right about that.

In early 1977, Tom Duxbury, my Group Supervisor at Jet Propulsion Laboratory, had a wonderful idea. On June 19, 1976, the Viking 1 spacecraft went into orbit around Mars, and shortly thereafter, on July 20, the Viking 1 Lander landed on the surface of Mars. A second spacecraft, Viking 2 reached Mars orbit on August 7, 1976 and the Viking 2 Lander also landed successfully on Mars on September 3, 1976. A spectacular mission followed from these four craft, two orbiters, and two landers on the surface of Mars. There are not many of us who can ever forget the unprecedented look of the Martian terrain at the two landing sites in pictures taken by the Viking 1 and Viking 2 Landers; the Martian red rocks spread over an alien, yet beckoning landscape and breathtaking Martian sunsets, that so resembled Earth's.

Tom, in his ingenious way, had figured out a way to locate the two Viking landers on the surface of Mars, in pictures taken by the cameras on the orbiters, to a higher accuracy than could be found any other way.

In the same way the Viking Landers were too small to be seen in pictures taken by the orbiting spacecraft of the surface of Mars, the driver of a car on Earth driving further and further away from a passenger they have just let off, can eventually no longer see the passenger standing in the road behind them. The passenger becomes just too distant a point to see or resolve with the human eye. This concept is called spatial resolution.

The smallest feature the Viking orbiter cameras could resolve or be able to see on the surface of Mars from Mars orbit was larger than the size of the small landers. Another way to state this is that the landers were beneath the resolution of the cameras and could therefore not be seen.

Tom envisioned that when the much larger shadows cast by the two moons of Mars, Phobos and Deimos traveled across the surface of Mars (the same way a cloud in the sky can cast a shadow on the surface of Earth), the orbiter cameras could easily see and take pictures of those shadows of the moons. If these shadows happened to pass over the two landers on the surface, then pictures of the shadows might be taken at the exact time they were right on top of the landers. You might not be able to see the lander in a picture taken by the orbiter, but if you could take a picture at the exact same time a lander went into darkness underneath a moon shadow, you would know the lander was somewhere underneath it.

In the example of a car driving away from a passenger, you might not be able to see the person you had driven away from if you got too far away, but you might still be able to see a large house the passenger walked into when you let them off.

You could say that you knew where your passenger was to the uncertainty of the size of the house. They were somewhere inside that house, and depending on how well you knew the location of that house on Earth, you could be closing in really well on the location of your passenger on Earth, at a moment when you couldn't even see the passenger.

In this way, this experiment utilizing all the Viking spacecraft in a cooperative effort, the two orbiters and the two landers, and the shadows of two moons on the surface of Mars, could be used to locate the positions of the landers on Mars.

Tom submitted the idea to Viking Extended Mission for consideration. Tom Duxbury and I would become co-investigators in the Viking Guest Investigator Program during the Extended Mission, if the experiment were approved.

When Tom received word the experiment had been accepted and we were on the Extended Mission, he drew a couple of diagrams, like stick figures in children's drawings, showing me vector geometry with respect to the Sun, the moons of Mars, the Martian surface, and the shadows. He handed me the diagrams, and said, "I am very busy. Go and do this." He had turned over, completely, a high visibility project of science investigation to a young investigator while leaving his name and reputation on this experiment to my mathematical, engineering, programming, and science skills. Tom had very good reason to do this.

When I accepted JPL's offer to become a full-time Engineer in 1974, I took off running from the point I had progressed a year before as a temporary summer employee. I performed the research, implemented and used for data planning, computer programs for the prediction of Earth-based observations of Jupiter, Saturn, Uranus and Neptune. I documented favorable planet, moon, and star opportunities for photographic plates to be taken from Earth, to be used for orbit refinement of the planets. I produced the means for identification and reduction of the observations.

I did utilize the software for plate reduction going from raw measurements to celestial coordinates. I performed the reduction of plates for the improvements to the orbits of Jupiter and the Galilean Satellites, Io, Europa, Ganymede, and Callisto, necessary for the upcoming Voyager mission to Jupiter.

This processing involved mathematical modeling of coordinate system transformations, and atmospheric properties that affected how the light from the images appeared when passing through Earth's atmosphere, among other considerations.

I performed a calibration of an observatory telescope with this program and began planning my first publications in the scientific literature from the work.

I began utilizing a Trajectory Geometry Program system for the prediction of spacecraft television pictures. With this software, I performed an in-flight calibration of the Viking cameras using about 200 star images taken by the Viking cameras. This work was published in *Applied Optics* in December of 1977.

Once I joined JPL in 1974, Tom and I became members of the Viking Flight Team, and we reported on Lab every day, instead of the Crest Building, to an area right next to the Viking Science Orbiter Imaging Team area, where all the orbiter imaging science was accomplished.

While working, we would periodically get up from our desks and observe never before seen images from the Viking Spacecraft, as we watched imaging team members peruse these images and marvel. It was during this time period that I met a senior engineer at the Laboratory named Louis Friedman. His co-founder of The Planetary Society some years later, Bruce Murray, was director of JPL at this time. It would be another 21 years before I would run into Lou Friedman again.

As members of the Viking Flight Team, Tom and I assisted the Viking Orbiter Imaging Team in the planning of processing of Phobos and Deimos pictures, and in data reduction of camera pointing angles and a revised estimation of Phobos' orbit. This required Image Processing analysis and was in preparation for the first time a Viking orbiter would encounter or pass very close to Phobos. These results were published in *Science* in 1978.

I also did work on better correlating what we saw on Mars to exact Martian latitude and longitude coordinates.

Tom had very good reason to believe that I could handle my first-ever autonomous implementation of an experiment on Mars, but it was still a very important step for me as any researcher. I began work on the project. I made the predictions when the shadows of the moons of Mars would pass over the landers. I made the predictions therefore, for when orbiter pictures of those shadows should be taken, and when sensors on board the landers should be checked to see if they became dark in broad daylight on Mars, as the shadows passed over them.

All of my predictions were translated into commands to the spacecraft by the sequencing teams for Viking. On October 11, 1977, nothing was left to do but wait and see if my predictions had been calculated correctly and if this experiment was going to work. I had only minutes to wait.

I entered the room where the data from the Viking 1 Lander would be returned. There were many technicians at work there. They acknowledged that they knew who I was, that I was the Investigator who had brought them here to do this work, and had made this experiment happen.

Before any pictures would come back from the Viking Orbiter 1, before any other form of confirmation that my calculations had been right, the Viking Lander 1 would tell the people in this room if the Viking Lander 1 had gotten dark in broad daylight on Mars, as though night was passing over it, under the shadow of Phobos.

The time was rapidly approaching for this event that either was just a calculation on a paper that I may have bungled or a real phenomenon happening on another world as I sat in this room, and I was terrified.

I actually remember looking for the nearest door to where I was seated. I have never done anything like that in my entire life, before or since, looked to find a door where I could escape from complete embarrassment from the other people, if something I did went wrong. And I would have, right out the door without a word.

I had never done anything this large, on a scale like this. It would be sort of difficult if this failed to gracefully say to the technicians about what had been programmed by my commands to the spacecraft, what I told it to do, never mind, don't worry, was just a big mistake, see you later. I held my breath waiting for word from Viking Lander 1. I wasn't sure I was even breathing at all.

Dave Curkendall, and J Frank Jordan, who had been Supervisor of The Satellite Orbit Determination and Planetology Group in Section 391 when I first came to the Laboratory and later became Section Manager, very senior men in my Division at JPL, took every opportunity to come and speak with me from the moment I joined the Lab as a degreed Engineer in 1974. It boiled down to the fact that people doing the type of work that I was doing all had advanced degrees. They were pushing me over a precipice of perspective in their eyes that I need to climb, to start moving down the other side, along a smooth career path to longevity.

For some reason, the thought of graduate school did not appeal to me, although I did not express that to them. I was certainly an astronomy-and-origins-of-the-universe type, and planetary science, the study of the planets exclusively, per se, was never what spurred me on all through my youth. There seemed to be more too it, however. A connection, I didn't understand.

By the time I fully understood the connection to my past about leaving JPL and not being able to return, and therefore losing my career in formal science, I had not yet mourned for the loss. The mourning over the horrific events of my childhood would often come last in memory.

I remember sharing the revelation with my son Ryan. On October 31, 2007 a former supervisor at the Lewis Center for Educational Research and I visited an area of JPL, one floor above where I had made my discovery of volcanic activity on Io, in Building 264 there. My former supervisor from the Lewis Center and I had spent the day in mission operations for the rovers Spirit and Opportunity on Mars.

At that time, I walked through the same halls where I had made my discovery in watching rover operations, albeit same building but different floor; similar layout and appearance. It was the same area, though, exactly, where I had many dreams over the course of Ryan's youth, returning to JPL there, and not knowing why I was there or what I was doing.

When I returned to the office by the end of the week, I printed out one of the pictures my former supervisor and I had taken for the Lewis Center when there; one for work purposes.

It was then that I told myself I must post that picture in my office at work and look at it always and never take it down. I knew by the oddness of this thought, it had something to do with my past.

I then mourned the loss of my entire engineering career to the parallel universe that had taken it away from me. When I told my son about this, he said, "Mom, you always talked about that dream the entire time I was growing up." I had not realized until that moment, that I had shared that lament over all the years of his life.

When I would travel on business, or any form of travel, Ryan would always remind others in the family in my presence too, "Mom always thinks she is going to die on any trip she makes."

———————

A couple of times, over the years as I raised my children, I had health scares. I lost hearing in my left ear and my sense of balance and had to undergo a stapedectomy at the House Institute for Hearing in Los Angeles, in 1992. I had a biopsy on two cysts in my left breast in 1994, which fortunately both turned out to be benign.

At these times, I would tell Gibson Reaves, I learned for the first time in life, when I had to stop, that I was running at all.

Gibson and I had remained close. He and his wife Mary had attended every significant celebration of milestone events in my life. Gibson had become family. Gibson's widow Mary and son Benjamin even attended my wedding to David Meyer on August 2, 2008, after Gibson passed away.

I was so motivated at all times in my life about work and family that I actually had never even noticed I was moving so fast until these health conditions, which had to be dealt with, slowed me down temporarily. This was sound self-discovery and in a way allowed me to realize how much ground I had been covering in a day, or any year, and that I had been making such remarkable strides all my life.

For the first time, I could see the still ground beneath the fantastic journey with respect to astronomy and space exploration I had been making. It was the farthest thing from anything I could have even dreamed during the vast, vast majority of my life, that overall I was doing anything but running toward goals.

If I had been told the truth about me was that I was running away from anything at all, I would never, never, never have believed it. As far as anything I knew, whatever "animal" it was that might drive a person to run from something had nothing to do with me. Maybe there were people who were like that. I hadn't an identity problem of any kind. I knew my life, I knew my history and exactly who I was.

I acquiesced in not too long a time to the higher wisdom of getting an advanced degree. Late in 1974, I took a graduate level course in Fluid Dynamics at UCLA, and did not enjoy it. I was very sensitive to the atmosphere at UCLA, which is why I hadn't gone there as an undergraduate. It's a fine campus, but I still had no feeling of connection with it, and the purely planetary science emphasis wasn't going to hold me hard and fast enough to the discipline, as I had suspected. Once the class was over, I had to make a decision.

Dave Morabito was continuing on straight through at USC toward his Masters and ultimately his PhD in Electrical Engineering. He did this while working as an Engineer at JPL too. Dave had started at the Lab through me, and for a short time also worked for Tom Duxbury. We had no mobility to travel anywhere for graduate work for me, therefore and because I was pursuing the advanced degree somewhat as a formality, Caltech in Pasadena didn't make too much sense. It would consume me and my work at JPL was already doing that.

Since there was no heart-felt goal that was driving me forward and really none that could be obtained by my need to remain near USC for David, I picked the logical thing to do. I loved computer science; it was an enjoyable passion and always had been. It made perfect sense for me to get a graduate degree in that field, and to pick it up at USC. Beyond even that, classes were televised right into JPL, and I could attend interactively without even driving to the campus. It was an ideal solution.

By the fall of 1975, I had begun graduate studies in Computer Science at USC. I walked up the steep streets of the JPL complex, higher into the hills, where one might see a coyote or a deer, although JPL split the rugged terrain with its signs of civilization, concrete walkways and some smaller buildings.

But, this building was high up enough to have untouched California desert hills on several sides, climbing to the top of the precipices around it. I was always completely alone participating in my graduate classes this way, at a desk in front of a television monitor, except for the presence of a JPL overseer, a technician in charge of keeping the interactive equipment going.

The cameraperson at the other end in a classroom at USC was obviously trying to keep things interesting for people like me, attending remotely. Once in a while, that person would pan the camera around the actual classroom to show the students listening, as well as the professor. On one occasion I saw a student or two asleep at their desks during the lecture. That didn't help, although I got A's in both classes that I took.

In the spring of 1976, I took a course called Compiler Design. This course taught how computers took high-level language coding (user friendly language such as Fortran or Pascal), and broke it down into assembly language, and then ultimately of course to machine language, which was combinations of 1s and 0s. The method of teaching compiling was to have the students actually write a compiler. This project was even to understate, massive. I found myself alone in a televised classroom center at JPL, with no team to join.

The students on campus were breaking into teams, and this type of isolation virtually made this project beyond what any one person could do in a semester.

Tom Duxbury was aware of the situation. It vaguely occurred to me why a group of students in the class at USC would want to include a complete stranger who they had seen perhaps only once or twice for exams on campus, in their group.

Tom told me that he was actively seeking another student who could jump right into the work that I was doing and take off running alongside me.

I went straight to campus for the next meeting of the class. I told Homa Taraji, an Iranian national studying and living in the United States, that there might be a job opening at JPL for which she might qualify if the most suitable candidate, after application. Homa told me the same thing. There might be an opening in her group for which, if I were qualified to help, I might obtain. Both of us were highly qualified, and I had found my group.

Homa was a tiny person, like I was. She was dynamite in so many ways. She was not only very beautiful, but she already had a couple of Masters Degrees she had already earned at different universities. She was in the process of picking up her third Masters Degree in Computer Science at USC when she did qualify to work at JPL. There was only one other student in our compiler writing group.

Homa eventually began working for Tom alongside me at the Lab. I always recall when I try on dresses at dress shops one of our characteristically fun-filled times together. Homa was considering dresses at an exotic dress shop, when the bodice of one of the dresses caught her eye. It was an odd dress to be sure. She said to me complaining about how large it was on top, in her wonderful Iranian accent, quite perturbed, "Just how big are these American breasts!"

That wasn't the only generality that Homa fashioned in our adventures. We were both young, both attractive, both in the prime of our youths, and we dressed immaculately. Homa introduced me to knee high boots with thin leather and thick price tags that we would wear with our lovely clothes, as a fashion statement. We bought the finest make-up brands in the high-end department stores. We were something together, but I think Homa was something more just on her own.

Homa had lived in Germany for a while. I don't think there was a person among us at JPL, after she joined the Lab, who was close to her who was not aware of the worldliness and rich-in-philosophy aspect to her character.

A generality she proposed that I couldn't have agreed more with was that there was no such thing as an American brother. She told me that in other cultures there could be relationships where men could truly be a friend to a woman like Homa or myself. I couldn't believe this amazing revelation. From what she was saying, it was theoretically possible that I might be able, somewhere outside the United States, to have a male friend.

Neither Homa nor I had ever had an experience of working closely with, or going to college with an American man who did not, at some point, want more out of the relationship. Homa and I would say this phrase often about there being no such thing as an American brother and laugh out loud.

When Homa came to work for Tom Duxbury, that made a total of three of us doing exceptionally good stuff in engineering, including someone Homa and I worked with on a part-time basis at the Lab, Adriana Ocampo, who was in the Earth-Moon Physics Applications Group of the Section when I started at the Lab in 1973. Adriana went on to receive her PhD in geology afterward, and did wonderful work in bringing space science opportunities to third world countries. Homa taught me a little bit of the Persian language. The word for "little person" or "little one" was pronounced "Koochoolu." Homa, Adriana, and I became known to Tom as the "Three Koochoolus." On the engineering front we couldn't be beat.

Life on Lab was idyllic, if that is meant to mean working many hours beyond full time. It wasn't always necessary to be on Lab first thing in the morning. When Dave Morabito and I first moved to La Canada, the apartment manager, who was seldom sober and had driven his car past his own parking spot right into the building one occasion, accused us of having Banker's hours. He wasn't present when we would return home at night, at 8:00, 9:00, or 10:00 PM or later as the rule and not the exception.

There was no such thing as an eight hour day, but the days were filled not in the frantic way that seemed to accompany the personal computer revolution, where the mentality began to give more and more work and responsibility to fewer and fewer people, with less and less in the budget.

This was the Golden Age of space exploration and everything was right at this time, not wrong. The days were packed just right. Yet, lunches were some kind of odyssey away from the highly technical work. Here the problems of the world were discussed and reduced somewhat to engineering problems, by myself, Homa, and our male Engineer counterparts. We would linger at a round table outside long after our food was eaten, usually with Tom.

I still found that I could not break down the impersonal nature of my co-workers, even those I felt closest to. There seemed to be some kind of a wall that defied really getting to know them. As much as I cherished these long lunches outside the JPL cafeteria in the California sun that allowed us to collect our thoughts and return to the technical work that dominated our lives otherwise, I eventually came to resent them for what they were not.

Perhaps it had something to do with the age difference between my co-workers and myself; I was indeed from the next generation. Somehow I didn't feel that I totally belonged in the engineering world, all of me, my heart as well.

There were no such boundaries for Homa and myself. We were always having fun. I remember following her in her car one day in mine, and watching her literally come up and down in her seat bouncing to the beat of music I knew she was listening to. I could follow along by the beat of her head rising up above the seat back. It was fantastic!

She forbade anyone to drive in front of her. Which meant, literally, that according to her no one had the right to ever be in front of her on the road. Of course, someone is usually driving in front of anybody in a car, so driving with her meant moving past these sinful transgressors who were in front of her who had no right to be where they were, one at a time.

Then, came time for traveling to Lick Observatory for measuring star images on plates that had been taken for use on the upcoming Voyager mission. In a dark room, Homa and I would isolate these star images mechanically with a machine (the Lick Gaertner survey machine), and tell it to take the measurements. The astronomer at the observatory must have asked us twenty times over every solid hour of this one day Homa and I did this work if we needed a break for the hundreds of star images we dealt with individually in the dark. Neither she nor I needed any break. By the end of the day we had directed the machine to the better part of 5000 stars' positions to be measured. There was nothing that we couldn't do easily and well. We had youth and a great deal of smarts on our side.

By the time she and I went to dinner in a really nice area in Santa Cruz, it was time for laughter; probably from too many long hours spent in those dark rooms. We spent our time in hysterics about a co-worker name George who was so serious that instead of coming from Missouri as we knew was his home state, we decided he must actually be from "Misery." After dealing with nearly 5000 stars, it seemed particularly funny at the time.

That went on until we were laughing so hard we nearly fell out of our chairs a couple of times. We weren't drinking, but went on disrupting the entire restaurant ad infinitum. Our waiter spent this sad and unfortunate evening for herself, circling the table of the two ladies killing themselves, on the verge of throwing us out, until we could collect ourselves just a couple of minutes before we were nearly evicted, to begin laughing all over again.

Homa and I turned in our compiler written in Pascal to the Compiler Design class. The number of lines of code in that card tray rivaled some of the computer programs we worked with at JPL. She would later marry an Iranian physicist, who got his PhD in New Jersey.

Years later, I would visit Homa on a memorable trip to see New York when she was living in New Jersey after having left JPL. For right now, everything was right in our world, our work at USC and our work at JPL.

When I got the opportunity, however, to be a Guest Investigator on the Viking Extended Mission and Tom turned that experiment over to me for its implementation, I stopped graduate school completely. One of the teachers I had during the brief graduate work I had done said when I told him I was leaving, "Then USC Graduate School in Computer Science is losing one of our most gifted students."

––––––––––

My world at JPL was completely distant from anything my parents knew or understood, although they totally accepted and applauded it.

My mother's sister, my Aunt Nora, who lived still in Vancouver, however, would constantly try to get her arms around it. She would ask during visits or on the phone, what I did. I would tell her I was an Engineer at JPL, and she would repeat the question.

She meant what did I do everyday; how did I spend each day at work. It seemed a hopeless exercise to walk her through a typical day of equation implementation, coding, debugging, running data, attending meetings, etc. It never made any sense to her.

As far as she could gather, each day I was launched to the moon and each day I came back, from what she could grasp. It had no substance in any world she had any reference to, and she was fairly well read.

On October 11, 1977, I could have told my Aunt if so inclined that I was in a room looking for the exits out of the corner of my eye to see if a spacecraft on the surface of Mars became dark under a shadow of a moon of Mars, Phobos, passing over. That is why it never made any sense to share the specifics of my work with my Aunt. How could anybody really grasp that is what one does for a living?

The technician looked at a reading and cheered. "It's dark," he said. "The Viking 1 Lander just got dark." I closed my eyes in the chair where I was sitting in that room with exits whose placement no longer mattered to me. As an experimenter on the Viking Extended Mission to Mars, I had just done what needed doing, a successful experiment on the surface of Mars.

––––––

I began to remember the aspects of an existence that was basically a criminal affront to any form of human behavior. This was what was inflicted upon me as a child.

In sessions with Connie McDonald in 2008, I remembered I had assigned animals as a baby to the characters in a saga that would ravage the mind and body of a child, who would later scream to David Meyer, at home one night, when remembering the edges of this universe, "It would have been so much better if I had died!"

I recovered what my daily life was like at home, with a mother like mine. The animals that I assigned to the various players would ultimately be either viscous dogs or cats, or birds with sharpened beaks, all of whom would attack at the lower portion of my body in savage rampage; a place that cannot be seen when a child is clothed. To my father I assigned the role of a zebra, flighty, but with teeth; the symbolism of which would thread through my memories, and land upon my mother in my first symbolic vision of her as an abuser, clothed in a zebra print dress.

I had recovered images of my grandmother, my mother's mother Rose, from the back of her, with out of body horrors I experienced, the exact conformation of her body, which I could never have reconstructed from family photos. Each relative who was involved did a particular horrific thing to me, a rape of some kind with a cross or a male member; I am certain of my grandmother, my grandfather, and quite possibly other relatives.

Although these memories have never fit into a complete ceremony, they stand out in vivid recollection of horror, and the soup of a purple sea at the base of Hell. I have an impression of which relatives may have been the worst.

When it came to clergy, there were men in robes, even a Bishop, who dressed in jeweled finery on his robe, attacked me as a baby. I was able to ascertain which of them was manifested in the symbolic caricature, which had initially descended down the ladder in to a cavern with no lower boundary as to the pain. Over time, I would find the bottom of that boundary and Hell.

David Morabito and I decided to give up our apartment in La Canada after less than a year. The manager, who was inebriated most of the time, kept coming into our place when we were out. I developed allergic asthma to our cat, and giving the cat away seemed easier if we were headed to new surroundings. We moved into an apartment on Los Robles Street in Pasadena, only about a fifteen-minute drive from JPL.

I really didn't like the apartment we selected. It didn't seem to have any personality, but I couldn't clearly pinpoint what about it was unacceptable, so we settled on it. We spent time with both our families, applied as astronauts, specifically Mission Specialist Astronaut Candidates for the Space Shuttle program, and took up jogging for a while.

There were thoroughly enjoyable days spent at parks or family events with my family or in gatherings with his. His sisters graduated USC. One married and had a baby. There was what felt like a full life in the presence of others, our family and friends, but not somehow between the two of us. I called my gynecologist, who was a doctor two generations older than I, and asked for help to resolve the issues that were making me so unhappy in my marriage. I didn't know how to verbalize these issues. I asked my doctor to recommend a counselor we could see. He sounded horrified that such a thing needed asking, these were different times when people really didn't speak about such thing, even not so long ago.

Perhaps that is why the gynecologist sounded so completely distressed that he knew of no one to recommend or that he knew of the problems, I wasn't sure which. It was a ridiculous shortcoming of the day. This call reinforced the hopelessness I felt. When I put down the phone, the last defense I had against the erosion of my marriage with David, disintegrated. The deep love we shared for one another that had not changed over time, I learned, was not enough.

My marriage and for the moment, my life seemed to have come apart. In the saddest of ironies the collapse unfolded as David and I changed our external circumstances and bought a beautiful condominium. It was the emptiest showplace I have ever seen.

Homa opened the doors of her apartment to me when David and I decided not to be married anymore. I remember not leaving her guest room for one if not two entire days. I took a car trip with my two aunts on my mother's side and my Uncle Gerry to try to sort things out. I was devastated by the ending of my marriage and for not knowing how to better handle things when they weren't working out.

Years later, when I made the decision to have children I visited a fertility clinic headed by a world-renowned fertility doctor near UCLA. The doctor took the role of bringing children into the world very seriously. He wanted to know why my first marriage had ended.

As I sat in his large office before his desk, I said, "My husband and I were very young when we married..." He interrupted me when I began to tell him about this and said, "That is not a reason." I started again, with one of the many things I had been thinking since the marriage ended. To a like response on my part, the doctor said abruptly again, "That is not a reason." I tried again and the doctor said again, "That is not a reason" and this went on in the same way again and again and again.

When he had done this six times, and I was more mortified from frustration than in any other exchange in my life, from somewhere inside me I yelled about my mother-in-law, who had seemed to cause us some problems during the marriage and then uttered, "We never had a chance." The room fell silent. I never forgot it.

All of my other relationships, until meeting and marrying David Meyer in 2008, however, had no such logical connection to the present. Only to the past. I would later learn that it was impossible for me to look any bad character flaw in people who were in personal relationships with me, directly in the eye. From my past, I was too afraid of what I might find. I have been awed by remarkable people I have known in my lifetime such as Gibson Reaves. I had no personal requirement that the people who were at the very heart of my personal life would have any such qualities at all; in fact a closer statement was that my past strictly prevented any such discretion at all, until my past was known, and its effects could be overcome.

The Voyager 1 spacecraft was launched September 5, 1977, Voyager 2 shortly before that on August 20, 1977. These spacecraft were as close to the Grand Tour, the planned voyage to view all the planets in the Solar System, as would happen in our lifetimes. If all went well, these spacecraft would visit the giant gaseous planets known as the Jovian planets, Jupiter, Saturn, Uranus, and Neptune.

By the spring of 1978, I reported to a new group supervisor Dr. James McDanell at JPL. Something exceptionally noteworthy had happened. After all these years, Chuck Acton, whom I remembered from sitting on trashcans in Tom Duxbury's office five years before, made his decision to take a summer off and go and pump gas at a gas station or do whatever it was that he had been envisioning in reliving summers without much responsibility, like those of long ago. There was an opening now for Cognizant Engineer for the navigation of the Voyager spacecrafts using pictures taken by the spacecraft.

The Optical Navigation Image Processing system, a dedicated minicomputer system, also known as ONIPS, was losing the person in charge of bringing the project to completion for the work of navigating Voyager.

I had already done some work for the Voyager mission. I had done a pre-flight calibration of the distortion we could expect to see in pictures taken by potential Voyager flight cameras. I had actually developed the model that would be used to determine distortion in pictures that would be processed by the ONIPS MODCOMP IV minicomputer, using dark marks etched in the camera for this very purpose, called reseau marks.

I had researched formulations and design, and implemented a computer program for the prediction of good opportunities for Optical Navigation pictures based on satellite (moon) to satellite and satellite to star proximity. All of the pictures for Optical Navigation required at least one of the moons of Jupiter against a star background in each picture. Before the Voyager spacecrafts had even launched, I had created a pre-launch picture schedule needed for the Optical Navigation.

I had become completely familiar with conventions and accuracies of existing major star catalogs in the development of a Star Catalog Software System used to generate small star files necessary for the on-board navigation of Voyager. I produced four Engineering Memorandum in 1975 at JPL to document this work.

While Chuck Acton began the summer he had been dreaming about as a renewed child of the world, I was offered the position he vacated of Cognizant Engineer of the Optical Navigation Image Processing System in the summer of 1978.

I accepted the position and began the intense work of getting the software set in shape to perform the countless intricacies associated with finding the centers of the objects in the pictures of the moons of Jupiter against a star background that the Voyager 1 spacecraft would take. Some of these pictures would over-expose the moons of Jupiter in order to be able to see the much dimmer stars in the pictures. This would result in something called geometric blooming or artificial enlarging of the appearance of the size of the moons in each picture.

Of the many challenges ahead, included among them, I had to create mathematical models for how the satellite images would appear, so distorted, in each pictures. It would be difficult to find the centers of these "warped" images to the sub-pixel or picture unit accuracy Voyager needed to encounter or pass by Jupiter and its moons to the precision needed to accomplish the mission.

These pictures of the moons of Jupiter against a star background were translated eventually into the position of the spacecraft with respect to the moons, and were combined with other kinds of data, and then ultimately to TCMs or Trajectory Correction Maneuvers that would set the spacecraft along a corrected and accurate path.

Days ahead would be filled with this type of analytical work based on mathematical modeling of empirical observation in test data, and working closely with Joe Donegan, the ONIPS Cognizant Programmer, to make sure the uncounted equations in this program set were all accurate, as well as getting to know the many pieces of ONIPS hardware that filled an entire room within the Navigation area for Voyager. I began this work eagerly. I had no idea I would make history in the process.

The discovery of the volcanic activity on Io took place ironically four days after the Voyager 1 encounter with or arrival at Jupiter, after the excitement of the encounter had died down, and most people undoubtedly believed that the wonders that Voyager had showed us in the realm of Jupiter had already been revealed. This is the historical account of that day, March 9, 1979.

Jupiter is a gargantuan world, and the cameras on Voyager began to see more and more of Jupiter as the spacecraft approached the planet in January and February of 1979. Jupiter has no solid surface. Jupiter is a gaseous world that has clouds instead, storms, and lightening. The biggest storm that has been raging for hundreds of years, the Great Red Spot, would hold the diameters of several Earths within its perimeter.

But, now as Voyager approached we were seeing the cloud patterns at a level of detail beyond what anyone in the history of Earth had ever seen. These visions of Jupiter would appear on the JPL site-wide monitors, as the pictures came back from the spacecraft.

What human artist could have drawn these cloud patterns? None could, anywhere at anytime in art history; the intricacies, the swirls, points and folds composed of outer planet material as the Artist's medium of expression; the beauty nearly beyond the mind's capacity to absorb.

I would glance up at a monitor to see Jupiter, rushing in the performance of my work, but stopping because I felt compelled to stop, absorbing what of the beauty of Jupiter's cloud patterns my mind would allow me to absorb, and thinking once again, no human artist...

And then there was Jupiter's moon Io. No one could have imagined Io; no one could have drawn Io either or conceived of how Io would look, with very small exception. No one could have envisioned a real world where its surface might look like an orange kept too long and covered with a burgeoning, whitish parasitic mold, or a bizarre pizza pie where the chef got carried away with too many varieties of cheese, some tinged in blue.

I'd never seen this world before, the way its surface looked. No one had until Voyager encountered Jupiter and showed us. Galileo had seen Io in 1610, but as a dot in his telescope on Earth circling another planet, with three other dots doing the same thing. These are the Galilean satellites of Jupiter: Io, Europa, Ganymede, and Callisto, discovered by Galileo.

These are planet-sized worlds that held a secret even beyond the one that confined Galileo to house arrest for the rest of his life after seeing them. Not only did they prove in 1610 that the Earth was not the center of the universe, since they orbited around another center, violating religious doctrine at the time, but the existence of the outer ones, the three beyond Io, made Io into something beyond imagination.

The changes in gravitational force caused by two orbiting outer moons, in a tug-of-war with giant Jupiter on this body, flexed Io until it heated, flexed Io until it became a world that had no explanation for what the scientists on Voyager saw once Voyager was close enough to reveal Io.

On very few occasions did I return home for any amount of rest, no more than four hours a night during the encounter phase of Voyager 1 with Jupiter in February of 1979. This was true right up to the encounter with Jupiter on March 5, 1979.

On March 4, at 11:20 AM, I walked down the stairs of my condominium in Pasadena at home preparing to return to work, and caught a glimpse of a press conference emanating from JPL, where I would be within the hour.

My images of Io for Optical Navigation were over-exposed to capture the delicate and much fainter star images in the frames. I could not see detail on the surface of Io in my pictures and was working too hard for navigation at that point to concentrate on what the scientists were seeing in their color pictures of Io.

I caught the image of Io on my television as I came down the stairs at home. I stopped where I was. Amid the reddish and whitish hues of this inconceivable "moldy" looking world, was a massive heart-shaped feature.

The scientists were proposing that the surface of Io might not be too old in geological terms, much younger than the four billion years of the moon's existence, and much younger than the surface of other moons, because this surface was smooth and not cratered. I began weeping. This was a gold rush for the world, what Voyager was showing us. We had found gold that would capture the textbook pages of the next generation and redefine our knowledge of the outer planets in the Solar System. Tears rolled down my face at the sight of a world more unexpected than imagination itself, as I looked upon that ugly heart-shaped feature. I would remember this later. It was as if I had been gazing into destiny.

Those of us performing the navigation for Voyager were in a team. We were all member of Frank Jordan's Section at JPL, and one of the seven groups within it. I was still working under Jim McDanell, but for Mission Operations for Voyager all of the navigation engineers fell under a different hierarchy.

Our Nav Team Chief was Dr. Edward McKinley. Ed was a very formal man, and always looked dressed up even in leisurewear, immaculately pressed plaid shirts and kaki pants, which he wore routinely to work. He had a large smile that was still somehow projected formality.

Second in command was Ed Tavers. Ed always looked so comfortable that I felt like he was walking across his living room every time I saw him rushing here or there in the Nav area. He liked to wear cardigan sweaters and loafer shoes.

The optical data from Voyager, pictures taken by the spacecraft, were not the only data type used in the navigation of Voyager. This is a spacecraft-based data type. The pictures were taken by a camera onboard the spacecraft.

The optical data was combined with radiometric data, an earth-based data type, in which radio signals are sent from the Earth to the spacecraft to determine distance to the spacecraft called range and doppler, which is relative motion along the line-of-sight. Both types of data went into the spacecraft orbit determination process. Both types of navigators, optical and radio were present on the team.

Jim Campbell and Steve Synnott headed the orbit determination effort, in long hours combining radiomentric and optical data solutions to produce the final spacecraft orbit determination. Jim Campbell was an extremely friendly person, with an infectious smile, whom I admired for his diligence, but did not know well. Steve Synnott was an avid bicyclist and outdoorsman. He would later become known for the discovery of many moons of the outer planets in Voyager data. He struck me as intense.

I respected Steve for his technical expertise. I was cognizant over the Optical Navigation Image Processing System, a MODCOMP IV minicomputer, which was housed within the Navigation Team bullpen area in the second floor of Building 264 on Lab. Joe Donegan contributed immensely to the creation and maintenance of the ONIPS software. Joe Donegan was an intelligent, thoughtful, and refined man. So, there were only three members of the Navigation Team, working with the optical navigation data extraction, Joe, who reported to me with respect to ONIPS, and Steve, who was above me.

There were two areas partitioned off within the bullpen that held the entire team and their desks. ONIPS was housed in a corner diametrically opposite Ed McKinley's office as Nav Team Chief.

My desk was right outside the door to the ONIPS glassed-off area, and Steve Synnott's desk was right behind mine. The ONIPS area was filled with the central processing unit of the minicomputer, two computer monitors, a magnetic tape reading device, hard-disk storage device, a printer, a modem and other equipment. The minicomputer had to be cooled. Cold air blasted from beneath the floor twenty-four hours a day, in a cacophony of horrendous noise. Over time, dressed warmly, I got used to the wind blowing and the deafening noise within the room.

Above us on the third floor of Building 264 was the Science Imaging Team. This was a team of investigators from around the country, gathered at JPL to carry out scientific studies through pictures taken by Voyager for science. The team was headed by Dr. Brad Smith of the Department of Planetary Science at the University of Arizona. Brad Smith had a very stern demeanor, prone to not smiling.

Deputy Team Leader was Dr. Larry Soderblom, a geologist at the U.S. Geological Survey in Flagstaff, Arizona. Larry was very businesslike, but friendly as well.

Other investigators had been on the Viking Orbiter Imaging Team, such as Joe Veverka, from Cornell. Approximately 20,000 pictures were taken by Voyager 1 for science during its fly-by or encounter with Jupiter. These images were mutually exclusive from the only 130 pictures taken by Voyager 1 for optical navigation purposes.

These 130 Optical Navigation pictures were taken over the month of February 1979, leading up to the encounter. They were pre-planned. I had participated in determining these picture opportunities early in my career at JPL. In these pictures were one, rarely two, of the Galilean satellites of Jupiter, Io, Europa, Ganymede, or Callisto with several stars in the background. They were taken with the Narrow Angle Camera on Voyager 1, which had a field of view of less than half a degree, at 960 millisecond exposures, so that I would be able to detect stars that were reasonably bright, down to an effective visual magnitude of 9.5.

At this exposure three out of four of the moons were between two to four times overexposed. I had to find the centers of the satellite and star images to sub-picture unit or sub-pixel accuracy. A pixel on this Voyager camera represented 10 microcradians.

Overall distortion varied from picture to picture and had to be calibrated by my computer software. Star images had to be filtered to find their centers, and satellite (moon) images were scanned by the computer radially outward, removing geometric distortions from their edges or limbs, some because of the overexposure, in a process that was called limb-fitting.

Other members of our Voyager Navigation Team included Jerry Hyder, Margie Medina, George Rinker, and Stan Mandell. Jerry Hyder was an extremely handsome man, tall, thin, with dark hair and a sculpted face. He worked on editing the raw radiometric data, with Margie Medina as assistant. I was aware that Jerry was a contractor for JPL, single, and conducted what seemed like an active social life. He had told me that he and many of the people he knew on Lab would always show up for Happy Hour at a local cantina in Pasadena on Friday nights.

Margie Medina was a lovely Hispanic lady, devoted to her children, and proud of her ascent to the type of work that she did. Ultimately, her husband, who was not in any technical field, left her for a younger woman. In her own way, which I totally respected, Margie never got over this. I didn't blame her for the impact this had on her life. She was such a meaningful person that it was hard to envision that her husband could have ignored the long history they had together in the life they had established raising their beautiful daughters.

George Rinker was a studious person, extremely staid and bookwormish in appearance. Over the years, I recall seeing George's wife, also a JPL employee in the Section, socializing often and usually without George who was back at the office late into the night. They seemed complete opposites, but somehow it worked.

Stan Mandell was a dedicated engineer who worried about everything, drank coffee without abatement all day long as if trying to drown the smoldering embers of his concern. He was a young man and died within several years of the Voyager encounter from cardiac arrest.

I came to work to perform the optical navigation image extraction at all hours of the day and night throughout February of 1979, instead of any sleep, and often before the sun would rise. I walked along the path from the entrance of JPL, on a pathway that led to the second floor of Building 264 at the rear.

Just above it, higher up the hill was the SFOF building, or Space Flight Operation Facility Building, the proverbial one that people associate with mission control – each engineer at a named station in front of a computer. The very first light of day was emanating from the East.

I watched my feet, able to see them through the near darkness one such dawn mid-February as I made my way to the Optical Navigation Image Processing System in Building 264. Very suddenly and surprisingly, I recognized something familiar about this moment of being completely alone crossing the Laboratory.

This was the dream that Ray Bradbury had talked about when I was an undergraduate at USC. This was what I had fallen asleep thinking about every night for four years of college and all the years before that. I wasn't myself going into space. But, my life's mission was in space as I walked here.

A small spacecraft representing humanity in the realm of Jupiter was what brought me to this destination, to perform the critical Optical Navigation for the spacecraft at the hours when people normally sleep, when astronauts might dream of a next day's flight. As I looked at the beauty around me, in stars fading from view, at that still, breathtaking moment in time at JPL, I knew my life's path had intercepted my dream.

––––––––––

I would get the chance to mention to Ray Bradbury about his inspirational talk at USC, and the words that had stayed with me long past college, and what I had gone on to do. After his presentation at USC when I was an undergraduate, I along with many other students followed him over to the Student Union Building and sat at his feet to listen to more of his moving thoughts. He told us that the world was not going to end before our homework was due the next day, sorry, but it just wouldn't, and he urged us to follow through.

It was a star-studded night inside the famed Pasadena Playhouse in 1999, and Ray had written a work just for The Planetary Society to perform as a reading, called *An Evening on Mars*. Ray hosted the evening to a capacity-filled playhouse as a fundraiser for The Planetary Society. He was in his late seventies at the time, and I was asked to help escort him backstage during rehearsal for the play. He was able to walk on his own, without using a walker.

Alice Wakelin, my co-worker, and I were each on one side of Ray helping him up the stage stairs from the front row of seats at the Playhouse. As we made our way behind the stage curtain, I mentioned to him long ago, a group of students at USC had followed him across the street from a lecture hall to the Student Union Building, and that I was among those students. I saw a light go on in his eyes. He remembered the occasion, apparently.

I told him about the work that I went on to do. He smiled broadly. That night in 1999, at the Playhouse, I met a lot of my heroes. I had a chance to tell these people, who were performing at the reading, some as a favor to Ray; that I admired them. One was a favorite actor of mine, Charlton Heston, whose movie *Ben Hur* inspired me throughout my life, as it still does today. It is the greatest American film of all time in my estimation.

I met Nichelle Nichols that evening, whose role on *Star Trek* as Lieutenant Uhura was lauded by Martin Luther King Jr. and told her of my admiration for her. A favorite actor of my son's, and a very friendly and personable, John Rhys-Davies also performed that night.

Another close friend of Ray's is Angie Dickinson, the legendary actress of *Rat Pack* vintage and fame. I would meet Angie Dickinson shortly after my discovery when she rushed up to me on Lab at JPL, and told me that she recognized me and knew all about me, that her daughter, who loved space exploration, had told her.

I saw her daughter on Lab moments before this happened, a young, sweet girl who wore the thickest glasses I had ever seen. My mother had told me about Angie Dickinson's daughter's health problems, which began at birth and included problems with her eyes. My mother was always following along with the lives of movie stars.

When I saw the little girl on Lab, in the days after the Voyager 1 encounter of Jupiter when the press was everywhere and my discovery had brought me fame, for some reason, I guessed correctly whose child she was, in part because of what my mother had told me. It seemed so ironic that a movie star of this stature rushed up to me and said she recognized me.

I have never seen anyone look closer into another person's eyes, perhaps simply to take a good look at what can appear in some lighting as a very deep blue, than Angie Dickinson did on our meeting. Twenty-four years after my discovery, in my professional capacity for The Planetary Society, I would host Ray Bradbury's 83rd Birthday celebration, in another completely magical evening that rivaled or perhaps even exceeded Ray's *An Evening on Mars* at the Playhouse in its novelty. It was wonderful to see Angie Dickinson again there, who never forgot a meeting and was completely gracious, after all those years. I cried for her in much later years, when I learned that the daughter she had cherished and nurtured through greatest difficulty all her life, took her own life in adulthood.

In 1973, in a vast lecture hall at the University of Southern California, in a class I attended because I was a Teaching Assistant for the Department, Gibson Reaves gave me the greatest gift any scientist could ever receive. He taught me history. This was not the only occasion he mentioned this one historical reference.

In 1967, at the University of Cambridge in England, a young woman named Jocelyn Bell made the discovery of pulsars, a type of dead star. She saw something anomalous in the data she was analyzing as part of a team.

Her thesis advisor, Sir Anthony Hewish told Bell not to get sidetracked by those "little squiggles" in her data and to continue on with her work. She did not take his advice. She went on to make the discovery. Ultimately, Sir Anthony Hewish was awarded the Nobel Prize, in part for the discovery.

Jocelyn Bell may not have received a Nobel Prize for this discovery alone, but she was not credited with it. I loved astronomy so much that as I sat in this lecture hall, I was certain that kind of injustice would force me to love astronomy less. I vowed at that moment, I didn't under any circumstances want to end up like Jocelyn Bell.

In 1995, I contacted Jocelyn Bell Burnell, now married, to thank her for the inspiration her story had provided in my life. Ultimately, it provided real guidance to me in real time as my discovery unfolded. She graciously responded to my letter in appreciation, but neither she nor Dava Sobel, the author of *Galileo's Daughter* who met both her and me personally, would ever claim that she had been cheated out of credit for her discovery.

As a young PhD candidate looking forward to a lifetime of participation and publication in the field that she loved, Jocelyn Bell didn't believe that she should have been further credited, despite her independence and, against advice of her direct superior, pursuing the anomaly she noticed to historic result. It was Sir Fred Hoyle, the famous British Astronomer, who was afoot at the time of her discovery, who clarified that history that she should have been given full and independent credit, and Gibson Reaves, as he, spoke up in strong voice about the significance of what this young woman had done. She had made this discovery. She had borne what is a significant theme in the history of scientific discovery, the resistance to new ideas, and the mis-assignment of credit that can follow.

———————

Jim McDanell gathered the members of his Group at JPL together just prior to the start of Mission Operations for Voyager 1 in January of 1979. It was on the eve of turning us over completely to our Nav Team environment. Jim was a very quiet man with milk toast skin. He told us that he had made sure that if any of us died during Mission Operations, the mission of navigating Voyager 1 could still be accomplished.

Connie McDonald guided me through one of the most difficult sessions of my life near the end of 2008. I told her when I arrive for this session that I have been thinking persistently, for some time, "Weep for me Mother of God. Weep for me."

I begin screaming during this session when I realize the blood on my father's face around the area of his mouth is my blood. I am screaming and crying, when I see that he was wearing white that day, and the red blood that covers his mouth, is mine. I do something in a session that I really had not done before. When I erupt with this knowledge, I am so afraid and taken aback that I cannot control my arms from flailing in the horror.

Afterward, Dave is giving a planetarium show that evening at the college, and I try to go there to assist him with selling tickets, as I normally do. I turn the wrong way down a familiar street and cannot make it to the planetarium. I don't really know where I am. When Dave comes home, I am terrified at the extreme level of this memory, how powerful it feels in our universe. The power of what is coming through to me from the parallel one is growing with time.

I literally am sick in bed nearly the entire weekend. Dave is beginning to talk about visiting Nebraska where his family is for Christmas. I am trying to tell him for a variety of reasons, I don't think that I can make the trip. There is my concern about Ryan's health. In the spring, his wife Michelle had hit a car while driving, and Ryan's injuries from that accident pushed his injury that had disabled him off any scale in terms of what he endures from pain. He cannot move now, from where he lays on the sofa downstairs. I am worried about the care Ryan is receiving as well.

This is compounded with another issue. Travel is always difficult for me because of my past, but I try in vane to convey to Dave the seriousness of what I am feeling now in memories from the past. I don't know how to put it into words; I don't know what's happening. What is happening is not good.

Dave and I have volunteered to work with the High Desert Astronomical Society in showing the heavens with telescopes to Ft. Irwin families of deployed U.S. soldiers around the world. As he and I drive there, the following weekend, along the path we take to the Calico campgrounds, I remember the image of an old fashioned razor blade, the kind that rusted in razors.

Calico is a place my parents had taken my brother and me as children after we came to the United States, and along our often-taken trek to Las Vegas. It is an old deserted gold miner's town, replete with restored general stores, jails, Indian statues, etc., and absolutely charming. I took Ryan there too when he was a little boy, and took a picture of him standing where I was pictured as a young girl, beside the wooden Indian.

In the dark of this car trip along the road to Calico so very long after that, I remember it was a razor blade that my father used during the ceremonies to get my blood, from a place that was always targeted, that could not be seen when a child is clothed.

I beg my father as he does this, "Daddy, let me die."

At Dave's home in December of 2008, prior to our trip to Nebraska, I am reaching for a door in his bedroom. I am very much afraid of what will happen when I open the door, what memory will be revealed to me. I am interrupted by a phone call from the Los Angeles County Counsel for the Public Guardian. My mother, who has suffered total dementia in old age now, is being cared for by a man who is trying to take advantage of her situation.

I am learning all I can about what has happened concerning my mother with whom I have had no contact, except through reports from my brother Gary, about incidental visits she has taken to see him where he lives. With new information about her situation coming from the County Counsel, Ryan speaks with his grandmother on the phone.

Since Ryan has dealt with the elderly in his type of work prior to becoming disabled, he understands that her long term memory would survive intact much better than her short term memory with dementia. She admits to Ryan in this conversation that Gary was hit in the head in Beach Grove. The only other person who has ever stated this is me, and not to her at anytime since I remembered what happened to Gary on that beach. Gary has no recollection of it, and with a brain injury that severe, his memory has been erased.

She says when Ryan appears to be pushing her, and since she can no longer recognize his voice as her grandson, in dementia, "Linda falls down a lot." The reference is in response to pressure that he is putting on her to admit some of the things that I have remembered.

She says, "Linda went to the bad end of a party we took her to, and then behind a closed door. We had to take her to the hospital after." Ryan says, "Why, what happened to her?" She says she doesn't want to talk about it.

I reach for the closed door in Dave's bedroom. I closed the door in the Planetarium at Victor Valley College where I teach Astronomy, once I finished my lecture there only some days before this, after all the students had left. I locked it and my heart was desperately in my throat. There was something behind that door. There was something that corresponded to what I remembered a year before when we had traveled to Texas and I had sensed the presence of the most fearful entity that could ever inhabit this universe. I had later seen an eye, an eye of this creature.

My mother had put what I believe was a leopard print fabric over my head just prior to my attack on Beach Grove, as I lay on that bed. Just in the way the sun had been occulted by that truck in Texas, when I remembered the presence of that entity, all light had gone away before I sensed it, as she covered my head. She had told me not to scream. Later in another horrific and returned memory at Dave's home, I saw the eye of a creature who had yellow where there should have been white. At first, I believed the eye was likely the leopard print that my mother had covered my face with. Now, I no longer believe that.

When I locked that planetarium door, days before, whatever I had sensed in that room when my mother attacked me, was on the other side of that door. In the battle for my soul, which my parents began so long ago, God won. I love God and nothing, no matter how hard it tried, will ever change that.

———————

Dave helps me with the memory that is emerging that day in his bedroom, after I speak with the County Counsel. He helped me the weekend before, when I had recovered the memory that told me, that "I am for It." I was being sent to It.

In Dave's room I remember that my little arms are tied above my head, and I am hanging from there, behind that closed door where "they" have taken me where these ceremonies are performed. I am being beaten, and I am spinning each time they send another blow into my body, spiraling downward. I can see the image of darkness in the hole through to a destination that no one would want as their life was ending. I am spiraling downward, and downward and downward.

I am in Dave's arms, and am quietly whispering, "Save me," over and over again.

T.S. Elliot wrote the world ended not with a bang, but a whimper. I have no idea the profound effect this memory of being beaten has on me. It has a much stronger tie to any impact on me than far more dramatic memories have had, in the sense of the quiet way in which I begged to be saved. I am spiraling downward, and I am not sure I will live through these memories or this Christmas season.

I tell this to Connie, but I do not think that anyone can well imagine how bad things are for me now, and everybody believes I should travel to Nebraska with Dave. Connie and I have a session. I remember a red ball with a thick rope in it, which was forced into my mouth during the beating, so that my screams could not be heard. The rope was apparently so the ball could be later removed. The beating is done by a man who is in a red costume as the Devil. I can see the line on his forehead that the costume makes where it intersects his head. He slithers along the ground with thin legs in that costume and has some representation of claws for hands. Others who take turns beating me are in costume too, but he is the only one in red.

Dave and I are driving days later, when I remember. There was a crucifix on the wall of the room where I was beaten. I had asked Jesus to save me. I get the returned memory on a weekday at home, that God did save me from my downward spiral, from going through a door that was far more devastating than any door made by human hands, and lifted me up. God had been there once again, because I had asked Jesus to save me. I weep uncontrollably when I realize that God had been there, again.

Later on, my father did drive with someone to the hospital, with me folded in a blanket afterward, as I recall was the case at the end of all these ceremonies. He took me to the hospital there locally. As we are driving, he looks down on me in the blanket. I see contempt in his eyes, as though he had to run to the market to pick up something he had forgotten on a first trip, and it was a waste of his time that he had to go back again.

I Have Been Where You Are

On the morning of March 9, 1979 when I woke up, I had actually considered not coming into work. This was four days after the completely successful Voyager 1 encounter, or arrival at Jupiter. I was very far behind on my rest. During the 28 days of February, the data had been pouring down on us like rainfall. There would be times when I knew I had exactly four hours out of the next twenty-four to sleep, and I simply couldn't sleep at all because I was just too nervous and excited about the importance of the work I would be doing for the navigation of Voyager.

I knew the frames I would be processing today would be used for something called post-encounter satellite ephemeris reconstruction. The spacecraft was looking back over its shoulder for one more look at the satellites of Jupiter, and we would use this data to better improve our knowledge of the orbits of the satellites. There was no timeliness constraint on this work, and it was not for the post encounter Trajectory Correction Maneuver, consequently it was not extremely important.

Still my dedication to the work was so deeply ingrained that the thought of not coming in was just wishful thinking, a sort of daydream about more sleep after more than a month without it.

Although the job for Optical Navigation of Voyager 1 had been completed by the day before the encounter, on March 4, 1979, it was time to gear up to watch the encounter pictures come in. This was an enormously pleasurable experience, but a marathon in itself.

No sooner had I arrived at ONIPS on March 4 to see if the scientists had captured the small moon of Jupiter Amalthea in their Narrow Angle camera pictures based upon our improved orbit, which would be very much to our credit, and they had, then the door to ONIPS flew open violently and two members of the Science Imaging Team rushed in, Dr. Edward Danielson of Caltech and University of Hawaii Astronomer Toby Owens.

Ed Danielson had a QEDR tape in his hand. QEDR tapes contained the pictures taken by Voyager for Science or Optical Navigation. They were generated in the Space Flight Operations Facility building behind Building 264 in the Mission Testing Imaging System area. For Optical Navigation pictures, these tapes were hand-delivered to me by messenger from across the street.

Ed Danielson and Toby Owens had come to me for verification of what they believed was a ring of Jupiter. The Image Processing Facility used by the Voyager 1maging Team was across the street the other direction from where we were. It was, therefore, a remote location, and ONIPS apparently came to the scientists' minds when they urgently needed the kind of capability that I had at my fingertips.

I placed the picture on my system and performed a linear stretch on it, an image processing technique to increase the contrast between gray levels ranging from white to black. The ONIPS room filled up with people from the Navigation area. I later saw a videotape of what took place during a movie presentation at the Von Karman Auditorium at JPL, so unbeknownst to me someone had a video camera in the room. There is some really impressive footage documented by JPL of that scene in the ONIPS room.

There we sat, and appeared probably for the first time clearly anywhere on my ONIPS monitors, the ring of Jupiter. In the footage I saw, my hands were dancing in front of the monitor, pointing at the newly discovered ring.

I was absolutely thrilled to be present during the discovery of the ring of Jupiter, and to have been some small part of it. My most indelible impression of this event, however, was the incredible force and powerhouse of energy with which the scientists had come to ONIPS, and then the incredible force with which they left. As if someone had run the film backwards, the chaotic smashing about of the entry was repeated as they took their QEDR tape and fled.

Very soon afterward, Steve Synnott and I found something on our desks. It was an autographed picture of the newly discovered ring of Jupiter, one each signed by Toby Owens and Ed Danielson. It was not known before the Voyager 1 image that Jupiter had a ring.

Voyager 2 would ultimately photograph a ring system at Neptune as well, and confirm one at Uranus, adding to the knowledge that all the outer planets were ringed.

The order of the universe was not disturbed by the discovery of Jupiter's ring. Scientists were doing science and when they came downstairs from the third floor to the second floor of Building 264, however rapidly, into the domain of navigation engineers, the brief visitation was commemorated by autographed pictures. The gift was nice. I think Steve Synnott might have shrugged at me when he looked at it.

I arrived at the Nav Team area at my desk at 9:15 AM, March 9, 1979. The MTIS QEDR tape containing the four pictures I would be processing today, the first of these post-encounter frames, was already on my desk. It had probably been placed there by a runner at 6:00 AM. The pictures had been taken by Voyager 1 the day before.

I was aware in advance there was a high phase angle in these pictures. What that meant was the angle between the direction or line-of-site to the spacecraft from the moon, viewing direction, and the direction or line-of-sight from the moon to the Sun, incident sunlight, which would light the moon, was very high. This was the viewing geometry. Moons and planets do not shine by their own light. They shine only by reflected light from the Sun, unlike stars. Our Sun is, of course, a star.

When we see a full moon in the night sky from Earth, it is because the Sun is directly behind us as we are viewing the moon, and directly opposite the moon. That full moon on Earth represents a very small or zero phase angle; the angle between the viewing direction of the moon, and incident sunlight.

The smaller the phase angle in any viewing geometry, the larger portion of the moon that is lit; hence a zero phase angle leads to a fully lit, or full moon. With such a high phase angle, approximately 124 degrees in the viewing geometry of these post-encounter frames, the moon of Jupiter would appear to the spacecraft camera to be far from fully lit, in fact, like crescents or crescent moons.

With only a partial limb or edge of the moon lit, unlike the full moons we had used for the orbit determination, the computerized limb-fitting process would be undermined and impact the accuracy of my center-finding and therefore the usefulness of the data.

By the time I got organized and copied the pictures to ONIPS' 50 megabyte disk pack, it was 10:00 AM. I displayed the first picture on ONIPS' monitor. There was nothing in it, it was devoid of a satellite. This had never happened before in an Optical Navigation picture, to have missed capturing one of the images of a moon of Jupiter. I was very surprised, and I quickly considered what might have happened would be a pointing problem, the direction that the camera was looking at the time was inaccurate, or a timing problem on the spacecraft. If the time the picture was taken was incorrect, then the geometry was changing so rapidly with the spacecraft moving out of the realm of Jupiter, the moon could easily have been missed.

As I displayed the second picture, Steve Synnott walked into the ONIPS room. The picture was of Io. Io was in fact a crescent, just as it would be with a known high phase angle as we were expecting in these post-encounter frames.

The dark side of Io, the unlit side of the crescent, the larger portion of the moon, was also visible though just faintly above the blackness of space in the picture. This is because light from the Sun was bouncing off Jupiter and back onto the dark side of Io's surface. This happens with Earth's own moon as well. When Earth's moon is a crescent because of the geometry of the viewing light will bounce off the Earth and back onto the moon's dark portion not illuminated directly by the Sun. This dark portion of our moon can therefore be seen above the blackness of space, but fainter than the crescent itself.

Steve and I looked carefully at the crescent image of Io. We both knew that our center-finding algorithms depended upon a fully lit satellite to do high-accuracy work. There was no favorable geometry for viewing the satellites of Jupiter as the spacecraft looked back over its shoulder one last time, as it flew by. Yet, these frames were all that was available to us dictated by the circumstances pulling away from Jupiter.

Steve was always highly focused on whatever he was considering in front of him. I watched his eyes zero in on the Io frame displayed on my monitor. Neither of us at this moment was showing outward signs of exhaustion to an untrained observer, but had either of us had any demanding work of any kind, that exhaustion was within us both. The relative unimportance of this work matched a kind of automatic and after-the-fact following through state we were both existing in after the pre-encounter work that had the intensity of a hurricane.

That thin crescent of Io reaffirmed as we gazed at it that all of these post-encounter pictures were essentially useless. Steve and I agreed on it. Steve got up and left the room.

Regardless of its usefulness, I got to work on processing the picture of Io because I didn't want to leave a job undone. I performed what is called the registration of the picture, in which I aligned a graphic overlay of the way we had planned this picture, what we expected to see in it, interactively using a joystick. Joysticks are the way children control their interactive game systems. They move virtual spacecrafts or cars around video games with a hand-held controller, which can occupy kids for hours. Joysticks were not that commonplace in 1979, and my computer system was hardly for gaming.

Such a graphic overlay always allowed me to know where to start looking for the star images in the picture, which were too faint to be seen without some computer enhancement to bring them out through image processing. The two stars predicted to be in the picture with Io were a 7.2 visual magnitude G5 star, which refers to its brightness and spectral class, which is a temperature and color indicator, and a fainter 8.3 visual magnitude G5 star. The star names or identifying numbers represented a catalog designation of AGK3-2006 and AGK3-10021 respectively, although the usefulness of that information is basically just to designate them with a name.

I moved the interactive graphic representation of Io, which was just a computer-generated circle of the correct size over to the actual crescent of the moon on the monitor using the joystick control.

Given that, I knew the 7.2 visual magnitude star fell into the upper left hand quadrant of the picture. So, I needed to zero in on that quadrant to do some image processing and bring out the faint image of the star. It is the actual location of the star and satellites in these pictures that yield the information I was looking for.

Before the fact, or what is called apriori, I could only approximate what the pictures would look like, based on a location of the spacecraft and an orbit of the moons that all needed refining. The true positions of the moons and the stars in the Optical Navigation pictures held the information for those results to be eventually derived.

In zeroing in on that upper left hand quadrant of the picture and with a linear stretch to enhance the contrast in that quadrant, the image of the star jumped out at me, and became brighter than the darkness of space that surrounded it. Yet, it was very far from the computer generated graphic of a little box that had this star's name on it, on the overlay.

Since I had placed the overlay directly upon Io, I was once again very surprised by one of these post-encounter frames to see that the star appeared so far from its predicted or apriori location. In all 130 Optical Navigation frames I had processed the positions of the stars were usually predicted better by the navigation programs. Once again, I thought that the picture might have been taken at a different time than planned, or some kind an orientation problem existed in the direction the camera was pointed, or perhaps the overlay itself had been drawn with an older spacecraft predicted position.

Even though these frames and this work was low priority, I did not feel immediately comfortable with any of these explanations as to why the star would be so far from its predicted location, and given the fact we had missed the satellite in the first picture completely, everything about these post-encounter frames seemed foreign to me, nothing like the precise and flawless work that I had done pre-encounter which had been part of the spectacular success of Voyager 1 at Jupiter.

I was thinking I was relieved on the one hand these frames were unimportant, but upset on the other hand that my desire to do this job was being undermined by these various peculiarities. I thought, "Oh well, I'll go and look for the other star."

It was at the moment that I displayed the lower left hand quadrant in which the 8.3 visual magnitude star was predicted to be in and into which the image of Io mostly fell, and I performed a linear stretch to enhance the dim signal of the star, that I noticed the peculiar marks to the left of Io. I have never since or to this day remembered anything about the star I was looking for after I performed the enhancement that brought out the bright marks beside Io.

I succinctly asked myself, "What's that?"

In the same way, not aloud I answered myself, "It looks like a satellite behind a satellite."

It did indeed appear, this large bright anomaly like another moon peaking out from behind Io.

My mental process wouldn't stop, and I was insisting to myself in the absence of any new information that I find out, when I asked myself immediately again, "What's that?" Once again, my mind automatically concluded, "It looks like a satellite behind a satellite."

Since I couldn't know at that instant, what was clear was that we had captured something unintended in this picture and that is always exciting! I jumped up and went to get Steve. Steve came very quickly to the monitor. When he saw it, this good-sized anomalous protrusion beside Io, he said, "Jesus, what's that?"

We both agreed it looked like another satellite behind Io.

Steve went to get one of his data products, a Trajectory Geometry Predicts output. Characteristically, he pushed the pages of the oversized printout back one and then the next until he found where he wanted to be looking. At the time this picture was taken, there were no other of the Galilean satellites predicted to be anywhere near Io, not even the little moon Amalthea, which would be only 5 pixels in diameter at the distance of the spacecraft at this time. This object, if indeed represented the full sphere of a moon, would be approximately 20 pixels in diameter.

I told Steve that the timing of the picture might be wrong, what I had been thinking prior to finding the anomaly. I had noticed the time tag or what was called the FDS count of the picture was one count off, predicted from actual. The predicted was 16481.10, and the actual 16481.9. I had heard that the spacecraft was having a timing problem after the encounter. Perhaps this was an indication of that, I went on.

Then, I thought perhaps the large crescent satellite in the picture wasn't even Io; as in all my pictures, most of the crescent was saturated, or overexposed, and no surface detail was visible. But, then I realized this moon crescent was indeed the right size for the graphic overlay I used in the registration process, so that meant this was Io and not one of the other Galilean satellites.

As I expressed these thoughts to Steve, I became suddenly aware of the level of exhaustion I felt. What was happening here was no longer some form of routine following through with rudimentary work. Steve was wearing his everyday striped polo shirt and casual pants. I had on one of my everyday shirts and skirts that kept me warm inside the ONIPS area. But, each of us was slowed down, belabored by the simplest acts of moving around. Steve looked spent. I knew I was too. I realized almost horrified that I was having trouble thinking. Steve and I had talked about this yesterday. He said his brain felt numb.

Despite that, Steve managed a quick back-of-the-envelope computation. An object at this range or distance from the spacecraft, which was four-and-a-half million kilometers away, of this apparent size, if it indeed represented part of the full sphere of a world, would be a world with a diameter of one thousand kilometers. Such an object would not have been able to hide from discovery from the Earth. It would have been seen and discovered by an astronomer somewhere on Earth, as Galileo had discovered Io. Steve caught his breath. He said, "It can't be a satellite. I would be ridiculous and impossible not to have been seen from Earth."

I responded, "Then it's an Io flare."

I was joking.

A disturbance on our star, the Sun, produces flares that rise very high off the surface of the Sun. Since Steve had eliminated the possibility of the anomaly being a newly discovered moon of Jupiter, then my mind had done the logical thing and correlated the phenomenon whatever it was with Io itself. Yet, the protrusion that otherwise did look spherical, was gigantic with respect to the size of Io, about fifteen percent the radius of Io. It was too large a phenomenon to be emanating from Io.

Psychologically, your brain can't look at a saturated, overexposed crescent, an entire world like the Earth in crescent lighting and decide that a hefty good-sized object off its limb or edge has anything at all to do with that world. It's too big, too mind-boggling a possibility. Not even a tired brain could conclude that by looking at the anomaly I had found.

Steve listened. He said, perhaps pictures for science planned by the Science Imaging Team were also taken at that time, and the scientists above us on the third floor were on the verge of making some kind of a discovery as well. He said he would look in one of the sequencing products to see if any other imaging had gone on at this time. Steve left the ONIPS room.

I was now alone with the image of Io and the anomaly. I sensed the significance of what was in this room. I knew I had something here. I knew it was important. I sensed that I was seeing something that no human being had ever seen before.

My heart pounded. For the first and honestly only time since, I allowed myself some genuine heart-pounding excitement. In the long term, the significance of the discovery would come to far overshadow anything else. In the short term, I had a very bad feeling about how difficult the hours would be ahead. This was my time with my discovery; the only time that has ever belonged to me and this discovery. And, I cherish it. It stays with me always. It was the stuff of dreams.

I paced back and forth. I glanced at Steve through the windows that encased the ONIPS area to watch his progress as he spoke to the Nav Team Chief, Ed McKinley, and appeared to be working. However, I saw Steve leave the Nav area.

Fifteen minutes passed since he had seen the anomaly in the picture of Io by the time he returned. The first thing I noticed was that he was carrying a carton of milk in his hand. I was thinking, carton of milk… The only place I knew anyone could get a carton of milk this time of morning was the JPL cafeteria. There seemed a disconnect between what I was thinking about this image of Io and taking a trip to the cafeteria.

I rushed out of the ONIPS room over to Steve. What had he checked? What had he found out? I questioned. Had any other imaging for science gone on at that time this picture was taken?

Steve said, quite deliberately, "I haven't been working on it. I haven't talked to anybody. Look, I'm not very excited about this. It could hardly be an undiscovered satellite with a radius permitting observation from Earth." He went on to say, therefore he had dismissed the image entirely after having left only minutes before.

My reaction to this was personal shock. Steve was all about technical expertise everyday I had ever known him. No matter what was happening anywhere in the world at this moment, I realized I could never have done what he just did in dismissing the anomaly in the picture of Io.

I had never before considered that any of the people who surrounded me with their profound technical backgrounds like Steve, could be any different than me in the sense of their comprehension of the reason for all of this work we were doing, their grasp of the rarity of an anomalous observation.

I thought about being a Guest Investigator on the Viking Extended Mission, working more directly with the science of the moons of Mars, afforded the luxury of dealing first hand with the natural wonders of planetary exploration.

I had been present in the Viking Orbiter Imaging science area for two years, with my desk and Tom Duxbury's located right next to the Team, where I had wondered about the smallest detail of every picture and taught myself not to go on without trying to at least grasp what I did not understand in the pictures of Mars.

I had participated in the collection of knowledge of Mars' moons Phobos and Deimos with Tom Duxbury since beginning at JPL. And, as a college student in Gibson Reaves' Extragalactic course, I had remembered not so much each specific name associated with every discovery in the field, but rather that there was a name, and the countless discoveries, and what was just waiting to be discovered in space. Gibson had taught me the history of astronomy.

Yet, Steve's reaction seemed surrealistic to me and inexplicable. I could only characterize it at this moment by a fundamental difference between Steve and I. The difference was the carton of milk.

I couldn't help but wonder what was waiting for me in the next minutes or hours ahead. I began to mentally prepare myself.

I was unsuccessful at expressing my intuition to Steve. I was pleading for his support. As head of the Optical Navigation sub-Team, I relied on Steve, he was the person directly above me. I caught myself just short of saying, "Please be excited about this."

I reminded Steve he was about to determine if any other imaging had gone on at the time of this picture. Steve seemed willing to do that. Steve located a final sequencing product. We determined that no other imaging had gone on at that time.

We went on to explore the timing problem that I had mentioned about the picture in trying to explain the various things about it that seemed unusual. As we talked about it, I recalled this had happened on one if not two other Optical Navigation frames last month, to have an FDS count differ from predicted, and in the heat of the work and the time constraints I had neglected to mention it to Steve. That seemed crucial now in the context of an oversight that might have caused an error, albeit, a small one in our navigation solutions.

It was important that Steve and I consider this immediately. It turned out the error had affected only one previous Optical Navigation picture, and it was important to correct our future solutions for this one picture.

When our attention returned to Io, we discovered that the frame had indeed been shuttered 38 seconds earlier than predicted, 1979 March 8, 13 hours 28 minutes Greenwich Mean Time. This could still in no way account for the presence of the anomaly, although it completely explained the larger than usual difference between the graphic overlay and the relative positions of Io and the one star I had seen.

Even though we were working on the image, Steve's enthusiasm was still sorely lacking. I kept thinking that by my experience with Steve Synnott to date, it was as if 364 days out of the year I would have been willing to risk my technical life on his judgment one hundred percent. But, not this day, not even close, there seemed no judgment or discernment at all from him.

As I watched Steve and fully recognized my reliance on him as I stood in the presence of an anomaly in space, a one in a trillion occurrence, I felt as if I was alive in a nightmare, moving in a slow motion dream, with a great opportunity just out of my grasp.

―――――――

I was aware before my discovery that Jerry Hyder, a JPL contractor and Navigation Team member, had a Friday night group he liked to hang out with. One Friday night when I was at work between the Voyager 1 and Voyager 2 encounters with Jupiter, Jerry, whose desk at JPL was not in the Nav area, but close by and who was often in the area, asked me if I wouldn't like to come along with the group to Happy Hour at a bar in Pasadena. I told him that I would love to come along.

Years after I met Jerry, I would see the movie *Play Misty for Me* starring Clint Eastwood. Although the similarities that I saw in Jerry had nothing to do with the movie plot, the character that Clint Eastwood played reminded me of the man that I met at JPL. Jerry was a bachelor in that very same way you find Eastwood in the movie, enjoying life to the fullest. Clint Eastwood walks and talks so much the way Jerry did back then, they were both tall and lanky and extremely good looking. I see Jerry in that character as I met him back on the Navigation Team.

Jerry's group of friends at the Lab who met up with him on Friday nights was not at all like the groups I hung around with at the Lab. In fact, everything about my interest in Jerry originally was perhaps my over-compensation for a first marriage that did not include the chance for my young husband and me to really be out in the world, studying all the time. I was probably reaching far to the other side.

Jerry could hold a conversation with anybody. He was, as it turned out, completely dedicated to his children and a wonderful father. In applying for his security clearance over the years for engineering work after his JPL contract ran out, the chief stumbling block was that the official investigators of his life could never find any friends other than family we ultimately associated with, with the exception of a special few. We spent sixteen years together with our children. That was our lives.

Jerry had holes in the back pocket of every single pair of pants he owned, all of which were polyester in that day. He owed this to a green MGB car that had something wrong with the driver's seat, which produced the holes in his wallet pocket. You could see the ground go by under the rusted-out chassis by your feet as you drove along. He'd fly through the streets in complete darkness in that sports car; a new world for me, a town called Norco, inland of Pasadena, and a good hours drive away from JPL.

Norco was like the old West with no streetlights, and horse trails and complete refuge from the fame I would earn from my discovery, which had a frightening edge when I began to be stalked by the person who had been calling and talked once to Joe Donegan at JPL. I had loved certain westerns as a child, the *Rifleman* and *Rawhide*. In a way, it felt like Norco where Jerry had a home was a secluded place where I very much needed to be.

I had multiple opportunities to learn Jerry's worldview while we were dating. There were things that he said or alluded to, that told me he did not view relationships as I did. But, I was a star with a much different life than anyone I knew actually. Our lives included trips to Canada for filming of talk shows, celebrities such as Linda Gray of the TV series *Dallas*, and Robert Walden of *Lou Grant* being especially pleasant upon meetings, and Donna Mills popping pills backstage before her appearance on camera with Alan Thicke.

On a live monitor in a green room once, I saw my entire family, who had come to see my appearance on the show with bags over their heads, because they were in the front row in the audience and being used by the "Unknown Comic" in a routine of his to make people laugh.

Appearing on these shows always made me nervous. After seeing this in the green room before my appearance I nearly couldn't go through with it.

I clearly wasn't in a category where Jerry lacked respect for me, or so I believed; we had wonderful times at work and at very special events to do with my discovery. But, I had enough information to know I was in over my head with him, and there was nothing I could do about it. I needed to be away from the Lab eventually after all, I had some haunting feelings about that past. This part of my life seemed less intimidating to me somehow. It was about the work of family and raising my children. That was all at the time that I knew.

Jerry had spoken on and off about his two sons. They spent a lot of time at the house next door in Norco with a mother who had children of her own and babysat for Jerry. Jerry would make comments about them that they were difficult and somehow it didn't bother me a bit, I wanted to meet them. When I did, I learned that Jerry was clearly joking about what he had said. I won't forget the look on his face when they walked into their own living room from the babysitter's house when I was there. I will never forget seeing them for the first time.

The only other time in my life that I have been so overwhelmed with a child's beauty was the day my son Ryan was born two years later. Those two sons of Jerry Hyder's, Brett, 11, and Jason, 6, walked in the room like angels floating on air, and I knew my life would never be the same again. They were the most beautiful children that I had ever seen.

I left JPL in 1981 to go to General Dynamics in Pomona, California. The commute would not be so far from Norco as JPL, and because I felt I wanted to have a child of my own, I was sure that it would be scandalous at work for me to be expecting a child and not be married to Jerry. We had been living together since August of 1979.

I can remember the fear of moving into Jerry's house I felt that summer knowing how sadly my first marriage had ended. I was under a microscope at JPL and was still famous and could not imagine having a child under that kind of scrutiny.

The work at General Dynamics was purely defense, and I found the military atmosphere on the facility depressing. To retrieve a single printout from one computer run on thermal target characteristics of black body radiators, which is what I was working on, I had to walk to a different building than my office each time. On the way one day, I was nearly hit by a very large plank during construction they were undergoing. I got back to my office and the phone rang. The fertility clinic I had been visiting called and asked me if I was sitting down. I said, "Why?" And they told me, "You are pregnant!"

General Dynamics was so difficult a place to work that when I decided to leave after a few months, my young officemate looked horrified when I told him. He told me that he had been assigned by our supervisor A.J. Martella to spy on me and determine if I was happy in my work. He told me I had done excellent work, but that he couldn't tell that I was unhappy and therefore he was probably in trouble for not having forecast my leaving. I nearly fainted hearing this.

I moved to the Electro-Optics Division at Ford Aerospace in Newport Beach working on defense once again, specifically target detection via image processing pattern recognition. I was so fearless during my pregnancy that my doctor invented a 0.25 centimeter dropping of my baby one checkup late in my pregnancy to get me to start maternity leave prior to the baby's arrival. The commute to Newport Beach was significant and it made more sense for me to wait at home until the baby arrived.

On November 12, 1982, Ryan Deen Hyder Morabito was born. On September 25, 1984 Jerry Hyder and I were married in a small civil ceremony with only the baby present. Eventually we dropped the Morabito from our son's name.

Ryan is facing experimental surgery now for the misfortune that has been dealt to him during his life, from a surgical error and the car accident he was in with his wife. It seems over his life he has never been given the chance for any length of time to have his dreams take flight on this Earth.

But, he has accomplished in my opinion more than most people have in a lifetime. He was accomplished in his field of care for the elderly at the time of his misfortune that disabled him, and has powerful expertise in electronic scanners and the world history, specifically the history of World War II. Because of his wife's family's circumstances, his children, my two grandchildren have faced a highly difficult situation which could expose them to abuse. Ryan has stood in the face of that, and protected them with every ounce of his remaining strength.

———————

Early in 1999, working for The Planetary Society, I flew to NASA's Ames Research Center in Moffett Field, California to attend a landing site selection workshop for NASA's planned Mars Surveyor 2001 Lander mission to Mars.

This mission to Mars would never fly. On September 23, 1999 NASA's Mars Climate Orbiter spacecraft would be lost due to a navigation error. Later that year, December 3, 1999, the NASA's Mars Polar Lander mission was also lost when it attempted to land on Mars.

Although the entire Mars architecture or planned missions to Mars was redone by NASA because of lessons learned from the losses, and the Mars Surveyor 2001 planned mission was cancelled, the program that I was working on for The Planetary Society called Red Rover Goes to Mars went ahead in conjunction with NASA's Mars Global Surveyor mission already in orbit around Mars.

This Red Rover Goes to Mars program was privately funded, since The Planetary Society is a non-governmental organization and could therefore not take NASA money. The program took shape and form with a very small group of individuals beginning in 1997, Lou Friedman and myself from The Planetary Society, George Powell, an independent contractor working closely with us, who had originally conceived of the idea for the program with Lou Friedman years earlier, and Brian Wilcox of Jet Propulsion Laboratory.

My attending the landing site selection meeting at Ames made sense for The Planetary Society. I would attend many such meetings to do with the upcoming Mars Surveyor 2001 Lander mission before its cancellation. The Planetary Society was serving as the outreach arm for the mission in the largest educational effort ever associated with a planetary exploration mission.

At this meeting, scientists who were pre-selected for the various science teams on the mission would give their best arguments as to where the spacecraft should land on Mars to perform the type of science they felt was most valuable. They and JPL engineers would also present arguments as to the safety of any area being considered for a Mars landing.

The list of things that have to be considered in landing on another world is not small. The decisions from these meetings would greatly impact our program and what students around the world should be learning about Mars in order to be considered for active participation in a real NASA planetary exploration mission.

When I attended these Mars Surveyor 2001 meetings, I was always surrounded by the faces of people I knew from another capacity, my many years at JPL.

At lunchtime, we were instructed to join together with anybody we could find who had a car and knew the area to find a restaurant. A young man in his twenties seated next to me suggested that I, along with two other people allow him to find us a place to eat. I had never seen him before the meeting. It sounded good to me.

When we got to his car, I happened to be the passenger who sat in the front seat beside this young man. I later learned he was doing post-doctoral work on Mars analog research. To study Mars, scientists often work in remote places on Earth that have extreme climates that resemble the conditions on the Red Planet. This was the important work he was engaged in. Before he started the car he turned to me and expressed what was probably one of the most significant results of my discovery in my estimation, to inspire the next generation to go into careers in science. He said, "I know who you are. You are why I'm here."

I am at work at the Lewis Center for Educational Research, beginning in early 2007 in Apple Valley. I hear the train whistles day after day, long before I ever consciously notice the double train tracks along Highway 18, leading there from home. The train whistles fill me with foreboding, with horror, every time I hear them. Early in our relationship, Dave Meyer and I attend star parties and celebrations with the wonderful folks of the High Desert Astronomical Society. One such party takes place near train tracks. The train powers by us. I am filled with the anticipation of knowledge I do not want to have.

On May 21, 2008, I am pulling out of the driveway of Dave's home, when I see a bell tower, clearly. It is from the vantage point of my father's arms once again. I feel the sense of walking through large green manicured lawns and gardens of endless expanse. I have always had the sense of statues of Christ and the Virgin Mary in my mind. Jesus is three dimensional. Often, often clothed in purple.

I tell Connie on May 24, 2008, that I have asked Dave to not search the Internet for the tower that I have seen. I know it must be at a place where monks stay, because of the chanting and how they are dressed all in robes in my memory, somewhere in the vicinity of Vancouver. When I get home that night, I sit down at my computer and tell Dave I am ready to look.

When I search on bell tower and Vancouver, Westminster Abbey comes up. I see the tower that I saw in memory earlier in the week, exactly. It resembles a tiny tower at the Mormon Church near the Lewis Center, but the one at the Mormon Church is only like a small caricature of the Westminster Abbey tower.

I do not feel panic or horror when I see this tower for the first time in memory earlier in the week. I wonder why not; if this was the place of the horrors I have endured. I later learn the tower was not built before my second birthday, and that my parents had possibly done once again what they did with the Beach Grove area; perhaps they took me back, afterward, albeit after the ferry was built, to the same place that had held a much different time.

I tell Dave, look for railroad tracks, look for tracks! when he gets on Google Earth on his computer. Double railroad tracks are just outside the boundary of the Abbey grounds.

I do not have any confirmation whatsoever that this is where my abuse took place. I only know that remembering the tower there was one of the most significant memories I have ever had, and recovered in the process of the memories that returned to me from a parallel universe. [2]

I do research, and find that the Benedictine Monks who settled there, did so within months of my birth. I do research and find that they were settled just outside the primitive location of my mother's childhood before she was born. I know my mother's

---

[2] It would be several years before I would understand the connection of this memory to the place of my abuse.

family contends to be Jewish. I know my mother clung to this identity as a shield for what she really was. Who could possibly suspect the most vivacious, beautiful and devotedly Jewish woman by identity of crimes for which people have spent their entire life in prison? It is the perfect shield. But, there was a witness. A witness who came through time from another universe to tell her story. It was me.

———

I was always very friendly to the engineers and scientists at JPL, regardless of who they were and if I knew them well or not. If I saw them in the hallways coming toward me, I said hello, whether or not they ever answered me. Many did not. I had a supporting reason as well.

I had trouble wearing glasses, because I could not tolerate the weight on my nose, which would cause enormous discomfort and headaches. Although my vision had been perfect up until then, from the moment I was prescribed them as a child in junior high school at Sears Department Stores Optometry Office, where my retinal hemorrhage had been uncovered, I always got prescription glasses, but never wore them.

For my years at JPL, I was able nearly to the end, to escape wearing glasses. Ultimately I tried contact lenses. But, since I was nearsighted and only my long distance vision was affected by my declining sight over time, it was usually safest anyway to say hello to whoever was very far in the distance, before I could be sure who they were. When that person got just a bit closer and I noticed they happened to be one of many very senior scientists on the Voyager mission, my hello often went unanswered.

After March 9, 1979, I said hello as usual to people I saw in the hallways outside the elevator in Building 264. I noticed the strangest thing when I did.

Suddenly, I got an excellent acknowledgment and a returned hello; every single time.

If the discovery did not change me, it appeared to have changed many other people.

———

JPL gatherings on Lab were always enjoyable. They, like lunches, represented a break from the technical work, but they were even better, usually they represented a demarcation in time when a real rest was coming such as Christmas Holidays or the end of a huge milestone in the work.

The Voyager parties on Lab were beginning after the Voyager 1 encounter at Jupiter. I could just taste the relaxation and the ability to put it all behind me for a while.

I entered the room at JPL for the first of these celebrations with the champagne flowing and the promise of that kind of letting one's hair down. I took a champagne glass. Someone I didn't know well came up to me and complimented me on my discovery. I thanked them. Then they went on to tell me the reasons why what I had done wasn't so great really in their opinion. The next person came along, with a similar greeting.

I kept looking around for someone I could lose myself with and talk about a great deal of nothing for a while. There was no such person. The people in the room came up in streams of recognition, some nice, some not, and there was no end.

I left the party without something I didn't even know I had until I lost it. My anonymity.

———————

When things died down in the days after the discovery, I walked into the Nav Team area and was pleased that only one of twenty of our team members was even present that early, and that it was quiet.

Stan Mandell walked over to me as I was readying to sit down at my desk. He handed me a piece of paper. I took it. It was blank. I said, "Stan?" He handed me a pen. He gestured, and said, "Sign it, please." I said, "Stan, no!" and burst out laughing and handed it back to him.

He handed it back to me. It was like a hot potato.

I handed it back to him.

Finally, I said, "Stan, no, it's me!" meaning just me, just your co-worker.

He handed it back to me. I autographed it.

———————

We answered our phones on Lab with a statement of our last names usually, instead of saying hello. Like most using that convention, when that phone rang, I said, "Morabito."

I'd received several calls now from a man who possibly saw my picture in a magazine similar to *People* magazine that was on the stands shortly after my discovery. It was a good picture of me, and the article had a personal slant.

I was getting fan mail too by this point. One letter from Europe came from a man who claimed to be the illegitimate son of Albert Einstein. He sent a tome with the proposition that we should have children together because they would probably be very smart.

Coincidentally, I had never spoken to the man who kept calling to reach me. Each time, my Group officemate just across the hall from the NavTeam area, the offices we had under Jim McDanell, Joe Donegan took the calls when I was away from that desk.

When I returned to the office one particular day, Joe looked pale. He said, "Linda, this person who has been trying to reach you, I urge you to be careful." I asked him why. He said, "He won't give me his name. He won't say where he is calling from and I have reason to believe that the times he has called, he is calling from different locations. I recognize the type of person he is. I am urging you to be careful."

Joe took a newspaper article from his wallet that was obviously very old. He had carried it with him his entire life since childhood, I learned. Joe allowed me to read the article. It was clear that Joe knew what he was talking about, that he recognized a type of personality that had a devastating impact on his own life many years before. Joe said, "He said he would call back in an hour. I think he is waiting at some location to place that call to you." Joe looked up at the clock. "That's about now," he said.

I sat down. Shortly, the phone rang.

Instead of saying my name, I said, "Hello."

A male voice answered and asked if I was Linda Morabito. I heard in his voice what Joe had heard. I told him no, I was the secretary. He sounded like he didn't believe me. I asked if I could take a message. He told me no. I asked if there was a number where he could be reached, he said no, that he moved around a lot. And then he said in the most icy tone I had ever heard, "This is you, isn't it."

I told him like my life depended on it, that it wasn't. That I was the secretary. And, then I demanded to know if there was no place he could be reached, did he plan to call back. He said he didn't know. He sounded defeated.

For many years after, I would never tell anyone who I was on the phone, until I found out who they were and if I knew them, especially at my home after I left JPL.

––––––––––

On July 6, 1979, the JPL-wide publication, *Universe*, featured me on its front page and credited me with the discovery of the active volcanism on Io. When I got the copy of the publication, I was at my desk just outside the ONIPS door. I looked at Steve Synnott at his desk behind me and said, "You know when I came to JPL, I could never have expected anything like this."

Steve responded, "A lot of people around here are very unhappy about this."

My response to the people who do not know the discovery story, what really happened, and feel that I should not have been given the attention or the credit that I did is that people should receive credit for the work that they do. On March 9, 1979, that is the work that I did. To borrow from the words of William Herschel on his discovery of Uranus: "It has generally been supposed it was a lucky accident that brought this volcanic plume into my view; this is an evident mistake. In the regular manner I examined every Optical Navigation frame of Voyager 1, it was that day the volcanic plume's turn to be discovered."

––––––––––

The exhaustion that I felt, and the lack of acknowledgment from Steve Synnott that this anomalous observation was worth investigating; Steve had said after he had gotten his carton of milk from the JPL cafeteria that he was not very excited about the anomaly in the picture of Io, was not going to stop me. I decided to do something on my own.

I telephoned Tom Duxbury. I wanted to make sure that what was appearing beside Io was not merely an artifact of the camera. There were such things that appeared in every picture taken by spacecraft vidicon cameras like Voyagers', if you knew where to look for them. The Viking "cheerio" as we had called it during the Viking mission was a prominent artifact in one of the Viking orbiter cameras and was about the size of this object besides Io.

The object beside Io, the anomaly, itself had the properties of a crescent, more brightly lit around the edges; a little like a ringed cheerio of breakfast cereal notoriety, which is how the Viking cheerio had appeared. Tom confirmed on the phone what I had noticed during the encounter, that there was in fact a Voyager cheerio too, but that he thought it was closer to the upper left hand side of the field of view. This reaffirmed what I remembered as well.

I told Tom I was seeing something in an OPNAV frame I didn't understand. Tom said, jokingly, "Perhaps you have discovered a galaxy with a hole in it." I was relieved by his humor, and the conversation ended that way. This touched on how much better it was to play this down, primarily because of just how quickly word spreads. It dawned on me now, that I had no control over this situation whatsoever, and how easily it could slip out of my control before I had a chance to find out what needed to be done to understand the anomaly.

There was the larger issue. I knew of no path to walk on to have this situation proceed as it should. I had no prior knowledge of a discovery coming out of an engineering setting at Jet Propulsion Laboratory. The Science Imaging Team made science discoveries. What path could recognize ONIPS as a viable area from which to push forward to completion an analysis of the image? A path that would result in the preservation of a record of these events, so that what had already happened here, or what was about to happen here; that one day it would be known what had transpired. This path represented the way to survive this experience for me, and I knew of no precedent for it.

Two hours had passed now since I had first seen the anomaly. However awkwardly, Steve and I had now explored all of the timing and technical geometry considerations of the frame. We were still sparring about Steve's lack of enthusiasm when the subject of what to do next came up.

I looked to Steve for the next step; I worked for Steve as a member of our OPNAV sub-Team, and I felt I should defer to his judgment because of this. Steve had an outstanding quality for speaking up for and clearly stating his accomplishments better than anyone else I knew at the Laboratory. If anyone could protect this discovery, Steve could, I felt. This was the one day of the year, however, when that was not true. He said, "You have done everything you can," and he said to call Ed Danielson of the Science Imaging Team. I did this because I was told to.

I placed a call to Ed Danielson upstairs. The administrative assistant in the Science Imaging Team area was a friend of mine and she told me she would leave Ed Danielson the message to call me. She told me as well that he might be at the Image Processing Laboratory across the street.

I placed four calls to various numbers at that facility and each person who answered there had never heard of Ed Danielson. It was interesting the way they all said, "Who?" rather indignantly.

I looked around when I'd gotten off the phone. Steve had disappeared. I presumed he went back to the cafeteria. I was right. It was after twelve and lunchtime. I had not eaten all day and had not eaten much the day before. A good analogy for Mission Operations seemed to be war at that point. I was fighting back a good measure of physical weakness by this point, but nothing was going to stop me now. I had to do something.

I placed a call to Peter Kupferman, an astronomer, who interfaced a lot with the Imaging Team, but was not a team member. I did not reach Peter with the first call, and even though I left no message for him, he called me back minutes later although I do not know exactly how. I told Peter I was seeing something strange in an OPNAV frame.

Peter, if anyone, could conclusively eliminate the artifact theory, as he was a camera expert. He was the one person I knew who could determine if any quality of the camera could induce the appearance of the anomaly, thus not representing something Voyager was actually imaging. Peter told me he would come right down, and he showed up a minute later. I pointed to the image on my monitor.

Peter said, "Oh my God!" and moved very close to the screen. He asked me if he could call Andy Collins, the Voyager Experiment Representative.

Andy Collins was known to us Optical Navigators as a good guy, because he was. His job was to interface with the scientists as the bridge between the engineering world at JPL and them. He seemed to be one of the few people who realized if there is no Optical Navigation there is no science! I told Peter it was okay to call Andy.

Andy Collins, who had a wonderful boyish quality, came down to the Nav area eating a cheeseburger. I do not believe that "Oh my God!" was a quote for Andy, but that is what his face was saying. It was the most incredible experience watching Andy Collins look at the image of Io. He was acrobatic about it.

He sat on top of a table in front of the monitor, crossed his legs, looked at the monitor and at one point he lay down on the table on his belly and looked at the monitor, all the while taking bites out of that cheeseburger; his face still spelling out, "Oh my God." I watched Andy and the cheeseburger. I have never been so jealous in my life of anybody having anything than I was of Andy having that cheeseburger. I envisioned headlines, as I watched this amazing sight, OPNAV Analyst Dies of Hunger While Making Great Discovery.

What Andy did say verbally first, was that he would need digifax hard copy of the picture. This told me that the picture would leave the ONIPS area. I protested that I did not want the picture to leave the room, because honestly I did not know who my friends were. He seemed to understand. But, Andy said that ONIPS was not capable of the type of image processing that needed to be done, that the IPL facility across the street could do. I told Andy my system could do anything that IPL could do, which was of course not true and I could not appreciate suggestions of taking this out of my hands.

We all sat down, Andy Collins, Peter Kupferman, and I and I performed some basic "look-see" capabilities that ONIPS could do on the image. Peter definitively told us that what we were seeing was real, that whatever this anomaly was, was not camera induced.

The largest single revelation that came out of this work was from exploring the portion of Io's surface that was receiving reflected light off of Jupiter, the portion darker than the bright crescent of Io. The brightness or DN level (Density Numbers ranged from 0 for black to 254 for white associated with each pixel in the frame) of the dark portion of Io, was at the same level or brightness as the dark portion of the anomaly; the portion of the anomaly that was also not bright, bordered by a brighter crescent shape of its own.

This matching of the brightness levels gave credence to this observation as though whatever was happening in space in the realm of Io was in some way receiving the same degree of lighting from the Sun as was Io. Between this and Peter's assessment, this observation was gaining credence. To deal with something that has never been seen before is to have nothing to equate it to. First for the human mind, to know it's real.

Andy suggested taking the picture away again, and I refused again.

The rest of the conversation was Andy and Peter taking turns with one another in different expressions of "Oh my God!"

Steve Synnott returned in the midst of all of this. My confidence in his ability returned automatically, from long habit. But, I said, "These people are a little more excited than you were." I looked him squarely in the eye, and asked him in that way to take over. I was headed to get a cheeseburger.

I called Gibson Reaves at his home in Palos Verdes Peninsula on the evening of Sunday, March 11, 1979. I got Mary Reaves on the phone. She told me Gibson was in Fresno, California and gave me a number where I could reach him. When I called Gibson in Fresno, I told him that I had discovered volcanic activity on Jupiter's moon Io.

It would not be out of the ordinary if that discovery had taken place and I was simply aware of it and not involved directly, and to be calling Gibson about it. Gibson was aware that I was part of the Voyager navigation work. So Gibson asked for clarification. He said, "YOU did?" I said yes, and he asked again just to be sure. "YOU did?" I said yes.

By mid-day, the next day the *Fresno Bee* would carry the story, as would all major newspapers around the world. I would begin a trek into a world that included television work, appearing with celebrities, and what was ultimately too the manifestation of personal unhappiness for me in my private life on more than one occasion. Jealousy over the discovery would often enter my interpersonal and professional relationships.

Gibson said of the discovery, "Linda, write everything down." In a letter dated March 15, 1979, I wrote what happened the day of the discovery minute by minute to Gibson on 11 typed pages, single-spaced. Gibson placed that letter in the archives at USC where it remains.

In late 1990, another documentary crew located me at my home in Norco, California where I was living with my husband, Jerry Hyder and our children, and set a date to come out and film me. The documentary maker had spent the previous so many days at JPL, filming there.

When the documentary maker arrived at my home, he took me aside and told me that Dr. Edward Stone, now director of JPL had told him my discovery was the largest ever to come out of Jet Propulsion Laboratory.

I would be featured in several documentaries over the years to describe the discovery, including two episodes of PBS's *NOVA*, "Jupiter & Beyond" in 1980 and "To Boldy Go..." in 1990, as well as PBS's *The Infinite Voyage*, "Sail On, Voyager" in 1991.

Dr. Edward Stone and I were named together, as deserving special recognition by *Aviation Week & Space Technology* for our accomplishments in 1979.

In 1987, Gibson Reaves suggested to E.L.G. Bowell at the Lowell Observatory in Flagstaff, Arizona that Asteroid 3106, discovered by Bowell be named Morabito, which was adopted by the International Astronomical Union, in honor of my discovery.

I received a Certificate of Appreciation for the discovery from NASA as well as three NASA Group Achievement Awards for my work on Voyager.

———

My years at The Planetary Society from 1997 to 2004 set the stage for my journey through time.

On February 15, 2001 I was at Malin Space Science Systems, from where the Mars Global Surveyor spacecraft, in orbit around Mars, Mars Orbiter Camera was controlled.

Four days before, during this same week, one of the most incredible of my career, I was at Los Angeles International Airport meeting nine students coming from around the world to work at Malin Space Science Systems to command the Mars Orbiter Camera. The students were from six different nations, the United States, India, Hungary, Poland, Taiwan, and Brazil. Their names are Zsofia Bodo, Kimberly DeRose, Bernadett Gaal, Shaleen Harlalka, Iuri Jasper, Hsin-Lui Kao, Tanmay Khirwadkar, Vojciech Lukasik, and Vikas Sarangadhara.

Working to help me at the airport was Rachel Zimmerman, who assisted me on the project for The Planetary Society. She did an outstanding job. Later on, we would be joined by the students' teacher Paige Valderrama, who also worked for me on the program, and who performed like a sage with the children. This took place in a week that would change all our lives.

There were volunteers too, notably Kim DeRose, the only American on the team, the best in the United States of the many who applied for the opportunity, has an incredible mother Cathy DeRose, always willing to help. It wouldn't be all work and no play. The students would tour Los Angeles, be hosted by Robert Picardo on the set of *Star Trek: Voyager*, and make a significant discovery on Mars.

Lou Friedman, the Executive Director of The Planetary Society in Pasadena, California had a vision. He wanted students to participate as astronauts in a real NASA planetary exploration mission. The Planetary Society, an international membership organization, had as its mission to inspire the people of the world about space exploration. My friend, Adriana Ocampo from JPL, suggested that I talk to Lou Friedman when I decided to return to the world of space exploration after my marriage to Jerry Hyder ended.

Lou, along with George Powell of Visionary Products, and the LEGO Company had invented a computer controlled educational product called Red Rover, Red Rover years before. Rovers made of LEGO parts were "teleoperated" by computers equipped with Red Rover, Red Rover software, emulating the way scientists would explore remote worlds such as Mars, with rovers like Pathfinder's Sojourner, which landed on Mars in 1997. Lou Friedman's belief was that even when astronauts landed on Mars, they would still use rovers to explore the surface in the hazardous conditions outside a Mars Base; which included freezing temperatures, toxic air, corrosive and choking dust. Why not stay inside the safety of a Mars base and teleoperate rovers with cameras and command them to explore and accumulate knowledge about Mars? The astronaut could do all this and remain inside the relative safety of the base.

As was the original plan for this Planetary Society program, the students could live in a simulated Mars Base on Earth, and demonstrate to the world how the future of planetary exploration might be accomplished.

In August of 1997, Lou asked me to create a vigorous Astronaut Training program for students around the world for participation in the upcoming Mars Surveyor 2001 Lander mission. I took him literally. Astronaut training does not come at a low level of expertise. While I made sure that students in Africa and other nations that might have had limited resources had just as much opportunity as any others, by striking deals with *Science Magazine* and the LEGO Company for copying rights and donations of Red Rover systems respectively, I never even dreamed of scrimping on how vigorous this program would be.

As early as 1997, I began to gather teachers at The Planetary Society as well as consulting with space scientists for the most thorough and invigorating program I could devise. The teachers were experts on dealing with students and from them I would be able to learn what ingredients in the program could not be compromised. The most notable teachers who assisted were Sheri Klug of Arizona State University, who gave her time and support freely to this project, Steven Dworetsky of Los Angeles Unified School District and District Administrator Joe Oliver. Paige Valderrama, the students' teacher, would ultimately join Sheri Klug in working with Dr. Phil Christensen at Arizona State University.

I would literally solicit the participation of thirty-four nations on a volunteer basis, reaching in India alone, one million students. I wanted the finest student astronaut team that could exist. I envisioned that The Planetary Society's reputation in this project could be only as good as the experience actual Mars scientists on the mission had working with this team.

On February 11, 2001 after selecting them, securing their translators and regional and national centers, having their work judged by the likes of Donna Shirley and Matt Golombek of Pathfinder fame from JPL, and creating their training program in Mars science, they arrived already trained at Los Angeles International Airport.

I'm not sure Lou Friedman envisioned this much authenticity to the Astronaut Training. Later on he would tell me that when he looked at the materials that I wrote for the students selected in the second wave of the training mission, he couldn't believe how good the materials were. Yet, I have a feeling Lou didn't want the job to be done quite this well. It might have been better to scrimp, perhaps.

This program never did for The Planetary Society in return what the Society did for the world and the young people in it. The program, although it was manifestly what the Society was mandated to do in its essence, could not under my management or other managers later leverage the public's involvement into membership in the Society.

While membership in The Planetary Society continued to decline around a changing world, infrastructure created from impetus from the program, where there was no infrastructure before, was changing students' lives, putting them together directly with their national scientists as mentors, giving them unprecedented opportunities and exposure to materials that would steer them toward careers in planetary exploration.

I think the world benefited, if not the Society, from something I do not believe Lou Friedman could resist. I always had the feeling that more than even wanting to demonstrate to the world that students could live in a Mars Base on Earth and foretell a future when astronauts would explore Mars from a base that would also one day involve the world with each person at their own computer on Earth owning the data and the thrill of exploration, that Lou simply wanted as well to be directly on a JPL mission once again, under the auspices of his organization, The Planetary Society.

How much satisfaction is that, for a man who once was employed at JPL under strict government regulations to be able to come back with the largest space interest group in the world and beat JPL at its own game by joining it in an outreach effort previously reserved for government agencies?

I was part of Lou's plan, but in a characteristic interestingly way like my ex-husband Jerry, Lou often had trouble remembering what I had done at the Society over time (in my ex-husband's case the work I had done in raising our children), even when he heralded my many accomplishments, nearly to the exclusion of everyone else at the Society, for years.

I could never have guessed going in, however, but my astronaut selection process resulted in many prodigies from around the world rising to the top of the selection process. It only made sense, but I hadn't even envisioned the high level of these young people ages 10-16. Ken Edgett, a remarkable Mars scientist at Malin Space Science Systems, would ultimately comment that working with the selected kids was the same as working with many of the Mars scientists he knew.

On February 15, 2001 as the pictures of Mars came back to Malin Space Science Systems of the areas on Mars these students had selected with their own expertise on February 12, 2001, I, along with everyone else in the room, Ken Edgett of Malin Space Science Systems and Mike Malin himself, world-renowned Mars investigators, the students, their parents, the chaperones, the translators, noticed what appeared like an ordered structure in a corner of one of the pictures of the middle latitudes of Mars, which turned out to be monolithic boulders. One of the students, Shaleen Harlalka from India, at the last moment on February 12, three days before had suggested tweaking the pointing of this high resolution camera just a bit to capture an area that seemed a little more interesting than what he and his fellows had already selected.

By doing that, Shaleen and the other students who agreed, saw in high resolution what had never been seen before. Scientists would not be able to explain the presence of these boulders here. I can remember the feeling that shot through my heart when I saw what looked nearly at first like missing data on the large screen at Malin, too ordered to be part of the natural terrain.

It was instead the dark boulders on nearly white sand on Mars that looked like they were deposited there through a means no one can hypothesize.

The news through press releases from Malin Space Sciences Systems and The Planetary Society went rapidly to the press on February 16, 2001, who were on their way to Legoland for a press conference the next day, when President George W. Bush bombed Afghanistan. The press literally stopped their cars and turned around to cover what the new Bush Administration had done.

I managed the educational aspects of this program, which The Planetary Society called Red Rover Goes to Mars for five years. It was the largest outreach program associated with any NASA planetary exploration mission, and was announced to the world by former astronaut and Senator John Glenn at World Space Day on May 6, 1999.

––––––––––

The last ceremony I recovered in memory at the end of 2008 and the beginning of 2009 was so disturbing that I barely survived the Christmas season. Fortunately, through a series of only what can be described as difficult events, I did join Dave for at least Christmas Eve and Christmas Day in Nebraska. I thank God for these difficult events, no matter how hard they made life, because I saw my husband Dave Meyer's father, Ewald Meyer for the last time on that brief stay.

Dave and I had been married in August of 2008, in a perfect ceremony at Faith Lutheran Church by Pastor Brad Viken who had baptized me earlier in the year, Dave's long-time pastor. What would have made it truly perfect of course, was if Ryan had been able to move from bed at home, and to attend. Instead, in nearly hundred degree heat the day before the ceremony, a remarkable volunteer at the church Jay Graham had installed successfully a way for Ryan to view live on the Internet the wedding and hear the sound.

Our close family and friends were there. Dave's brother Mark, his sister Gretchen and her husband Bob were there, although Dave's brother Robert did not make it. Agatha Hou, a parent of one of the Student Navigators, Kevin Hou, from The Planetary Society program, was my Matron of Honor. Dave's parents were too elderly to attend. Twenty-six days later, his mother Cecelia Meyer would pass away. I thank God that I had the chance to meet her on the trip to Nebraska the winter before, and for the time that I spent with both his parents. Dave's family was an indicator of the type of man he is.

In Ryan's place, my grandson Robert walked me down the aisle and gave me away. My grandson Nathan, only 14 months old, walked the rings down the aisle by pushing a toy lawnmower; the only way he could walk stably at that age. I have never been so proud of both my boys. The wedding with my hero Dave, dressed in his Air Force dress attire was the stuff of life-long dreams. My other hero Ryan was at home. And my brother Gary, my hero, as well, had decided not to come. Such trips for him were far too difficult. He had married a beautiful lady Gina Dassance in the institution where he lived, many years before, and his precious wife, my sister-in-law had lost her battle with cancer in September of 2008.

By January of 2009, after a far too difficult memory of being beaten in the ceremony in which if not for God, I would have succumbed to my wounds and destination in Hell, another ceremony began to emerge. It was beyond anything that could ever be described.

I see the eye of a donkey with very long, wiry fur screaming in panic, as it does. It is on its side beside the altar. I think as I begin to remember this and its eye, "Lay open my heart and my God."

They slice it open while it is still alive in the way one would slice a pocket from fabric to create it before sewing it on to a garment. They did this while it was alive.

I am placed inside the screaming animal, and the pocket of its flesh is closed over me. There is nothing for me to do, but die.

Something has been happening for a long time since I came to Victorville. When driving, I would always recite what I thought was a prayer to myself. I would repeat countless times a day, to myself, "Merciful God."

It turned out not to be a prayer. It turned out to be something that I had seen on the day of my attack at Beach Grove. I had seen God, and He was merciful.

In that same way, on my final turn on large throughway streets home after teaching my night class at Victor Valley College, I would find myself thinking about Gibson.

Hardly a day goes by when I do not remember something that Gibson told me. He often said, "We are dinosaurs." He was referring to the fact that University of Southern California had absorbed the Department of Astronomy into the Physics Department because Astronomy had the excellent teachers and attracted the students and the Physics Department, which profited more by research at the expense of students, wanted those majors.

And yet, Gibson maintained his integrity and high-standards throughout this ordeal and throughout his lifetime. Dinosaurs are people who put integrity first. Integrity, as Gibson always said, is all anybody ever has. I remind myself of this for the hard decisions in my life that I have made where I put integrity first. I am prouder of nothing more in the conduct of my life, than what Gibson told me often, that *we* are dinosaurs.

But, this thought of Gibson at the turn onto the street, was not that. It happened dozens of times, before I ever began to wonder why I thought about Gibson Reaves going down this final, long stretch of road, an undivided two way highway with no city lights. The long stretch seemed to go right to the sky.

I have always wondered about my rapid eye movement. It has become two things over the years. First, it always signals the processing of memories in waking hours. Second, if I hear of any tragedy at all, anything in this world that has happened to people which represents extreme hardship or death, or unjust suffering, my eyes go crazy in my head. I begin to wonder if there is something that I know.

Finally, the little girl tells me about this event with the animal in which I am placed inside, and I learn from her that they destroyed me. I learn from her not to let them win. I learn from her that God does not want them to win.

I learn from her the meaning of my rapid eye movement in instances of hearing about tragedy, that, as she says it, "The worst things in all the universe can happen to people."

Then, she rises up. She ascends to the universe above the Earth, and I am shown the vastness of God who seemed so small when He had rescued me from my descent when being beaten and sinking down. I am shown the universe God is otherwise infinite.

And, I take the time to ask her some questions.

I ask her, "Who are you?

She says, "I am me."

I ask her, "What do you want?"

She says, "To sleep. To go home."

I ask her, "What can I do for you?"

She says, "Live."

I have learned that rapid eye movement is her language. She is a speck of God, of the entire universe, where she died.

When Connie hears about this she thinks this is symbolic, and that my memories are over, and that I let the little girl go, but I am deeply disturbed by this. At a time when Connie no longer believes that, we will later discuss how the little girl may have instead reported what she had been told, to live.

I weep often after this, and I cannot exactly correlate the image of her rising up to any specific memory. This has never happened before. Anything symbolic or otherwise that came through to me from the parallel universe has had a memory; one that I can match up to a place in Canada where I shall go one day, sit down on the ground, and weep for what was done to my brother, and possibly to another place where I shall go one day and begin an investigation; to succinct memories which can be confirmed through evidence and specifically not some process of the mind which does not connect to reality.

I am so concerned, I don't know what to do, and suffer wondering. It is then that the Lewis Center for Educational Research changes its direction and decides to no longer do much global curriculum development. I am their Global Curriculum Developer, and now I am leaving. It opens the door to leaving the place I had *symbolically only* assigned to my inhumane destruction through atrocity years and years before, and now I will remember how I left.

I am at Dave's home when I am weeping about something to do with Gibson. Gibson did not know me when I was being tortured as a baby. So, it makes no sense.

I had on a previous trek home turned down that long stretch of highway, once again, and this time there was no putting off the realization that I always thought of Gibson going down this road. My mind said in full realization, "Gibson."

When leaving the Lewis Center for the second to last time after all my goodbyes and a lunch, I felt my body accelerated upward overcoming all opposing forces of gravity, as I drove away, like several g's of attractive force. This is what I had seen from the outside of my body when I had remembered being placed inside the animal, me rising up along a corridor represented by that desert highway.

At Dave's home, I know and remember what was trying to surface. On a piece of paper, I write, "I have been where you are." I had been to where Gibson is now that he is dead.

"They" drove swords blindly into the body of the animal, running it through with swords that surrounded me in its flesh, the swishing sound horrific; the blood and guts and stench and horror and there was no way that I could remain alive.

In Connie's office I remember rising above the curvature of the Earth as a very small child, and being between the greenery of our globe and the Sun. I went to a place that was the greatest peace I had ever known. And, I begged God to let me stay, as I would beg Dave to not ask me to go anywhere lately when the memories were getting worse and worse and worse in a progression that has been honored in my telling of them in this volume.

It is the greatest stillness and peace I have ever experienced. And, yes, Gibson, I have been where you are.

Chapter III

The Edges of Space and Time

The cheeseburger I grabbed at the cafeteria just past mid-day on March 9, 1979 didn't last long. When I returned to the ONIPS area within minutes of having left to get the only food I had that day, the excitement was spreading.

Andy Collins, Peter Kupferman, and Steve Synnott were wandering in and out of the ONIPS room, along with maybe ten other members of the Navigation Team. There seemed no way to stop that. Peter kept repeating to me, "Don't let [word of] this get to the Science Imaging Team, or you will never get the credit." The more he said that, the more I worried. I still knew of no path to walk on to know how to survive the challenges that were coming. But, I did sense I was in exactly the right frame of mind.

I was so dug in, that everything that was happening around me seemed peripheral to the sole purpose of me taking this observation to the ends of the Earth to understand it. If that is what it would take, that is what I would do. Tom Duxbury showed up now too based on my earlier call to him. An animated discussion began between those principally involved.

Andy Collins had it divided into three possibilities. One, a newly discovered satellite of Jupiter, two, a newly discovered satellite of Io, or three, an Io-based phenomenon.

Tom Duxbury assured us that an Io orbiter was dynamically possible, in other words, Io theoretically could have a moon orbiting around it even if it were a moon itself. But, Steve Synnott and I had established so much earlier in the day that we did not feel we were dealing with a satellite.

Tom Duxbury mentioned that the Voyager cheerio was a dark feature and not a bright one, as the anomaly was, and I agreed. So, this was not the most well known artifact of the camera system.

Andy Collins said if it is an Io-based phenomenon we have better find the location of that phenomenon – could it be a cloud? Steve Synnott said coincidentally he had been at lunch with a group of people discussing Stanton Peale's article, Stanton Peale of the University of California at Santa Barbara, which had predicted a volcanically active Io, and had been published before the encounter.

Peter Kupferman said, "If it is a gas shell, this is what it would look like." When Peter said that I recalled my very first impression of the anomaly, or gas shell, if it was, which had its own crescent or way in which the sunlight was hitting it, was more consistent with an Io-based phenomenon, than a body beyond Io, which would in all likelihood be in the same orbital plane as Io. If it were another body beyond Io, the crescents of that body and Io would probably have been more similar in their orientation. That had been my instantaneous impression.

Andy's suggestion was to compute the sub-spacecraft latitude and longitude, which would be at the direct center on the image of the moon, and from there, compute the latitude and longitude of the anomaly on the surface, to see what we would learn. The whole Nav Team was milling around now.

No one understood what they were seeing, that is the degree of difficulty associated with interpreting this image. Yet they could feel that we understood more although we would not tell them. Some members of the Nav Team came close to wanting to congratulate me, but things seemed too uncertain.

I caught a glimpse of Steve Synnott talking with the Nav Team Chief Ed McKinley and Steve's own counterpart on the team, Jim Campbell outside the ONIPS room. Steve appeared to be expressing great discontent and looking at me. I went right over to him and he criticized me for having contacted so many people while he was away at lunch. I informed him I hadn't done that. I had only called Ed Danielson of the Science Imaging Team who had not even shown up yet, Peter Kupferman and Tom Duxbury much earlier. Steve looked completely shocked. He asked me why I had called Ed Danielson of the Science Imaging Team. I felt shock ratchet through my entire body. I said, "That is what you told me to do!" Steve said, "I did not tell you to call Ed Danielson!"

Hearing this, I believed this was some kind of a joke Steve was playing on me, which was the only plausible explanation, and I paused, waiting to hear exactly what kind of a joke this was. Steve said nothing, I couldn't believe it; he could actually not remember telling me to place the call.

I regained some composure, but in an instant ran out of the Navigation area and into the hallway. I slammed the button on the elevator and waited for an elevator car to arrive. I got in it and hit the third floor button. When the elevator doors opened, I walked into the Science Imaging Team area as though I belonged there. My friend was sitting at her desk, where she had taken the message much earlier that day to have Ed Danielson call me. She said, "Hi, Linda!" I smiled nervously.

I don't know quite how, but out of 50 mailboxes, my eyes settled on a yellow note slip. I grabbed it like I knew what I was doing. It said, "Call Linda Morabito at extension 5971." I took it with me and no one saw me do it. I came back downstairs. Steve knew what it was when I threw it into the trashcan behind my desk, between our two desks. We sat there completely speechless at our desks. I was staring into nothing and could see Steve in my peripheral vision doing the same thing for a very long time.

President Ronald Reagan's Advisor Edwin Meese decided to visit Jet Propulsion Laboratory while in California, as the Reagan administration was taking hold in 1981. Jet Propulsion Laboratory wanted him to see where the discovery of the volcanic activity on Io had taken place. The exact timing of his visit was not known. It was about as uncertain it seemed as the future of unmanned space exploration at JPL under the Reagan Administration.

Voyager 2 encountered Jupiter July 9, 1979 and Voyager 1 reached Saturn on November 12, 1980. Our Team had done the navigation completely successfully. Voyager 2 was slated to arrive at Saturn August 25, 1981. As many members of our team sat under the California sun at lunch in the summer of 1981, prior to Voyager

2's arrival at Saturn, we were discussing our individual plans for the future once this final leg was done. There would not be another Voyager encounter until Voyager 2 would arrive at Uranus on January 25, 1986.

A young Ed Riedel told us that he wanted to complete another degree and would be heading back to school. Some of the other members would find projects at the Lab to sustain them, possibly some defense work would intervene. I remember feeling completely dejected that the reward of Voyager was that less would be done in space. It was enough for me to want to leave JPL at that time. This was a milestone in the history of exploration, Voyager, and I sensed a long dry spell coming for the Lab and this kind of work.

In this same timeframe, Frank Jordan had been unnerving me, calling me at the ONIPS area and telling me that within minutes Edwin Meese and the entourage of Meese's own people and JPL people commissioned to support this VIP group on their tour was on its way. Then, he would call back, and tell me they weren't coming just yet, to wait.

Each call made me more and more nervous about something I was very accustomed to doing and that was taking the press and visiting dignitaries through what had happened on my computer to produce the sighting of the first evidence of extraterrestrial volcanism beyond the Earth.

This find was the Holy Grail, the unparalleled equivalent of "E.T.," Extra-Terrestrial, alien life. Because of my discovery, for the first time in the history of space exploration, there was a known-moon, another planet-sized world like Earth, where scientists could observe and study violently active geological processes. Such processes had died out long ago most places in our Solar System.

Frank called again and said Meese was approaching. And for once, he didn't call back. The entourage arrived; I met the members of the delegation and went through my usual routine. However, by then, Frank had me more nervous than at any presentation I had ever done at the ONIPS area.

The entire ONIPS system had been transported across the hall from the original Nav area in Building 264 for the Saturn encounters. The Navigation Team had things going so much like clockwork by then, that it wasn't necessary for us to all be within one bullpen to function as a team. ONIPS had its own room just by my office in Jim McDanell's Group, with pictures of the discovery image on the wall for the Saturn encounters. My picture sitting by my computer on the day Edwin Meese's entourage arrived was featured in JPL's End of the Year Summary in 2002, more than 20 years after my discovery, as well as in JPL 101, a historic introduction to JPL on its website.

I volunteered nothing about my future plans during the lunch over which some members of the Nav Team discussed their futures. I knew what I wanted to do, but could not share it with the group of fellow navigators, all men. My biological clock had gone off resoundingly. I wanted to have a baby. I felt that topic was too different than plans for advanced degrees and new engineering projects and that the mere mention of the subject might scatter this group from the lunch table.

After the Voyager 1 encounter, I had been spending time with, and taking airplane rides with Jerry Hyder of the Nav Team, who lived in Norco, California and had a private airplane at an airfield right next to his home; a small Piper Cherokee. As a pilot, he showed me more adventure than I could have ever dreamed, including a miscalculation, running low on gas over the Oakland airport, and being granted emergency clearance to land, since his airplane did not have the necessary instruments to land at that airport. It was a rushed trip to get Jerry's two boys to their aunt's house in Antioch, between processing data for the first Saturn encounter. I made it back to JPL just in time to do my work.

I had witnessed a meteor enter Earth's atmosphere over Los Angeles one night in a sight that lit up the sky we were flying in, in what seemed like a giant fiery explosion that then disappeared before our eyes.

In only four years, in 1983, I would get the phone call at my home from my brother Gary that he had been confused with someone who had committed a break-in in the area of my parent's apartment, where he lived with them, and the Pasadena police had roughed him up. He didn't sound right in this phone call to me.

It wouldn't be that long after that I would go to the hospital where he was eventually sent and have him ask me questions about our parents and some of our friends, to prove to him I was his sister. I looked into his eyes and they did not focus forward, it looked as if they were looking straight back into his head, although they were looking at me. His degree of mental illness was so extreme that ultimately without medication he would simply become catatonic.

In some ways, back then, this seemed to link his entire life, as if from my mother's initial comments and stories of his childhood that he was never right. But, with all of my education and scientific knowledge, I would never have believed it possible there was a link that bridged this tragedy directly to me, that I was no freer from lifelong effects than my brother, which had already begun influencing nearly every major decision of my life.

As wife and mother over the many years I was with Jerry Hyder when those were my primary roles, my accomplishments went unheralded. They included Birthday celebrations, huge Christmas dinners, vacation planning, entertaining family guests, shopping, cooking, cleaning, laundry, organizing sleepovers for the kids, helping at schools, nearly raising a few neighborhood kids too, taking care of the pets, and delighting in every accomplishment of my husband and children. I was available to my family at all times everyday, for anything I could do to be helpful.

My parents could never understand why I wanted to have children, three let alone even one. My children were remarkable.

Jerry's son Brett at 11 looked very much like a Hummel Figurine with light brown hair that hung straight down to his eyes, perfect skin, dimples on the sides of his eyes that were black as coal. He was very tall, and I can remember asking him once to sit on my lap just as a joke, because he was rapidly trying to pass me up in height, and there had to be one last time to know he was my little boy.

Brett always knew exactly what it would take to be entertained. He brought along a tape cartridge of the Muppets and Kermit the Frog singing precious tunes that made a trip to Lake Havasu, California in 1979 at least bearable. The monster truck of Jerry's we went in, nicknamed "the Mannoleechee" was a beaten up vehicle that was manifestly ugly and had no air conditioning. We traveled in nearly one hundred-and-twenty degree heat under wet towels. If it hadn't been for Kermit the Frog's singing I don't think I would have survived.

Brett would come out of his room each night when he had enough of his homework and proclaim he wanted either ice cream somewhere or a trip in the airplane. Jerry nearly always accommodated. We would all go down to the airport, pile in the small airplane and go into the night sky to see the jewels of the night, city lights, glisten beneath us.

Jerry's boy Jason at six demonstrated a life-long proclivity. Jerry wasn't much for housekeeping as a bachelor, not true for Clint Eastwood in *Play Misty for Me*, but otherwise the analogy held. I once found a small scorpion over by the drapes that were decaying in his dining room before some family guests of his were scheduled to arrive.

In a fully enclosed back room that was once a cement patio of Jerry's home, the kids had put an old mattress on the floor. I watched Jason, who had incredible almond-shaped eyes, and a very round face as a little boy that was irresistibly cute, do acrobatics on the mattress. From my vista, every time Jason hit the mattress, backlit by the many windows in the room, a cloud of dust went up into the air.

Jason's penchant for flying through the air, ultimately became a love of gymnastics, diving, doing double back flips on a trampoline, becoming a parachuting instructor and an ultralight aircraft pilot instructor by age 18, and then a professional pilot.

Ryan was a breathtakingly beautiful baby, who had gorgeous dark hair by the time he was in kindergarten, which started out very light. When he was twelve, he had a passion for chess and was quite good at it. I entered him in his first official tournament. I picked the U.S. Nationals, Game 60.

When we arrived at the two-day tournament, there were easily 100 adults, many of them grand masters. There were probably five children, all of whom were gone by the first rounds; except Ryan.

When Ryan arrived and he saw all the adults he started to cry and said he had never played an adult, except his Mom, and after all I'm just Mom. Then, he sat down to play. He tied for the top unrated player in the tournament.

It was a sight I will never forget when everyone was gathered around him for the final round and he was playing a man who was many times his age, and many times his body mass, and who was sweating profusely right up until the moment that little boy beat him. Jerry sat back from the scene and the crowd around Ryan, because he was crying with emotion over his little boy.

Whether it was Brett or Jason on the little league baseball field, or Jason flying ultralight aircraft, or Brett mastering drafting, or Ryan consistently being awarded for academic excellence; a Presidential Academic Fitness Award, honor roll trophies for every year of elementary school, or winning school wide writing contests, we had plenty of opportunity for pride.

We made many trips to Lake Havasu on the California/Nevada border. We would gather up the kids and allow our older ones to take a friend with them, sometimes a girlfriend.

Our house was a warm, friendly place, where our kids preferred to be with their friends a lot of the time. Sleepovers of friends took many different forms, from kids just sleeping on the ground if they had partied there with our eldest the night before once he was in high school, to our youngest asking us to run power out to the clubhouse that Jerry built in a tree at the far end of the property. I once climbed up the ladder to the entryway in the floor making preparations for kids camping there overnight, when I ended up nose to nose with a monstrous possum. I screamed and the possum ran.

I'm not sure which of us was more afraid.

Norco was a wild, open environment. One day after lightening had hit a bird and it lay in pretty bad shape and with Ryan's cat Starblazer eyeing it, I looked up in the sky to see the entire vista filled with black crows considering attacking Ryan. I urged him forward across our near-acre to get away from them like in a scene from Alfred Hitchcock's movie *The Birds*.

There were always reports of large cats coming onto people's property and killing animals. It was survival of the fittest in Norco.

With my youngest came a succession of pets and I learned how much I adored them and the special way he had for them that ultimately made him many friends in the animal world, from cats to goats.

In 1986, Jerry suffered a heart attack, which was a terrifying experience for all of us, from which he fortunately recovered. When our youngest was only four, he asked me one day after Jerry recovered and headed into the office again, if his father was going to die at work, where he'd had the heart attack.

Jerry had a terrible bout with kidney stones a few years later. He spent extended time at home recovering, and on one occasion also spent a time at home between jobs. When Jerry was at home for any extended period of time, or when we were engaged in a large family event for which I had done all of the work, he was amazed by how hard I worked everyday and seemed appreciative of what I did. Otherwise, he seemed not to be. After more than fifteen years together, a very bad time in Jerry's and my marriage seemed to be taking us over.

In August of 1995, with just our youngest son Ryan still living at home, we took the car trip that Jerry had talked about for years. We would visit national parks and this was our very first extended driving trip. The further we got away from our home, the worse things became. I separated from Jerry immediately upon our return.

I took the CBEST exam so that I could teach math and science at the local middle schools and high schools and keep pace with my youngest son's hours. I wanted to try to do for him what I had done for his brothers, to be there for him when he came home from school. I scored a nearly perfect score on the CBEST exam in August of 1995.

I had no identity in the real world anymore. I didn't have a single credit card in my name and no means of support or way to purchase a home for my son, alone. I had to begin again. This was just the beginning of the adversity of the years that would follow.

Gary had been institutionalized by 1984. After his breakdown, my parents did not seem to understand that his condition was permanent. That illusion in their minds was dispelled when they brought him to my home after he had been released the first time from observation because he was threatening harm to others out of fear of the loss of his mind, and I could see the madness in his eyes again when they brought him to visit me.

I told them to take him away from my house immediately and Ryan who was just an infant, and by the time they got him to their apartment, for a second time he became violent and had to be confined by the authorities.

In a Herculean effort, they got him into a stable environment at a facility in Los Angeles. After years of instability, and ultimately the involvement of a spectacular psychiatrist, Gary stabilized in the facility that became his home, where he met his beautiful wife Gina and married her in 1994. Ironically, Gary's confinement allowed him years of peace and stability, where in the outside world, my life became more and more difficult.

I had done school talks about my discovery over the years my children were growing up. They were uplifting events for the children whose day they touched with a subject that no child seemed disinterested in; space. I could talk about space to children in a way that answered the questions they had always wanted to know. Most children had questions after my talks that forced hands high into the air begging to be called on.

When I would leave the schools, I would look back at the building, and feel what a waste that every classroom had not attended the event that had been so exhilarating for just one class. I remembered this now, as I readied to move out of Jerry's home.

I began a business giving school assemblies. Ryan, who was twelve, was a genius with computers. He created his mother's brochures. I began with the principal of his school, and networked into a deal with Corona-Norco Unified School District that backed me in the business to all the surrounding school districts near and far in exchange for my volunteering my time to middle school girls in conferences put on by the school district to inspire them to become scientists.

It was a win-win situation and this is how I met Aban Daruwalla of the Naval Weapon's Station in Norco. Aban was a brilliant engineer whose team of engineers at the Naval Weapon's Station reported directly to the President of the United States. Her weapons systems were used all over the world. Aban made a career of inspiring young people toward technical fields and would fly to remote corners of the world on her own impetus to promote space science education in areas where there were few resources for that kind of exposure. She and I would continue to work well together during my years at The Planetary Society, and always remained friends.

By January 12, 1996, the local press was covering my first school assembly. Six years before, I had formed an association with a newspaper reporter named Kris Lovekin of Riverside County's *Press Enterprise* newspaper. Kris wrote the story about my discovery when she found out that I had moved to the area permanently. Later in 1996, I would be featured over a much wider range by that same reporter in a story about the ramifications of discipline problems in our public schools. In addition to the assembly programs I offered, I began substitute teaching for the school district. I was given a long term assignment in my son's junior high school that did not include the warning from the principal that the class had forced a long-term teacher into a breakdown and retirement and that a stocky and over six-foot tall teacher who had then taken over left, because he had feared injury from the class.

I was given this group of students.

Later on, in Centennial High School in Corona, at another long-term assignment teaching math, one student who was adult-aged attacked another in my classroom and attempted to beat the other student to death. I stood between them as long as I could to try to stop what was coming. It was impossible.

I have lived through days within school environments that were beyond anything I ever felt I would be exposed to in my lifetime. Gone were the days of McKinley Junior High School and Blair High School. Schools were battlegrounds, it seemed, where the parents had let go of the family structure and discipline within their homes and had left it to the teachers. I have served in that army. I have laughed with teachers in the lunchrooms and spent my time wondering how they could do it day after day. That was why I so thoroughly appreciated and admired the Lewis Center for Educational Research when I first went there, soon to be employed by them in 2007, for the work that they have done in their charter schools in San Bernardino county, giving new hope to the future of education and young people. All schools should be modeled after them.

Gone were the days too of Jet Propulsion Laboratory. I went incognito into a world where my gift was my love of young people. No matter who they were, how hard core or criminal, they were comfortable in my presence. I became known as the only substitute teacher in the district who could do the Calculus in the higher math classes; these students were on the fast track to college. I also became known as the only substitute that the special classes for students who could not be controlled in my son's high school, who could be called directly by the teachers to substitute.

The district person who assigned substitutes had all the authority to even send teachers home without a day's pay if they broke her rules. But, she allowed me to be called directly to do a job that no other substitute could do at the time; spend a day with the hard-core students. Their language never bothered me. Somehow, I saw down to their souls, which were always gentle. The kids knew it.

But, I wasn't earning enough money to keep my son and me in our home that I was able to get with Jerry Hyder's eventual cooperation. I would go back to the world of space exploration. When I left my long-term assignment at Centennial High School to do this, they found the teacher who replaced me in the bathroom before the end of the day throwing up. She couldn't make it through the first day.

Sadly, one day, I stood in front of the home that Ryan and I had found in Norco in November of 1995, which duplicated his father's home that we left. It was like a small ranch. I had two dogs, two cats, two goats, a bird, and a Savanna Monitor as pets for my son.

The neighbor, whom I spoke with only infrequently, listened to some problems we had been having with the beautiful home. When we had bought it we knew it was perfect for us, in the prestigious area of Norco in the Bluffs. The owners of many years had the home completely open to the outside air when we viewed it the first time. When my son and I moved in, we sealed it up due to our common pollen allergy problems. Both Ryan and I had begun to get sick, but Ryan even a lot sicker than I. My neighbor told me that day, "You know, they (the former owners) raised their children in that home and even grandchildren. They had a lot of people in that house. For some reason, they never used that back bedroom." That was the bedroom my son had chosen for his own.

In the winter of 1996, on the advice of the Riverside County Health Association, advice I had to literally bargain for, since there was no agency dedicated to helping people in their homes with mold problems, I was told to begin a search for cracks in the cement foundation of the home.

By that time, Ryan was so sick, we had moved to a hotel, and had run from the home as the water table rose in the winter months and the situation began to disintegrate. Fate had been so unkind from early years to my son.

We were only one city block from the Santa Ana River. A heating and air conditioning person found the crack in the plenum chamber to the central air immediately, complaining as he did that his eyes were stinging from a cloud of fumes that passed by us in the hall. He said, "What was that?"

The entire house would ultimately get the mold contamination by late in the winter as it had the year before. But, the bedroom my son had chosen would get it first. Jerry Hyder and I pulled back the carpeting in my son's bedroom to find the cracks that allowed us at some point to see through to the dirt below. When he pulled the carpeting back, I felt like my head would implode, since I too had suffered so much exposure to the mold by that point. Jerry did not feel anything until the next day, he told me later. He began to stagger while walking through Home Depot looking for the material to seal the cracks with. That next morning, when I got out of bed in the hotel where Ryan and I were staying, I staggered across the room until I could gain my footing.

I had the cracks sealed and moved my son out of that room and positively pressurized the house in the room where the problem had been worst. I spent ten thousand dollars repairing the house and on medical expenses for my son. We eventually enlisted the help of a physicist who understood the mechanism of the exposure and that given enough oxygen, the effects of the mold could oxidize and not be so bothersome, but in a sealed house the way we had lived with our pollen allergies, we never stood a chance.

I came to The Planetary Society this way, hired in February 1997. I am extremely youthful genetically, and appeared very much in my prime. My last remaining child at home had his health devastated by the mold in our home, I was so alone in the world that I literally had no one that I knew to drive me home from a wisdom tooth extraction that I needed, so I could not allow the dentist to put me out for the procedure, my father had suffered a heart attack in 1996 and was then in a car accident that gave him a compression fracture in his back, and my mother, who had never learned to drive a car was beginning to depend more and more on me, and I was still undergoing the formal divorce proceedings with Jerry.

As I began a new life that would take me back into the exploration of other worlds, my father began a journey toward his death. It was the way that he would die that created the porthole into a parallel universe.

Dave Meyer had comforted me and held me during the worst remembrances a human being can have. He explains to me that because he served as an Air Force pilot for more than twenty years, including two tours of service in Vietnam and on an aircraft carrier on loan to the Marine Corps for more than two years, he can handle stress like this in a much different way than other people can. It is true. I have seen him demonstrate to me often the remarkable way in which his mind works. He sees things much differently, from a different and calm perspective that is rooted in his heroism and in his faith. It is hard to imagine that this intellectual instructor of Astronomy who reminds me most of Gibson's teaching style when he teaches or presents planetarium lectures, is a man who defended his country and could have died many, many times for it. Perhaps what we understand most in common is that there is evil in this world.

I tell him it is a mistake, and I shout and cry this. It is a mistake that I was sent back. When I left the Earth inside that animal, and had known the greatest peace any human being could know, it was a mistake; because of what happens after.

I had been in Connie's office when I had seen what was at the end of the corridor road that led to the sky, which I had only first experienced from outside my body, rising up as a small speck of the universe, after I originally remembered the torture of the animal and me.

When I was finished recounting the greatest peace I had ever known, what I had seen at the end of this acceleration to the sky and was drying my tears, Connie told me, "I think you were sent back, Linda. This time, you were not given a choice."

In our church in Hesperia there are congregational members who are among the finest people I have every met, including friends of Dave's and mine who are closest to us. There are some in the congregation who are sure of every word of the Bible and everything that God has told us.

There are two things that I know now from the little girl in a parallel universe. One is that the evil that exists is so profound and in fact so directly manifested sometimes on the Earth, that if others had seen what I had seen, churches everywhere would have standing room only and people lined up at the doors unable to be accommodated because churches are only so big.

The other thing I know is that sometimes God does things that we cannot understand by words alone. It is important to recite the Bible's words and to know the Bible as the Word of God. But, we are only human. Our thoughts are only human. We cannot know God completely.

We cannot know what God had in mind when I believe a mistake is made.

For I will come back to Earth, my body removed from the animal now dead, on a cross, and what involves the deepest level of subhuman behavior people can exhibit; torture, rape, excrement and urine, performed on a helpless child who is but a baby.

––––––––––

It had been many hours since first seeing the anomaly in the picture of Io. My analysis of this image hadn't been stopped yet by anything, and although I did not know the path to walk on for survival that day of March 9, 1979, I was still walking, and therefore was being given the chance to find out.

With crowds still milling in and out of the ONIPS room, and Steve Synnott and I sitting there at our desks, Andy Collins walked over and asked Steve if he could call in the Voyager Project Scientist, Dr. Edward Stone. Steve granted that permission. Dr. Stone would become the Director of Jet Propulsion Laboratory in 1982.

For Ed Stone's exposure to the discovery that day, and again the next, and every day since, I have nothing but the deepest admiration for him and the most profound respect. Years later, I would watch Ed Stone literally run after a researcher compiling information on Voyager and say, "Come over here! Talk to Linda!" I didn't fit into the theme of his book and the researcher sort of ignored Ed. I was delighted, laughing with Lou Friedman at my side about what Ed was doing running after the man, and felt privileged enough to just be looking on. Although the interactions I have had with Ed Stone have been all too brief over the years, each one affirms the integrity of this remarkable man.

I believe Ed Stone knew what he was seeing in the image of Io right away when he arrived at the ONIPS area, although he did not say that. His eyes were literally twinkling, with no exaggeration, and he kept repeating to himself, "This has been an incredible mission."

When Ed Stone left the ONIPS area, saying and doing nothing more, the crowd finally dispersed.

Steve Synnott and I got to work. We were aware of one set of latitude and longitude parameters, for the heart-shaped feature on Io. It was longitude 250 degrees, latitude –30 degrees.

Steve made a phone call to get the sub-spacecraft latitude and longitude on the Io picture. It was 338 degrees longitude and –4 degrees latitude. Knowing the orientation of the picture, and that ONIPS inverts pictures from the spacecraft, I was able to do the computations in my head for an approximate latitude and longitude of the anomaly if it were on a gas shell on Io. I estimated 90 degrees further east in longitude and 30 degrees further south in latitude. That put the anomaly at 248 degrees longitude and –34 degrees latitude, too close to the longitude and latitude of the heart-shaped feature to ignore.

This moment evoked my knowledge of history and the story of Jocelyn Bell. I don't think I said anything very polite on this subject to Steve. There was no joy in this discovery at this point. I told Steve of the very real possibility that credit for this find could easily be taken away from us. I didn't want to love astronomy any less. I didn't want any more grief right now. Another thing I realized at this moment was that I had looked upon that ugly heart-shaped feature on Io courtesy of our backbreaking navigation only five days before, and actually wept. Now, it felt like I had been gazing into destiny.

Armed with this new revelation of a latitude and longitude of the gas shell, we were now hypothesizing it might be, Steve and I set out for the Imaging Team area to find Andy Collins and Peter Kupferman.

It was a fight to get people out of Andy's office so that we could shut the door, but once they started leaving, it is amazing how fast it cleared out. Not many of these people were scientists themselves, fortunately, or they would have wondered about our presence there.

Present were Andy, Steve, Peter, and me. I do not recall Andy's specific reaction to our revealing that the cloud was hanging basically over the largest surface feature on Io, but all of us were gravely serious throughout the meeting.

We established a plan behind those closed doors. Andy had an ingenious idea. The very software that had been used to find the centers of satellite images to a high accuracy on ONIPS, could now be used to limb-fit a volcanic plume, to find its center, thereby determining to a high accuracy the latitude and longitude of the ejection center. I would limb-fit a circle to the edge of the crescent of the gas cloud, and Peter would help me to determine the satellite based latitude and longitude of the ejection center of the cloud.

Ironically, at lunch, Steve had been sitting with people who were discussing Stanton Peale's publication that had predicted an "active" Io. The mechanism of the Io volcanism, as discussed by Stanton Peale in his article, was a gravitational pumping of the satellite induced on Io by the other Galileans.

Andy said ejection velocities and particle sizes of the eruption would have to be determined.

Andy strongly suggested again that he be allowed to make digifax hard-copies of the picture. This time I consented. He had been responsible for putting T. OWENS for Toby Owens, who I understand had believed in and campaigned for the long exposure picture that revealed the ring, on the digifax hard-copy discovery picture of the ring of Jupiter. It was the one that Steve and I had found on our desks after the image had been brought to ONIPS. Now Andy would write "MORABITO/SYNNOTT" on our discovery picture.

When Steve and I returned to the Navigation area, I went into the ONIPS room and I got to work immediately. It was late into the day now. Steve came into the ONIPS room and he was acting very restless, very much an outward manifestation of what I had been dealing with all day.

I probably could not conceal the hope in my eyes that he was there for me on this with his technical expertise. He said, "You will never forgive me if I go home." I thought about it and hesitantly replied that I guessed I would understand.

"No you won't," he said, and left anyway. He was right, I didn't.

I remember exactly where I was in 1988 when I read Steven Hawking's *A Brief History of Time* in which he described that the universe might have been zero-sized at some time in the past, but never had a singularity event in which the laws of physics break down. I was sitting at my kitchen table in my home in Norco. When the kids were at school during the daytime, I went back to the study of my original passion of the origins of the universe, cosmology.

What was significant about what Hawking wrote is that he cut across disciplines in his search for the scientific origins of the beginnings of everything we see around us in space, and our own world. Hawking, in a scientific treatise of his newest ideas at the time, mentioned God. He felt that if the universe was in fact expanding and contracting to a zero-size and then re-expanding there was nothing for a God to do; no set of initial conditions need be established by a God, as would be needed in a cataclysmic explosion that most astronomers believed had begun the universe.

This explosion, called the Big Bang, was the most widely held theory of the origins of the Universe by astronomers. It held that 13 to 14 billion years ago, the universe began with one large, cataclysmic event.

Hawking and other scientists were searching for a Unified Theory of Physics, one in which all of the natural forces in the universe could be explained. These forces that scientists observe, are 1) electromagnetic, which produces electricity, magnetism, and light, 2) strong nuclear force, which binds neutrons and protons together in the cores of atoms, 3) weak nuclear force, which causes sub-atomic particle decay, and 4) gravity, which acts between all the mass in the universe. In addition to looking outward into the vastness of space for the answers to the origins of existence, scientists were beginning to look at the smallest particles that make up everything in the universe, including ourselves, and how they behaved quantum mechanically.

At the highest pressures and temperatures at the moment of the Big Bang, scientists were able to get far enough along with their Unified Theory to understand that three of the four natural forces in the universe looked the same. Gravity, however, the force that holds the galaxies together, and keeps Earth in its orbit around the Sun, still eluded them in a Unified Theory.

Hawking's progression of thought was ironic. He had pioneered the work on black holes, stars that are so dense and collapse so thoroughly when they die and cease shining (cease generating thermonuclear reactions at their cores), that they collapse down into a singularity, a place where not even light can escape. Ultimately, Hawking decided that black holes weren't so black, that indeed light could escape from a dead star called a black hole.

Then, he took the next step by saying that not even the universe began with a violent explosion in which the laws of physics did not apply. It simply expanded and contracted over time along a fourth dimension that no one had considered before in this regard, expressing time as imaginary, which has a specific and definite meaning in mathematics. In other words, when Hawking looked at things in a way no one else had before, he managed to frame the entire past and present of the universe in a way that didn't require a singularity event, or a massive explosion, and in his estimation, didn't require a God.

I loved hearing a scientist talk about God, even if I disagreed with his conclusions. I enjoyed his historical references throughout the book and the merging of science and history. I have always hoped for a Renaissance of educational emphasis to sweep the world and move us forward in our understanding of the human condition. Hawking took a giant leap in my estimation by looking at things in a way no one else had done before.

Now, much more progression of thought has happened, and scientists look to an eleventh dimension to explain the force of gravity, and do not believe the universe will contract over time. But, Hawking still incorporates his no boundary principle and what is called Hawking radiation, or the escape of energy from a black hole.

I began writing speculative science after I read Hawking's book. I wrote several works of science fiction over the next so many years, *The Gods of Eden*, *The Mangod*, and one essay on the subject, which Gibson Reaves read, as well as the famed literary agent Scott Meredith, who was Carl Sagan's literary agent.

Gibson honored me with a response I will never forget. He told me, "I taught you the [classic] Big Bang theory, but I never believed it." He was awed. Scott Meredith told me if I got one work published of those I had already submitted for consideration to be published to call him immediately.

Baen Books held onto three of my novel manuscripts of these themes for 18 months with promises to publish. When I contacted Professor Shelley Lowenkopf of USC's creative writing department for advice, on the basis of being an alumnas of USC, he absolutely panicked and indicated that Baen Books had no right to delay publication that long.

His panic in a field, creative writing, in which I had no formal training, panicked me. I was instructed to tell Baen Books that I had "relied upon them to my disadvantage" and to send the manuscripts back to me immediately. When that happened, Baen sent me photocopies back with pages missing, not my original manuscripts. The situation escalated as it fell apart.

Years later, an author I respected told me I should just have left the manuscripts at Baen and let them get around to publishing them.

What did the parents of two small children born in Vancouver, British Columbia, Canada, want to do with their children? The short answer, for me at least, was trying to kill them. These are children they didn't want, had tried to abort one of them, and claimed that both were accidents. These were adults who could not imagine why I in adulthood would want to have a child.

In hiring the expert on Beach Grove, Tsawwassen historian Gwen Szychter, a possible scenario has emerged. Gwen Szychter visited the local Ladner Police Department in June of 2006 in search of the Delta records for the summer of 1956. The head of police there tells her that by my parents' demeanor, nothing would have happened necessarily for the benefit of their children, publicly. Back then, things were not done that way, the way they would be now.

In discussions with me, Gwen helps me envision a logical perspective by my parents. My mother had omitted me from any mention in this story; it took fifty years for me to know I too had cut feet from the terrain on Centennial Beach. It was so wise of her to do that. She had tried to kill at the prospect of discovery of what she and my father were doing. Omission to her was nothing.

What my parents had undoubtedly told authorities back then was a variation of what I had been told all my life. My parents might have said, two people took not just my brother for a walk, but my brother and me for a walk that day, and when they got back, the children were terribly hurt. One with a brain injury and the other raped and assaulted so badly with a steel cross that she could easily have died.

No one would have believed them at first, except to the extent that my mother's lies were seamless and she had been getting away with her lies for her entire life; and had perhaps at some time in her life gotten away with murder. When growing up, she had convinced an entire class that she had a photo of a manufacturing plant as a mandatory part of a report she had given in school. In the photo she had no such plant or plant workers were shown. But, by the end of her report, everyone in the class would swear to her that they could see this in the photo. In adulthood, if my mother ever transgressed by showing her true personality and an adult would ask and expect an apology, my mother would turn the situation around so devastatingly, that the other adult always ended up apologizing to her. My parents had the air of respectability, quality, and integrity about them, even when it was the farthest thing from the truth.

But, as the head of the police department in Delta said they would not have been charged with only logical suspicion back then. The doctor at the hospital we were taken to definitely did not believe them, and undoubtedly threatened them accordingly. My life and my brother's hung in the balance of what that doctor must have said to my parents.

The scenario has imbedded within it a key ingredient that has been missing from my understanding. I have wondered what circumstances stopped the physical abuse cold from the time of my brother's attack. If the sexual abuse were attributed to two strangers who escaped and got away, my parents would be forced to eliminate this activity from their lives completely to prevent future self-incrimination. We lived only a one-hour drive from where these events took place. The layout and circumstances mandated the end of the sexual abuse.

By, 2009, my brother Gary had suffered two serious health conditions that required extended hospital stays and nursing home care, where he remains now. In the most recent one, he nearly died of aspiration of stomach contents into his lungs when ironically fear over his physical health manifested itself as if he were somehow off his psychiatric medication, and sent him to the hospital.

His mental health issues when coupled with physical problems are some of the most difficult issues I have ever had to contend with. I did this during the last year, when so much else was happening as well.

Gary is one of the kindest and gentlest and most thoughtful people I have ever known. His love for me is infinite as is mine for him. His life in his love for his wife, and the love he has shown his sister, and the fact that he gave his life for me that day in 1956 by standing up to my parents are meaningful to an astounding degree. I have written some of my thoughts down in a letter that I will show him one day:

"When we did not find the type of parents who would keep us from harm, when we did not find a single thinking soul, we created them. We created the adults, even as children, who could raise us. We imbued them with qualities of respect for the things in life that should be respected, honesty and integrity, we gave them an intrinsic wisdom, we viewed them generous and altruistic, and then we put the faces of our two parents on the caregivers we had created. These qualities, particularly of gentleness and selflessness, were our own qualities. These are the adults that we became. We raised ourselves in the image of these gentle, good and thinking people. The vestiges we left behind of the two wonderful parents who raised us were holograms superimposed into our small world and never existed.

"I think we brought out the best in the two people who raised us over the very long run. We set the bar very high and they, to the extent possible, believed themselves these people. It served them to do this. Sincerely, I believe our father got well. He carried with him in the darkest place of his soul, however, the memory of a different kind of man.

"My heart now carries for you the Medals of Honor you have earned. Perhaps my entire soul is living homage to you. In your heroism are the deep roots of everything that makes this world tolerable. You gave your life and your future to what you believed was right. At age 5, you possessed more knowledge of right and wrong than two people who had lived decades more than you. Your daily life is more honorable than anything they ever achieved.

"I too have tried to live the best life that I could. Now, I must carry a burden of knowledge. The burden that you carried all of your life, the damage to your mind inflicted by our parents, you have done with grace and humility, an intrinsic sense of wisdom, and optimism. I hope to do the same. I hope to earn the sacrifice you made for me 50 years ago. It won't be easy, but nothing we have done in this lifetime, sadly from the time of our births has been that."

Joseph Dickson once told me that people with my brother's mental condition are not self-reflective, fortunately, to understand what their personal lives and limitations really are. During Gary's first of two extended hospitalizations for physical problems last year, I was riveted to know this is not the case for Gary. He scoffed when I indicated to him that he would get well and return to the happy life he had known at his home. It is much more than I can think about to realize that Gary knows what our parents took from him so long ago.

They took in a final act, everything that they believed they were entitled to. They took his health, his reason, his eyes; his normal place in this world. They took his future because he belonged to them. Gary did not live by any higher power than they. We were accidents to them, so they held no responsibility to honor that we lived. They inflicted so much physical injury on Gary, his brain and eyes, that Gary gave to me in his young act of heroism to try to stop them, all that he had in this world. He succeeded when they could not hide his injuries.

I can only believe that my mother was not too concerned when Gary was born, and not anything beyond a fine looking baby in terms of his appearance. I can only surmise that she wanted to come home from the ceremonies where she took me, and I believe Gary, with one less child, notably her daughter. I was very beautiful as a baby. That won't work for a Narcissist.

I can only surmise that my mother was determined to do the job herself when she could no longer rely upon the people who were summoning a power far more evil than they could possibly imagine no longer wanted to do the job.

Tragically for me, I would come to know the reason my mother had to try herself.

There is something in the face of the costumed man who performs the torture. I mean that literally. There is something in his face. I tell Connie, I know what this is. I have been trying to fight this for a long time. It is better just to say it. I believe I saw the residents of Hell.

In returned memory, I have seen what seemed like demons swirling through the air and fire, but I can to those dates only imagine the frantic intensity of these ceremonies, which would begin at least on one occasion with my blood flowing from my body cut with a razor blade. I have lost count of the number of memories I have had now of my own blood coming from my body and the horror that instills in a human being, knowing and seeing the damage to their flesh, most often from outside my body, where my mind would help me survive. The instances I have recounted in this volume were experiences of near death, far beyond merely out of body, however.

I am certain when I first see the images of my mother attacking me in full detail playing from end to end, that the images that I have of hands like claws and snarling of animals pertains to the practices of these people. But, what I do not think my mother knew was that she was but a buffoon of the evil she had summoned. I do not think she knew what a two-year-old child knew, that she was the clown, naked, moving her hips in ritualistic decadence to a sickly beat, who thought she was in charge, in the presence of the being who wants our eternal death. Perhaps because I was a child, so young, I could see or sense what she could not.

When I see what I do in Connie's office, I tell her that the man in the Devil costume is a fool. "He is a fool!" He had no idea what he was mustering. Human beings are no more a match for what he summoned that day, than we are for God.

Andy Collins had suggested upstairs on the third floor of Building 264 that Peter Kupferman work with me on the determination of the latitude and longitude of the ejection center of the place the volcanic plume was emanating from. When Peter came back to the ONIPS area, we worked for the next two hours.

As we began, navigation people came in occasionally to inquire. This was a strain on me, because I did not know what would transpire. I was so worried they would talk to the wrong person later that night, I didn't know what to expect at any turn.

Fred Peters, on one trip in, said, "You can't base a find on one picture in Astronomy."

"Yes, but we have correlation with something on the surface," I retorted.

"On the surface!" Fred said, astonished. I couldn't blame him, it was the initial psychological problem I had with the image; how resistant this discovery picture was to giving up its secret. The projection was huge, 0.15 of Io's radius, 250 kilometers above the limb of Io.

Fred said again that another observation would be needed for verification. I said, "It may not be there when we look again." I know Fred was stunned. I could only apologize to him for not saying more.

It was getting dark outside now, and most of the people in the Nav area had gone home for the weekend. This was an incredible situation because no maps of Io existed yet to correlate Io's surface features with latitude and longitude; with one exception, however.

At the very moment we were working in the ONIPS room with the image of Io, a preliminary pictorial map of Io was being drawn by a U.S. Geological Survey artist upstairs in the Science Imaging Area, whom I would later come to know was P.M. Bridges. She was airbrushing in surface features of Io with breathtaking perfection in what looked like a partially completed photograph of a flat projection of Io, coming together on a latitude and longitude grid.

Peter warned me while we were still in the ONIPS room not to show any visible excitement if some of our theorized ejection centers turned up on top of what could apparently now be considered volcanoes. It was good advice. I remained very calm.

Peter and I had no choice but to function in the following way: every time we would derive a new ejection center we would jump up, run upstairs, and ask the artist if we could please look over her shoulder, or could she just look and see if she saw any kind of a surface feature at a certain latitude and longitude. Then, we would go back downstairs to try to use different parameters for our derivations, derive a new center, and do it all over again.

A small variation in our model of the cloud virtually whose crescent alone was visible, produced large variations in ejection centers, but none too far from the general region of the heart-shaped feature on Io. We repeated this process so many times based on varying models of the cloud that eventually the artist wanted to know where we were getting these locations.

Joe Veverka from Cornell, a Science Imaging Team member, one of the few who remained in this area now, whom I knew from Viking, watched Peter and I come and go with much suspicion. At one point, he put his hand up and came very close to stopping us, but he hesitated, and didn't.

As we sat back downstairs in the ONIPS room in between trips, Peter verbalized what I was feeling at the moment. "The more you work with it, the more you think it's real." Working with data in a new discovery puts the discoverer in a very unique situation for interpretation of that data. I always pay special, close attention now to what the discoverers of any new phenomenon have to say about their original studies; such as the discovery of the Martian meteorite ALH84001 holding evidence that magnetite crystals are of biological origin. I weight their original analysis very heavily, depending of course on what they did, in my opinion of the chances for ultimate validation of the discovery, in comparison to dissenting opinions that follow.

The ONIPS software was not able to conclusively tell us what we were looking for, it was not designed for this work, nor did it perform at any point well under crescent lighting.

Peter and I eventually abandoned that approach and began working geometrically with the image. No model we tried got us far from the heart-shaped feature. When we had done what we could, Peter surprised me by telling me that Andy Collins had called Larry Soderblom, second in command of the Science Imaging Team earlier that afternoon to report the discovery. After a moment of consideration that didn't seem too bad. Obviously no one upstairs knew about the discovery, and Larry was at USGS in Flagstaff, Arizona.

Many years later, Andy Collins would be kind enough to share a little more insight into what did and did not happen that day. He had called Brad Smith in charge of the Science Imaging Team, who was back in Arizona, as he had called Larry Soderblom.

In retrospect, Andy had no choice whatsoever. The Science Imaging Team was charged with this mandate. Discoveries on the missions were their directive. They knew about Stanton Peale's article, it could not have been overlooked as it was in the world of Voyager navigation engineering.

Andy's communication with Brad Smith failed that day. I understand he heard from Brad Smith the next morning, who indicated he was aware that Andy had tried to let him know about something the day before. He asked Andy what it was that he had conveyed.

The hours and minutes of March 9, 1979, could have turned out more challenging than they even were by any turn of fate. But, it was a good thing for me there was no more than I had already handled. I called Andy at 8:15 PM after Peter left. Andy was at MTIS in the Space Flight Operations Facility. I was moments away from finding out I was simply too tired to even be able to form words of sentences anymore.

I would later hear stories of how evidence of active volcanism on Io had been discarded in image processing techniques that had been specified by the Team to the IPL, the Image Processing Lab at JPL, but I have no concrete verification of that whatsoever. Dave Pieri, who was a PhD candidate at that time, and whose wife also worked for the Lab until he received his PhD, shared one story with me directly.

He said he spotted evidence of an eruption in a picture taken for science and had it explained away to him by a scientist on the Team.

What was crucial about making the discovery when I did, was that there was an immediate opportunity to go back to look at Io with Voyager 2 on its way in less than four months, and reprogram the mission on an Io intensive basis.

Had the discovery continued to elude the scientists, the opportunity would have been missed and not come again for another sixteen years when the Galileo spacecraft went into orbit around Jupiter.

I met Carl Sagan for the first and only time eight years before I ever went to work at the organization he created with Lou Friedman and Bruce Murray, The Planetary Society. Carl invited me, and many others of the Voyager mission to a party he was holding at his home with his first wife to celebrate the successful Voyager 1 encounter with Jupiter in 1979.

I found Carl to be exceptionally polite and he included me in both his book and television series *Cosmos*, as the discoverer of the active volcanism on Io. He complimented me on my presentation in *Cosmos* the series. He seemed a very nice person.

His second wife Ann Druyan, a member of the Board of Directors of The Planetary Society, is one of those gracious people one never forgets. I would meet her periodically at Society meetings and events. I came to The Planetary Society in February of 1997, after Carl Sagan passed away December 20, 1996.

The Society was in the process of planning *Planetfest '97* when I was hired. *Planetfest '97* was a celebration of accomplishments in space and would be held July 4-6, 1997 at the Pasadena, California Convention Center, to bring thousands of people together to witness the landing of the Pathfinder spacecraft on

Mars. It was to be a technology demonstration for the public as well, highlighting the capabilities of the computer age with personal computers filling the convention center and the possibility of a live participation in the event for hundreds of thousands of people if not more, on the Internet. At the time that I was hired by the Society, five months before the event, no one had succeeded in locating a single computer for use during the event, and no one had raised any sponsorship money.

My job was to create "A Child's Universe" at *Planetfest '97*. This was a family event and for the first time at an event like this, the Society would cater directly to children in what was slated to be a wonderland of children's activities that allowed them to learn about space while just having fun.

"A Child's Universe" could easily have taken the remaining five months to develop just by itself. However, I asked for and was granted by Lou the right to try to bring in some sponsors for the event. I had never done work like this in my life.

By the time I was done, in three months, I brought in Ball Plastic, Earthlink Network, Gateway 2000, Home Depot, Instructional Fair, Kidspace Museum, LA Unified School District, Lockheed Martin, NASA Office of Education, Price Costco, Sky Publishing Corporation, Smart & Final, Sun Microsystems Computer Corporation, Target Pasadena, and URLabs for cash and in-kind donations totaling hundreds of thousands of dollars.

I heard Lou scream one day, "Every time the phone rings it's someone begging to give Linda more money for *Planetfest*, and we are paying her a clerk's salary!" which was true at the time. My phone was ringing when he said it.

Ultimately in one such call Sun Microsystems told me they were wiring the entire convention center for Internet participation for the world at *Planetfest '97* at no cost to us. I had called most of these companies cold to ask for their sponsorship. I would eventually sign Sun Microsystems to a nearly one million-dollar commitment to Red Rover Goes to Mars, but Sun suffered an internal collapse, which nullified the agreement. I had this talent for attracting sponsors, apparently, of which I was completely unaware.

The Pasadena Convention Center was filled to capacity with computers that I got for use for use at *Planetfest '97*. Lou fired his high-priced consultants who hadn't brought in any sponsorship. I told Lou after several months that was enough on my part or there wouldn't be "A Child's Universe" at all, two months before the event.

I started working around the clock without sleep to get "A Child's Universe" done, at one point actually getting a little sleep walking through a store that was donating to us one day. I had never had that experience before, napping while walking. I created 197 on-site activities for children over the three days of *Planetfest '97*, which involved a museum, a Japanese water rocket team, and public transportation throughout Pasadena as well.

One of the Pasadena Convention Center officials told me afterward that many events promise family attractions, then don't deliver for kids. He said "A Child's Universe" was the best that he had seen. I enlisted an army of what I called Angels, teachers from all over the United States, coordinated by Sheri Klug to handle the activity sessions for kids. If not for those volunteers and the over two hundred others who worked like actual employees of the Society, not even the supplies for "A Child's Universe" could have come into being.

I had a strong affinity for working together with people and creating team spirit. By the time I rested when *Planetfest '97* was over, myself and many of the staff, including my supervisor Cindy Jalife, had literally forgotten how to sleep. But, this work changed lives. That was the thing about The Planetary Society, its events and involving the public in space exploration always changed the lives of those people it touched. The Society was capable of doing good things for the advancement of space exploration often on a massive scale.

We had the time of our lives with this work too. I worked with Apollo 13 Astronaut Buzz Aldrin on producing the recording that people would hear when they called ticketron for tickets to *Planetfest '97*.

Space Shuttle Astronaut Story Musgrave called my home one day to discuss his participation with me, since I worked two days out of the week in my home in Norco with that very large commute, once I had repaired my home from the mold exposures, and Ryan and I moved back in.

At *Planetfest '97*, when Pathfinder landed safely on Mars and the first pictures of the Martian Terrain came back with a new generation of cameras and technology since Viking, the cheering of thousands of people at the event made me so happy Ryan was present. It was fun for Ryan to have his Mom doing this kind of work.

One day, not too long after *Planetfest '97*, Ryan saved our lives in the house where we waged our battle against the mold, by waking me up before our heater ignited, and was sending smoke into the hallway.

I knew I always worked too hard and slept too deeply to have woken up at all to have saved us if Ryan hadn't noticed smoke before any smoke detector went off.

I scrambled into the hall when he woke me and managed to turn the heater off instances before it ignited, the fire department later told me. I described what had happened in an email to the staff later that day that I entitled "My Hero."

Ryan was still suffering from the mold exposure he had, even then. Once I moved Ryan to Arcadia to get completely away from that home, a teacher of his at Arcadia High School would give him viral meningitis, and over the course of years, Ryan would lose the sight in one of his eyes, despite the fact that neither of the major eye institutes in Southern California could diagnose correctly that he had lost his sight from optic neuritis, common with meningitis, until his sight was completely gone in that eye. They accused this young man of not having a real loss of sight, until a neurologist at USC diagnosed him easily, and could not understand why the diagnosis had never, over years been made before.

Ryan, as a baby had nephrotic syndrome, kidney disease, from which he recovered with great difficulty after treatment at UCLA, which definitely saved him. Although the cause of nephrotic syndrome is not known, most doctors I have spoken with trace it to a Lindane prescription incorrectly given to our entire family, including the baby, by an aging family doctor long overdue for retirement. My boy has seen the most difficult of times in his life. My heart weeps for my son, whom I love more than life itself, everlasting.

By the time The Planetary Society had its first staff retreat to discuss its future and its past, after my arrival there, it seemed the primary topic of discussion during the retreat became me. Charlene Anderson, Associate Director of the Society, had her own ideas of how I should be utilized. They had never seen someone bring in sponsorship for events that effectively. Money was a huge issue for a non-profit organization, of course.

I felt like a lightening rod. I was already Lou's showpiece. As time went by, a typical introduction of me to anyone at JPL when we were on Lab together, as we sometimes were, went like this one with Lou:

When Lou introduced me to Matt Golombek, the scientist star of Mars Pathfinder's mission, and one of the nicest people I have ever known, he said, "Matt, this is Linda Hyder. She used to work here at JPL and discovered the active volcanoes on Io. She's working for me now. She's a lot more famous than you. No, wait, let me think. No, I guess not. No, no, definitely. She's a lot more famous than you." Matt, in his wonderful way, just smiled.

Lou loved all things Russian. He spent an enormous amount of time in Russia and would ultimately come to work extremely closely with the Russians on Cosmos 1, the first-ever solar sail mission. At times, in my early years at the Society, I wondered if Lou could tell that my grandparents had all been born in Russia and if that was why he seemed so enamored with me.

Andy Collins called me as the hours went later into the night and said to come over to MTIS in the Spaceflight Operation Facility. I did possess a red card that provided restricted access to the facility so that I was able to do that. Andy showed me the hard-copy digifax of the discovery picture he was making. He had done some stretches and high-pass filtering as well.

In the high pass filter product, I could see features on Io, the crescent was not completely overexposed, and a possible indication of brightening in the region of the cloud, indicating that the best model of its ejection center might be on the front of the disk coming at us, rather than originating from behind.

I was very candid with Andy about my concerns about the discovery, but mostly I talked about what the science meant to me. I was so exhausted now, the words sometimes didn't form correctly.

I told Andy this discovery was now part of me and could never stop here for me. In ways I could not have predicted then, that was exactly correct. I would indeed go on to head another discovery on another world accomplished by another generation on Mars for The Planetary Society.

Andy seemed a little speechless. He may have been able to tell how hard I was fighting to conceal what was past exhaustion now. In my mind, since I could come up with no further thinking of any kind, my position was threatened by incapacitation on my part.

Andy volunteered the fact that he had called Larry Soderblom in Arizona. I was glad he mentioned it. It lessened its significance. Depending upon whether Larry took the train in or flew back, we would meet either Sunday night or Monday morning, OPNAVERs and scientists in a spirit of complete cooperation.

Andy asked if he could call me at home over the weekend to let me know whether the meeting would be Sunday or Monday. Andy was being very, very kind. As he had surely known when he had asked me, he had my permission to call me at home.

I would receive another call at home in the coming week. The head of the Science Imagine Team, Brad Smith called one morning to weakly ask what was my background. I am guessing he had been asked by the press often, and had no answer. When I told him I was an astronomer, I heard an audible sigh of relief.

My parents had been waiting for hours for me to show up at their apartment for dinner. It was to have been a fairly routine day, so I had accepted their invitation the day before. I had called them repeatedly throughout the evening having to postpone my arrival.

When I arrived, I must have looked like I was not in good shape. My father asked fittingly, "Is this something we should be happy about?"

I said yes, but explained how easily the credit could be taken from me for the discovery. He then said that it was better to face the fight, than to have not had it happen at all. And then he added, "Do you realize you may have discovered the only other volcanically active body in the Solar System?" His grasp of the situation took me very much by surprise.

My parents began a journey of their own then, which would turn their world upside down with elation. They began buying newspapers, magazines, such as *National Geographic*, *Smithsonian*, *Scientific American*, and *Time Magazine*, anything that mentioned my discovery.

Time noted in its January 21, 1980 issue, that the volcanic activity on Io was the cover story on all the three aforementioned magazines in their January 1980 issues, total circulation 12,750,000. Rather than having the same volcanic eruption pictured on all three magazines be a nightmare, instead the magazines viewed this as confirming their good judgment, the story in *Time* goes.

My parents became celebrities in a sense, the center of adoring attention by friends and family. For many years, I held that the discovery was primarily important on a personal basis for me, in addition to the importance to science, because of the happiness it brought to them.

Everyone at The Planetary Society was supportive of my loss when my father died in 1999. One day, I was in Lou's office. He knew my father had been sick for a long time, so he didn't seem to think there was too much trauma associated with his passing. I mentioned to him that I couldn't have stood it another day to see my father suffering anymore than he had when he died.

I didn't know why Lou looked so stunned. No one had been able to tell by my demeanor those were the circumstances of my father's death. I had been a good soldier, enduring what might have openly broken another person. It made Lou stop in his tracks.

Ultimately, Lou Friedman called me into his office once when he learned of even some of the adversity I had faced over time.

He said, "Linda, it's hard to understand how you can have gone through some of the things that you have and have just kept on going."

I had noticed over time that other people sometimes seemed weak to me, weaker than I was. That they would give in or give up or cry at work or were known for their sadness or problems. I simply got stronger, more and more like a soldier in a war with each passing trial.

He asked me if I could explain how I had been able to manage the many things I had been through. I told him, "Lou, there was always a child involved, my son, and for him the buck stops here with me. There was no way no matter what was happening in my life to do anything but stay strong for him."

It was the truth. But, he had noticed outright what Joseph Dickson would notice later on. That kind of demeanor I possessed had its origin somewhere.

I loved working at The Planetary Society. When my supervisor, Cindy Jalife left in 1998, I was offered the position of Manager of Education and Program Development. The Planetary Society received the type of career dedication that I had shown all my life. The results were fantastic. One successful project followed another.

I had a deep affinity for the people who worked there and for the talented and remarkable people the Society interfaced with, from celebrities such as Bill Nye the Science Guy, who was on the Board of Directors to the parents of the Student Scientists in my programs and the students themselves. I had one evening out with Bill Nye, when the Society sent me to Seattle, Washington to head a workshop on the sundial that Bill and Lou Friedman were primarily spearheading be placed on the next lander mission on Mars, as a calibration target for lander cameras.

Bill asked me to accompany him in the evening after the workshop to a couple of destinations, which included his office in Seattle. We had a lovely time.

On that same trip, I ran through the streets of Seattle with Sheri Klug tryng to keep up with her boundless enthusiasm toward educating teachers about science and exposing them to the opportunities for their students to participate in our programs and others.

Steve Squyres, soon to be famed from his Mars Exploration Rover landers, Spirit and Opportunity, was always available to talk to teachers. Steve and I went back to the Voyager days when we had both been working as very young people on that mission. Scientists like Steve Squyres of Cornell, and Steve Saunders, Bob Anderson, and of course Matt Golombek of JPL, graced us with the time they were willing to devote to us, and made my job easier in reaching the Society's goals.

I brought a lot of warmth to my position at The Planetary Society, in a joy I get from interaction with people on a human level, and made a lot of friends for myself, and the organization as well.

I became an outstanding representative for the Society; speaking at places like before the United Nations gathering of UNISPACE III in Vienna Austria in the summer of 1999 to Teacher's Workshops at JPL and National Science Teacher's Association meetings about my discovery and how the work I was doing now could involve their students in space exploration.

Ryan and I traveled to Vienna on this business for the Society in a trip neither of us will ever forget. We both became ill in Vienna which made for a very challenging time, but eventually recovered enough to tour the city in an unforgettable day.

I hit home run after home run for Lou Friedman in the course of my work, including in Vienna battling with a person who interrupted JPL scientists including Charles Elachi who later became Director of JPL at a workshop the Society was holding in Vienna for the United Nations.

An entire auditorium cheered when I managed to finally silence the gentleman from the crowd who innocently threatened to embarrass all of these scientists who had traveled around the world at our behest to talk about planetary science. One of the most senior members of the JPL staff jumped up when I handled things this expertly and talked this man down from his disruption, yelled, "This is the best time I've ever had!" I had that effect on people in my work for the Society for a very long time.

When I returned from Vienna in August of 1999, my work on the initial materials for Red Rover Goes to Mars Student Astronaut Selection was also completed. I had worked so hard for so long, I decided to reward myself with a gift to the condominium. A drapery installer showed up at my condominium to install two special window treatments, which I had selected, and we never stopped talking from the moment he arrived. I asked him if my phone number were in his records and said if he felt like it he could call me sometimes. He smiled and said his name was Paul Kelly.

The Planetary Society never did place Student Astronauts in a simulated Mars base on Earth when the mission students worked with was an orbiter rather than the lander mission that JPL had cancelled when two of its spacecraft were lost. When the spacecraft were lost, the competitions already going on for Red Rover Goes to Mars around the world were continued in a difficult decision on The Planetary Society's part, of which I was very much part. The LEGO Company stood behind the Society in recasting this enormous student outreach project as a Training Mission.

Both phases of the planned student mission went forward with modifications, until ultimately students were placed in mission operations at Jet Propulsion Laboratory to conduct operations similar to those originally conceived for the Mars Exploration Rover mission, several years later.

From this effort, there are four students in three countries I still keep in regular touch with, some of whom are now studying at top universities. They and their mothers are life-long friends of mine.

I helped to honor Bruce Murray in a fundraising dinner held for him on June 8, 2002. I brought in over $60,000 for that event by myself. When it came to Ray Bradbury 83rd Birthday party that I put on at the Society August 23, 2003, it was one of the most widely covered events from the standpoint of the press the Society had ever put on that I had seen.

Andy's phone call woke me up at 9:00 AM. He told me that the meeting with the scientists from the Science Imaging Team would take place Monday morning at 9:30 AM. I decided I could generate some impressive computer products relating to the image to re-enforce my position as discoverer. I kept thinking what I would say to the Imaging Team during that meeting. I kept thinking of Jocelyn Bell and the history. If they wanted to hear that I knew that history, I would tell them.

I went to the ONIPS area Saturday afternoon to generate the computer products that I had thought to do. I dumped the entire image of the satellite and the anomaly, cut and pasted it together and was tracing out Io's limb when the door opened behind me. The entire Nav area was deserted when I arrived, and I couldn't imagine who it would be. It was Ed Stone, the Voyager Project Scientist. He asked me if he could bring Bob Parks down. Parks was the Voyager Project Manager. I said yes.

I did not introduce myself when Parks arrived, for despite their presence I was still so completely engrossed in the phenomenon itself, I could hardly contain myself in wanting to talk about it and share it.

I took off like a shot, displaying pictures on my monitor. All I wanted to do was share with them the wonder of what I was seeing. I wanted to know if they knew the cloud was over the heart-shaped feature and had they seen the digifax? No, they didn't know that. Their eyes glistened. I mean that literally.

I spoke technically and competently. But, not introducing myself was not a transgression of assertiveness in my estimation. It seemed natural and correct. The significance of the discovery far overshadowed me, and I did not feel I was cheating myself by allowing that statement to be made. They obviously knew what was done here, or they would not have come to see me.

They came to ONIPS, a viable place for this discovery to have been made.

Ed Stone volunteered they had commanded the spacecraft at high risk to turn on the PPS (Photopolarimeter) instrument and look back for traces of the cloud. It had apparently been decided just earlier based on Ed Stone's exposure to my discovery the day before. Ed Stone did not have to tell me that, but he did.

"If it's verified," he went on to say, "it will be a marvelous discovery."

At the time, I had taken that as a general statement. They went along their way and I continued where I had when they arrived.

Much later in the evening, I suddenly stopped what I was doing.

I remembered Ed Stone was looking me straight in the eye when he said that, and saying that to me.

———————

The Planetary Society tried several strategies to try to bolster its declining membership. In 2002, they brought in a Chief Operating Officer, Charles Nobles, with a background in business. Charlie was not up to the task of helping the Society, but I worked closely under him for his entire tenure there.

Through Charlie, the Society got involved in member benefits. I brought nearly 100 planetariums to the table willing to enter into a cooperative agreement with the Society and offer discounts to the Society's members. This was a difficult task because every planetarium is run differently, some often in conjunction with museums. Each was like dealing with a different entity entirely.

I had warmth and enthusiasm, traits I have exhibited all my life. The Society worked often with a man named Warren Betts, who had contacts in Hollywood and with news agencies. Someone at the Society once told me that Warren had asked to know where this Linda person had come from. What planet was I from, he wondered or so I was told, with my smile and enthusiasm expressed nearly all the time?

The Society took Red Rover Goes to Mars away from me after five years. I had been responsible in good part for the program being selected for the Mars Exploration Rover mission in 2003. Bruce Murray congratulated me on that accomplishment. I knew that the Society's reputation was hanging on how well these students did their work.

I had just hired Emily Lakdawalla as my right arm for the educational outreach. She was the fourth person I had under me for education in my Department over time. One had not proved satisfactory, another had gone back to formal geology, and third had clashed with Lou Friedman probably because he felt some ownership of the Society and was pushing for things to be done his way and against Lou's direction. People like that couldn't last at the Society.

All of these people, however, were technically competent and Emily was no different. However, when Red Rover Goes to Mars went to Bruce Betts, somewhat new to the Society in a leading position, Emily went with it. I had hired my replacement.

The Society by need had pushed me further and further into fundraising, but I had no formal expertise in this area. My expertise began and ended with enthusiasm about what the Society was doing for space exploration and this worked well for events.

I did not have expertise in corporate memberships, or in courting individual donors. I had always been too busy on projects for the Society to be included in anything to do with membership.

After Charlie Nobles left the Society, the Society hired Andrea Carroll as its new Development Director. Ultimately, Andrea concluded that there was no money for sponsorship in the current climate in 2003. I spent a year unaware that the Society had basically given up on getting funding, but the Society had overspent to the level of my salary on an event that Andrea Carroll could not fund. They balanced their budget in 2004, as they cancelled *Planetfest '03* in favor of a smaller version. They made the decision to balance their losses by sacrificing my position.

It was ironic that 2003 held events for me that were what the Society was best at. Throughout history, scientists of different nations and backgrounds have been able to overcome political differences that would otherwise divide them by the science alone. I choreographed and handled in late in 2002, a contest to select two students to do an astrobiology experiment for the Space Shuttle.

The Palestinian student, Tariq Adwan, was studying in the United States when he was selected. His family was under house arrest in Israel at the time. The other noble student was a fourth year medical student, Yuval Landau, at Tel Aviv University.

I had the greatest pride in working with these two young men and introducing them to the world of astrobiology through mentors from Johnson Space Flight Center and the Israel Aerospace Medical Institute, and a chance of a lifetime to share in some of Neil deGrasse Tyson's reflections about history.

But, with the financial difficulties, because I was in a sense targeted by the female fundraiser at the Society, for the entire year of 2003, this may have set the stage for what was to come. I understood that any work environment can be challenging, and I had faced my share of challenges, but it had been a very long time since my days of selling dresses as a young girl working my way through college that work had not seemed to be conducted on any professional level, as it involved the way I perceived I was treated during this time at the Society.

I would seek work over the next many months, incurring my foot injury in that process, and so many coincident losses. I seemed lost in the month of August of 2006, at one point, as if crossing an icy desert, trying to handle these so many hardships alone, and seeking a larger home for Ryan and his family.

I put our condominium on the market because my grandson Robert was sleeping in a tent in his parents' room. Unfortunately, I hired a real estate agent to represent me in the sale of the condominium in Arcadia, who was likely a sociopath and got me at the moment the real estate bubble was just beginning to burst, so I was easily misled by the local residential sales he selectively showed me. He cost me tens of thousands of lost dollars, endless worry and exhaustion, trying to make a move to place where my son and I hoped that life would get better.

I was moving to the city where a man named Dave Meyer lived, who would become the love of my life.

At 9:15 AM Monday morning, March 12, 1979, Steve and I were preparing for the 9:30 AM meeting with the scientists. The Nav area was full. The phone rang. It was Peter Kupferman. "You'd better get up here!" he exclaimed. "They've found volcanoes all over the place!"

I could hear people actually screaming in the background. "Everybody's gone crazy!" Peter cried. Steve and I marched out of the ONIPS room to the Nav area. I had my impressive computer product gasped tightly in my hand.

I yelled back at the Nav Team, "It's verified!" That was a good feeling. A cheer of elation went up.

When we arrived upstairs, rather than a meeting it was Pandemonium, the area filled with celebrating scientists pouring over pictures.

I could see Brad Smith, the head of the Imaging Team, standing in a corner of the crowded room, looking up at an unenhanced science pre-encounter image of a volcanic eruption. Large as life. But, no one had noticed it. Brad Smith looked a little bit sick.

When we came into the room, he would not look directly at me. He said, as if talking to the air, "Linda noticed it first." I thought of Andy and a type of work he had to do that may indeed have been very much a part of what he did so well throughout the mission, that had less to do with the technical issues, but rather human interactions. I knew I had survived.

In addition to bringing the discovery forward to fruition, I wanted to be able to continue in my field in the only way I knew that I could, without the bitterness about what people can do to one another as I had learned from history. Larry Soderblom wasn't having any problem at all. He said, "Don't leave town," and actually looked at me when he said it.

Frank Jordan aptly made the point later that Navigation should get a publication in the *Science* issue that presented the results of the Voyager 1 encounter with Jupiter to the world. L.A. Morabito, S.P. Synnott, P.N. Kupferman, and Stewart A. Collins, in the order of our involvement published "Discovery of Currently Active Extraterrestrial Volcanism" in the 1 June 1979, Vol. 204 of *Science*.

By then, a second volcanic eruption, which I had not even considered, was subsequently noticed on the terminator in the discovery picture, the boundary between day and night on Io. At the moment the picture was taken, it was projecting above the dark surface into the sunlight. The volcano of this eruption was eventually named Loki. I had discovered the volcanic plume of the volcano that would be called Pele, both Hawaiian Gods.

My eleven page letter which describes every moment of the discovery dated March 15, 1979, written to and because of Gibson

Reaves, who passed away in May of 2005, is signed "Your former student, friend, and admirer, Linda Morabito."

In early January of 2009, the office of the Public Guardian allows me to come into my mother's apartment, where she is no longer capable of living, and has been moved to a care facility, and begin to claim her belongings. The man who has become the conservator of her person, and the lady who is responsible for the inventory of her belongings are both present. Eventually, the conservator of her person will stop this process and try to interfere with my mother's wishes that her family have her belongings; by the time I enter the apartment her entire jewelry collection has been stolen.

At this point her conservator asks me if he can bring Marline's clothing to her, that portion of which remains in her apartment, which is not worn regularly by her. Ryan has advised me to take at least a couple of articles of clothing to remember my mother by. I walk toward the closet and reach for her clothing, but I cannot.

I yell, "I can't! I can't!" and I rush to the living room and grab one of my mother's stuffed animals and collapse to the ground hugging the stuffed bear and weeping. When I am able to stand up, I explain to the very kind lady who is doing the inventory, "That is not an adult weeping. It is a very hurt child."

She says heartbroken, "I'm sorry."

There were very good reasons why I could not see my mother over the time of my memories returning. Even once I was able to merge with the child that I was, sometimes in images of me taking the little girl's hand in mine, or the little baby's hand she was earlier in mine, or imagining pushing her toward me and us becoming one, even the adult in me has terror of my mother.

When my brother was hospitalized just last year, the conservator of her person would bring Marline to the hospital even when she had to be reminded several times that it was her son she was looking at in the hospital bed. I learned on one such occasion that my mother could no longer recognize me because of her dementia. Even in these brief, accidental contacts, nightmares would follow for many days. I am incapable yet of dealing with the horror that I saw.

There is something in this costumed man's face. I see then from the area of his eyes, perhaps that he cannot see what he has brought forth. I think I see in his eyes the validation that he is a fool.

At the base of the cross where this ceremony is taking place, like the counterpart of ghosts, but from the Devil, black figures whisk by. My mind fights as it had before to assign animals to these figures. My mind fights to believe they are black cats. But, they have somewhat human shaped heads, with yellow eyes, no legs and do not touch the ground when they move. The closest thing to them I have ever seen in this world since are to the corpses of burn victims shown on television, completely black and charred, but they are alive. One takes a stance with arms and legs that appear when the others do not have them and its arms at least are too thin to be disguised as flesh covered limbs, as the ridiculous costumed man's red tights on his legs always look and the absurd crawling motion that he makes. It takes its stand in the hallways of Hell; its stretches upward, and its eyes turn more the color orange, and in essence, it becomes flame and joins the fires of Hell.

A Canadian Talk show called the *Alan Hamel* Show was prominent in 1979 on the CBC National Network in Canada. They were visiting the United States to film, which must have pleased Alan Hamel to no end, since his wife Suzanne Somers of *Three's Company* fame resided in the United States. The Show heard about my fame and that I was Canadian born. They contacted me to appear at their outdoor filming location in Century City.

The other guests that day were Steve Allen and Mike Farrell who played B.J. Hunnicutt on *MASH*. I had never seen anything quite like Mike Farrell backstage. His hair appeared to be thinning and he combed it non-stop with a small comb from the moment he arrived there and even while he walked along to be escorted to the stage outside. It's as if he was battery charged and that's how he breathed, by combing his hair.

The show went very well and the producers wanted me back for more to talk about Voyager discoveries. I was still appearing on the show as their guest science expert in 1980, when Alan Thicke took it over. He would go on to do the ABC sitcom *Growing Pains*.

I appeared a total of eight times on these shows between 1979 and 1981. As I flew to Vancouver, where the *Alan Thicke*

Show was filming I saw the giant cloud of Mt. St. Helens eruption in Washington that had happened in May of 1980, and was still lingering in the aftermath.

Four hundred million miles away from Mt. St. Helens, there were simultaneous eruptions taking place on Io more violent than anything that had ever happened on Earth, which paled Mt. St. Helens by comparison, so violent that in its four billion years of existence, Io had literally turned itself inside out with volcanic activity.

What evidence is there of a parallel universe when it cannot be seen? Scientists believe there was a rapid inflation period after the beginning of the universe, when for a brief time figuratively speaking gravity became a repulsive instead of an attractive force. This period of rapid inflation is what scientists believe accounts for the universe as we see it now. Data from the COBE and WMAP spacecrafts, show some heat fluctuations in the background radiation left over from the Big Bang or the beginning of our universe, that indicate that the density fortunately is not uniform, the fluctuations basically formed us. The size and distribution of these fluctuations have yielded many of the answers we have wanted about the universe. Now too, scientists are thinking that parallel universes arise at the time of rapid inflation.

Steven Hawking holds on to his no boundary principle, even though scientists believe now that the universe will not contract into a big crunch. Space was made basically flat by rapid inflation, and is at a critical density with what is called dark energy winning over gravity, and accelerating our expansion.

From Steven's Hawking's no-boundary principle it can be extrapolated that the universe has no beginning, but has not existed forever. Parallel universes are believed to in infinite number in what is contemporarily termed a multiverse.

Bubbles arise in the fabric of space and time, and never connect, or show the existence of one another. Except perhaps, I contend, when they collide.

My parents enjoyed a destination over their earlier years in Pasadena; the Huntington Library. When we moved to the United States, my parents become lovers of art and beauty. In our visits to the Huntington Museum we often saw the paintings, Lawrence's

"Pinkie" and Gainsborough's "Blue Boy." This is the ideal of my parents, perhaps, the ideal of beauty I held on to for all the years that fit so nicely into my amnesia. In my home are some shade of pink and blue nearly everywhere.

Evidence of a parallel universe that came into being because of my past, that is specifically indirect, is captured in an image of my parents standing in front of the pink and blue paintings of a boy and a girl. Even though my parents are side by side and both there, the beauty of the paintings does not change and cannot be diminished. My parents cannot alter the beauty, no matter what they are. This, after years of Hell is the image my mind wants to retain, and that is why I need those colors before my eyes, to remind me, I believe, that it is possible to survive what my parents did. I had called my brother a prince once in a session with Joseph Dickson. It was the connection my mind had made with Gainsborough's painting of a young man untouchable by my parents, dressed as a prince might be.

In early 2008, when driving with Dave, I am overcome with what I was dealing with back then; what kind of people my parents were. I had taken responsibility for overprotecting Ryan as a child, not knowing or being able to remember what I was protecting him from, and had apologized to him in adulthood. But, now I sensed that I should never blame myself for that ever again. Even when I did not know it, I was protecting Ryan from the most horrific evil I had ever known could be on the Earth. These were the people my parents were and the evil they were aligned with.

Ryan had once told me, "The purpose of death is to make life important." Not even minutes before, I had just seen those words stated as part of a new drama series on TV, but Ryan had not seen it, he was out driving. As a little boy, he once told me that he believed the Internet should hold places that people can go, like stores or malls when they can shop, at a time when the only thing the Internet meant to the average person, initially was email communication. He is able to settle on things directly, like no one else I have ever known.

Despite failing vision in one eye, Ryan got a job at a mortuary, assisting with funeral direction and helping the family and friends of the deceased, as was his passion. He applied to and was accepted at the Mortuary Science program in Cypress College, the only such program in Southern California. With sometimes no study, he achieved the highest grades on the exams, which were much on the level of pre-med preparation that had ever been achieved in the history of the program, sometimes getting 100% on them.

Even after he had completely lost the sight in his left eye, he came back to rediscover his love of helping people, specifically, the elderly. In November of 2003, he became office manager of a retirement home in Arcadia, the same city where we lived. He would clock out after days of the most hectic activity, handling everything that arose with 15 people working under him and then helping the residents on his own time with anything else they needed after he clocked out, and they loved him.

He had straight "As" at Arcadia High School when major illness had struck again for the third time before he was seventeen; first the nephrotic syndrome, severe mold exposure, and now the viral meningitis. The viral meningitis he caught from this teacher didn't affect his ear or hearing, as it had hers. It hit his eye instead. I shall never as long as I live, be able to understand what doctors over six years missed, when his optic neuritis was finally diagnosed, and how they could have put my son through the sorrow of his young life by telling him the optic neuritis was "in his head," as well as the grief of the harshness of the illness that viral meningitis brings it its wake, that once again put Ryan completely out of school and away from his peers.

When he got back to school, it was as if he was generations older than they. He choreographed video projects using video equipment with voice over music and written video annotation when such things were not accomplished easily or done by high-level software. As a young boy confined to home from mold exposure, he had helped the FBI track down some people via computer who were hacking into America On-Line. He had computer businesses in the Internet Revolution that brought in a thousand dollars in a day, when he cared to participate in them. The money was not the motivation, the novelty was. He created a computer project on World War II, which, to inspire the interest of the audience, pictured him sitting on his bed with the evil instigator of the Holocaust, Adolf Hitler. The evening audience for the presentation of students, parents and families were laughing so hard, they couldn't remain still in their seats.

He had knowledge of radios and electronics and began the first radio club the High School ever had, creating its charter. He identified and presented a book to his teacher and his teacher's father he had in his possession which had a photo taken by his teacher's father, a war photographer from World War II, of which they were completely unaware. In visiting his own grandfather in the convalescent hospital where his grandfather later died, I would often find Ryan as a young man of these early years, talking with other patients, veterans of World War II. Ryan would ask the ancient war veterans where they served and what action they had seen, and he could converse with them as if he had served alongside them.

After nine months on the job at the senior care home where he worked, on July 5, 2004, at nearly midnight, he went into emergency surgery for acute appendicitis, which would lead to the risk of death from the extreme pain he suffers or the experimental surgery he now faces as a last resort.

After my journey through time, I can understand the impact to my life caused by my parent passed to another generation. My lifelong tendency to want to protect my son, what I transferred from worry over what happened to my brother, had manifest itself in a level of concern over what Ryan had undergone that was proportional to the devastation in my early life. If my reactions were in proportion to the level of worry over my son from this dark and hidden past, I can imagine what I was like at key times in his life when calmness and possibly even doing nothing for just even moments would have been the wiser course. I have evidence of my journey through time in the way I must have been through most of Ryan's trials. I added to his suffering. I could not, no matter how I tried, contain my intense need to get help.

Ryan faces his fate of dealing with his misfortunes in quiet reserve and a sense of fatalism. He is a remarkable father to his two sons. When his emotion shows in the few times he has broken down, my heart disintegrates into pain.

I have more direct evidence of a parallel universe from a little girl. After her brother was hit and she was hospitalized, God told her that things would get better, and again when I relived this. Much later on in her life, when life got very challenging for more than the past decade, she grew into a woman who heard God tell her that things had changed and that they were difficult once again. God knew what had not yet happened; the entire plan of her life.

Ryan and I developed some form of premonition for a short period of time during which his circumstances and trials made his well being and health decline far too much, recently. I wondered about the value of this, and then remembered that he had insisted his wife and children come home before a certain time one day, because he had been dreaming for days about a car accident at a later time which would claim all their lives. They came home and broke the plans they had otherwise made. Perhaps there was a great deal more to this very brief gift we both received that seemed to be born out of tragedy for a short while, than having more evidence that time has neither the nature nor purpose that science yet knows.

I have traveled through time to memories that were locked away behind a door so that I would not be destroyed as a child. When the memories emerged, they emerged completely intact just as the child saw them so long ago. More evidence of an aspect of time we have not yet considered fully.

I have been blessed on one occasion in adulthood with a vision of Jesus.

When Connie briefly believed that I had symbolically let go of the little girl, until we realized the far more tangible nature of this final memory and final ceremony, she said something about the death of this little girl. She said, "One day you will see her again." Although that is a sweet statement of faith, it also encapsulates the infinite sorrow I have for this beautiful little girl. If I could indeed hold her in my arms, I would weep for her for all eternity. I suppose that is why it was better that it was not possible for me to truly touch her until one day, like in Connie's cherished analogy, I will see her again. She is but a tiny child, who has been in the presence of God, on the boundaries of our comprehension of space and time.

The ceremonies have in common the horrible Satanic ominous beautiful Christian melodic chant. It fills the chamber where they take place, and the entire choir is present, many, many men in robes. Everyone who was part of where ever they took place, was present, in very, very large numbers. My mother's family has sold their souls to these people, who were in disguise as servants of God. Undoubtedly it happened long before I was born.

Sadly for me a Benediction, not necessarily in English, happens at the end. A tragic, broken child hears the celebration of the torture of her body with the culminating chant and a Benediction at the end. I recognize this only by the familiarity of the cadence of the Benediction when my precious Pastor at church gives this at every service.

On July 18, 2009, I weep because my father, who is deceased, was one of them. I weep because I remembered Gibson at the base of the road pathway to the sky, and not my father. I have not been where my father is, I have been where Gibson is. I know my father's fate and what a good man he became ultimately. In a fleeting moment on July 18, 2009, I fear for my father with the memory of the kind of love children have when they worry that something bad might happen to their parents. I face what I have known for sometime in my heart.

————

My father has a knife, which they must have given him. He walks up to the child as they watch, lying on the cross, who has been brutally raped, covered in excrement and urine, and who just died shortly before, and he cuts her at her genitals with the knife. He is wearing green and has his circular glasses on.

At the age of two, when everything has been taken from this tiny child, including her humanity, I yell, "Kill him!" "Kill him!"

It is the first words I have ever spoken to these beings.

To the best of my knowledge, my parents are not asked back.

Daddy! Daddy! Daddy! Are you one of them? Daddy, no! Daddy, you don't know what I do! Daddy …

————

When I am freed, a little, naked girl cries on her knees, bleeding, and as alone and as small as any child can be, and vomiting from the innards of the animal, the excrement, the blood, the horror. She cries, inconsolably, "Mommy, Mommy."

My mother heard what she had said, and has made the decision at that moment that she will have to kill her herself, in a rural area away from the big city, called Beach Grove, which may have reminded her in that sense of where she grew up, and what she had seen done there before, or perhaps had done herself.

Epilogue: First

Imagine a universe in which a child knows her Mommy and Daddy are going to kill her, and you can imagine the need for a parallel universe. Once the parallel universe collided with my adult life, it is no wonder that the essence of my family as I thought I knew it disintegrated so rapidly. Decades of a life after the events that have been recounted here, once I began to remember, could not hold up to a foundation of horror even though it lasted only 30 months. The building on top of a poorly built foundation will fall much faster than anyone could have predicted by what could be seen in only one universe.

Fifty three years after what took place at Beach Grove and six years after I had begun to remember it, by July 28, 2009, I remember that I had certain knowledge that my mother would kill me, kneeling on the floor of that chapel as a broken child. I remember now that I asked Jesus if I could die, because I could not take the eternal sorrow of that knowledge.

A parallel universe began to recede from our own, as I remembered trying to stifle awareness to protect my mind, lost in an ocean of anguish, and then emerging on the beach where my brother had already been destroyed, and my parents had already carried out their intent.

As I watched the haunting vista of that shoreline at a place called Beach Grove, I remembered that I had changed, although it had remained constant in appearance. I had grown older with each visit when my parents took me back there.

For the very first time, time went forward from the moment of amnesia in 1956 at that same site. This is why I could never have fully merged with that angelic child from my location in time in adulthood; not until the moment I had remembered enough to know this was just one life. And so, parallel universes fade and recede from collisions that can make us certain there is very little we have ever known.

But, there is a price to pay for this knowledge and for fully becoming this child.

On August 4, 2009, the flood gates open. The details of a murder victim that have been held in reserve until now are recounted and re-experienced by the victim. I remember the molestation at home between the chapel and Beach Grove from the standpoint of gratitude that I was at least not murdered during these acts of atrocity.

But then, when the moment arrives, and it does arrive at the level of full awareness now, I cry in anguish to the universe, "No!!!!!!!" when the attack begins. What words can I use to describe what we have always wondered about; how a murder victim feels at the moment they know they will not survive?

At the moment of my death, I scream to Dave "Look at my eyes!" The rapid eye movement is off any scale that can be measured. My eyes vibrate so violently that my entire facial physiology is fluttering out of control as I sit on my bed and say to Dave if he is seeing what is happening to me. Then it stops and there is quiet.

I tell him my arms ache from "going to God" and being overwhelmed in God's presence. I scream the second loudest scream I ever have, when I return from God to the pain in my body. I clutch a doll I had already remembered only once, as I waited for morning and Gary's execution. In order of escalating horror, I remember the souls of the dead, ghouls, and the demon, specifically it, that my parents had "invited" to the killing. It is the loudest scream a human being can scream, and then I have new knowledge.

We cannot imagine the level of human suffering that the demon holds for human beings in Hell, because we are only human. The glory of God is all that stands between us and this, and the only thing that protected me. I know now that my first vision of Jesus may have been on the chapel floor, and I may have touched His face.

My son's fate because of his severe medical problems is now in God's hands as was mine. I pray for my son's survival. I want his legacy to have enough recollection by his children to reach them, for he like my husband and brother has a great legacy to offer.

The legacy I leave my son is a triumph over evil, a love of God, the largest discovery of the planetary exploration program, the discovery of the volcanic activity on Jupiter's moon Io, and the cherishing of children everywhere on this Earth. With more time in a universe far beyond our understanding, there could be other universes which offer each of us in our own way, our service to God.

Second: In Memoriam

In the dreams of children, they end on a happy note. In the nightmares of children, they end at least with no more than a child crying on a chapel floor. But, some nightmares cannot end there. Mine did not.

In March of 2010, I tell Connie McDonald that perhaps whatever I am about to remember will set me free. One dove is my brother... One is me... We are free... I chant to myself.

My mother did not just make the decision to kill me at Beach Grove - she did do that, but more, as I cried and vomited upon that chapel floor.

There was a reason I had vomited far beyond what I had remembered so far.

There are needles the monsters there used on us children. There were other children and I had remembered this after seeing the devastation to children in the January 2010 Haiti quake on television.

I had heard their screams only once, when I began to relive a powerful blow to my head with a sharp implement wielded by my mother on that chapel floor. There were needles in wood cases with primary colors of blue velvet that housed the gold nails that were often soaked with the blood of children, my own as well, and had plumes of ribbons in blood red attached to their tops.

I saw Jesus on that chapel floor. Jesus took me in His arms and I touched the face of the Lord. I saw the Savior of us all rise into the chapel ceiling, adorned in white, in the most glorious sight any human being could witness with Angels of the Christ about Him.

My mother wielded the nail a second time in a frenzy, that punctured my lip in a hole and the bottom lip swelled to a bulging size, and then she tore open my upper left arm, in a jagged wound where the flesh beneath my skin opened through the wound on both sides, and my fingers on that hand came to a point with a nerve like contracting. My father screamed her name, "Marline" so that they would not be held responsible personally for killing me. I lay down on the floor and a Bishop carried me away to be placed upon the altar.

This was not good, but was part of the ceremony. He drives a nail into my side. My face was held in the direction of a sight that no human being should ever see. A little girl about the age of three, came running naked, not able to know what was happening or what she should do. Her soft diffuse curls on her head framed blue eyes and there are only the words "The horror. The horror." to describe what this child is. Her lower face had been mutilated probably just as I had suffered my mutilation, but it was okay to do so as extremely as had been done to her, because she had been selected to die.

The Bishop took one of the swords that had been used to kill the animal and stood there with it, proud of the work he was doing and the power over life and death he deemed that he had. He took the screaming child's head off in one sweep of the sword.

There is horror on this Earth. Her soft curls touch the floor in a way that is not meant for the living. A woman, a mother, who is to protect her young by anything that decent people understand, guides me now to the child. This woman drinks the child's blood from the decapitated body, and licks her lips savoring the eternal youth she has been promised by the league of Satan, and dances around the still warm corpse that was once a precious human being. This woman is my mother, and part of the tiny child's headless body that lay there is forced into my mouth and I ask God to save me as I am drowning in the blood. Later, at the place where I am sewn back together, I see a scalpel and know if I can only reach it, I will be able to go the way of this little girl and be put out of my pain. I am two years old.

Baby Angel, little girl, I will see you in the Kingdom of Heaven. Little Girl, God was there for you to end your suffering as God was there for me many times. Jesus took you to Heaven and then reached toward me. In His eyes, I see the entire universe.

On May 10, 2010 I meet with my Pastor and his wife in the morning, with Connie McDonald at 11:15 AM, and at 1:35 PM, I call the Royal Canadian Mounted Police in the district of Mission and report the murder of a little girl that was so well choreographed that I know that she is in the Kingdom of Heaven with many others like her. One of her Baby Angels lived to speak for her.

Third: Important Dates

<u>May 10, 2010</u> I report the murder of the little girl to the Royal Canadian Mounted Police, Mission Municipal Detachment, Mission, British Columbia, Canada

<u>May 14, 2010</u> I submit my written statement to the RCMP, as they have requested, "What I Witnessed," Part I "Events leading up to the murder of a young child," and Part II "Beach Grove, Tsawwassen six months or less after I witnessed the murder of the young girl."

<u>July 14, 2010</u> RCMP requests that I have my abdomen examined by a doctor for evidence of a scar from my mother's stabbing of me, which was surgically repaired in Vancouver after returning home from the first ceremony.

<u>July 16, 2010</u> My doctor finds the surgical scar on my right middle abdomen two inches long, which was so faint that it was never seen by me before, and prepares the report for the RCMP. This is the confirmation of my account the RCMP was waiting for.

<u>October 21, 2010</u> The San Bernardino County (California) Sheriff's Department acting as a liaison for the RCMP takes my verbal statement of my account of the murder.

<u>October 26, 2010</u> I am commended by the RCMP after they have conferred with the San Bernardino County Sheriff's Liaison for having the courage to come forward. Sixty-two days later, my supplemental statement is given to the RCMP, about the murder of a second child I witnessed. A little boy whose fate was joined to the little girl's, united by the torture and execution they endured. The

investigation by the RCMP remains open, but is indefinitely on hold, due to the crushing weight of their daily workload.[3]

---

[3] Through the eyes of a two-year-old child, who saw more horror than any person can endure and numerous miracles, the tragic little boy was then made whole by the Son of God. Jesus knelt on one knee before the child, who stood upright beside his own corpse, in order to lay His hands where the child's eyes had once been, to take the little boy whole into the Kingdom of Heaven. As of February 8, 2011, I now realize that I can speak to a Gold City in the sky where Jesus walked in beauteous splendor and created the vision of small birds before my eyes, that were not real, but said to me "Such as these." to tell me where I was and that I too had not survived the ceremony with the little boy. A tiny little girl shook her head vehemently no thinking about her brother. I remember hearing the furious beating of wings as I was carried by an Angel back to Earth. And so now, I will come and speak to you wherever you are more than half a century later about the Gold City and the Son of God walking in sandals at His Home and the effulgence of His hair I could see as I followed Him to the park and tree where He spoke to me – lighting the way in Heaven.

Fourth: William Franklin Wolsey

At the conclusion of my telephone conversation with Corporal Foster of the RCMP in late 2010, I asked the Corporal if there was anything else he could tell me about my case or other possible reports which related to the crimes I witnessed and had reported to that date. Corporal Foster said, "Look on the Internet."

I said that I would, but assumed since I had already done an Internet search on Westminster Abbey and ritualistic abuse of children and had never found anything, with the exception of some ghost stories about a building somewhere in Canada, there wasn't any point. I wondered why Corporal Foster had seemingly sent me to a dead end with that suggestion. In retrospect, I believe I was not ready at that time to follow through on Corporal Foster's suggestion. On May 28, 2011, my mental resistance to doing this gave way.

I did a Google search on Benedictine Monks rather than the Abbey, and ritualistic abuse of children. William Franklin Wolsey came up, the Archbishop John I of Vancouver. In one instant of time, I knew I had finally found a reference to a Bishop based on a search related to my memories; my reports to the RCMP were filled with references to a sadistic and murdering bishop, and I sensed that this is what Corporal Foster had suggested that I see.

William Franklin Wolsey had no connection with Westminster Abbey itself that I am aware of. He purchased the Roman Catholic seminary the Benedictine monks owned in Burnaby just outside of Vancouver, which preceded their move to the Abbey in 1954. He had set up a school as well as a church in Burnaby at the mansion purchased from the monks, the Ceperley Mansion, named for its original builders. Some sources on the Internet state that the school was at least in part, an orphanage with live-in students. The dates when my ceremonial abuse began coincided with the dates William Franklin Wolsey was in what is known to some as the Westminster Priory, this Ceperley Mansion. This was that "other building" somewhere in Canada, which had come up only in secondary sources, as it pertained to ghost stories, and seemingly had little importance to what I had logically been seeking in the past. I had been seeking supporting evidence that my abuse had taken place in the Westminster Abbey, which I had never found. The monks had nothing to do with my abuse. The great mystery of my life had finally been solved.

William Franklin Wolsey was associated with the ritualistic abuse of children. He was notorious in Canada and in the United States. He had been front page news in the *Vancouver Sun* in 1959, as I would be so many years later for my discovery, and shortly thereafter his activities were covered in an article in *Time* magazine, as my discovery had also been. Ironically, my work on the Voyager mission had sent me to a location in California not far from where he later lived in the seventies.

Wolsey was no archbishop in reality. He became "Archbishop John I of Vancouver" through a strange medieval ceremony in England conducted by a former hotel waiter, according to the front page story in the *Sun*, published June 25, 1959. His sacred order was of course not recognized by the Pope. He was a bigamist, and a deserter of a wife and four children in the United States. He was a wanted man in the United States during the time he had run his church in Canada. But, his Temple of the More Abundant Life at the mansion had hundreds if not thousands of followers. His church assets were listed in excess of $1.5 million, a sum which he is believed to have extorted from helpless widows.

The tower from the Westminster Abbey was my mind's link to the Ceperley Mansion. Indeed like the ferry built at Tsawwassen, which linked my mother's attempt on my life to Beach Grove in the summer of 1956, there was otherwise no other way I could have known anything about where my ritualistic abuse had actually happened. If my parents had not taken me to Westminster Abbey, likely as I have believed when the bell tower was completed, I would never have seen the indications of what Wolsey had tried to duplicate in his surroundings. The pivotal memory of the completed Abbey tower was unique enough in all the world to bring me to this epilogue.

Wolsey surrounded himself with all things clergy, none of which he had rights to; ecclesiastical vestments on his person, "priests" who ran the school with him, a former seminary on a hill elevated above the surrounding terrain (like Westminster Abbey to some degree), and an altar in a makeshift chapel in the home. Double railroad tracks can be found not too far from the 23 acres of the mansion's property, close enough to hear train whistles, which to this day still fill me with terror. Perhaps I will know or remember one day how Wolsey was able to duplicate the one chant that was sung at the end of the abuse ceremonies. It may be as simple as him owning a long playing record of the monks as I had originally wondered aloud to Connie McDonald, if my mother might have owned such a record when I had first remembered the chant. Monks singing at the Abbey was likely something that my family saw and heard during our visit there. I had heard a chant before and of course had tied it to the monks.

Since finding this monster on the Internet, what I remembered with the aid and support of my husband, who never left my side through this horror, is beyond what can be sanitized by my mind.

On the day that I found him on the Internet, I contacted the Burnaby Village Museum to request a picture described in a photographic collection on a Heritage Burnaby website. It was emailed to me as an attached file to the email nearly immediately. When I opened the file and viewed the picture, I realized I did not recognize him. Over the next forty-eight hours, I realized the extent my mind had gone to, to block nearly everything that I had not remembered about him to that point.

Even before I had found Wolsey on the Internet, I had recently written to the RCMP that I had remembered something important about the incident when my mother had gone berserk after the first ceremony in which I was violently shaken but did not die. I had remembered that before my mother had placed me in the sink at our apartment and stabbed me, she had been screaming at me, "If it weren't for you, I would have all that money!" My parents would have collected an enormous sum of money had I died in the first ceremony. A far different picture of the basis for my abuse was beginning to open up in my memory. It is probably why I began the Internet search Corporal Foster had suggested when I did.

I am not yet aware how Wolsey became associated with my family, and specifically on which side of my family that association originated. I believe some members of both sides of the family became involved perhaps for more than just one reason, including the possibility of previous involvement with such practices.

I realize that my mother was a lifelong sociopath, and my father at that time was as well. Yet my father had only one goal, and that was to keep Marline in his life no matter what he had to do to accomplish that. My mother had only one goal, and that was to impress the psychopathic monster who had befriended them, to attract his attention and to let him know she was exactly like him. Those goals and the money my parents received, I believe now, were the primary motivation for my parents' participation with William Franklin Wolsey.

The interaction and synergy that this man had with my parents created the conditions of a perfect storm in the life of a tiny child. I have seen television dramas where people like him seem to make a plan built on targeting and tormenting one individual. I frankly had never heard of anything like that in real life. I have heard about serial killers, but could never have imagined that the murders of three children I witnessed may have had their origin in the mind of a monster who was at the same time trying to torture a baby, me, with each.

Without a single emotion, likely for money, my parents gave me for extended periods of time to this monster to live in his home with him. Every child there in his home with me, whom I loved, was murdered before my eyes.

I knew the little girl I saw killed in the ceremony I have described. I knew her well. She was a breathtaking child and was my friend, my first friend in life besides my brother. She and I lived in hell with Wolsey 24 hours a day. We survived like prisoners do. We found meaning in small communication with one another, in the love of one baby girl for another, and understood one another's agony and pain. What would otherwise be complete helplessness over our physical surroundings and abuse became a bond that was everything we had in life. We had one another to comfort each other, and this man could not control that.

As bizarre as it sounds, considering my age, I believe he knew he could not permanently break me, although at times he did. But, he knew he could not kill me either. The only way he could kill a child who had parents and was known beyond his school and was not orphaned was to do so by shaking me violently, which would leave no marks. I have re-experienced how hard one of his followers worked to try to kill me in that way during that first ceremony. When I did not die, Wolsey began a personal vendetta against a baby.

That is why my head was forced to the side during the ceremony in which little girl died, to make sure I saw Wolsey take the head off the beautiful little girl who had shared my life and my pain, and I hers. After that, he took me to some place on his property, outdoors. He carried a white material sack that he held at its gathered top in one hand, in which he had her headless body and her head. He led me to the top of a steep incline, what seemed like a high hill all covered in grass and he rolled her head down the hill.

When she was present in this way as a defiled corpse and her head rolled away from me down a hill, I realized that I would never see her again, she was gone forever, and I was completely alone. That had been his objective.

He raped me and I went into a fetal position not able to move and remained in that position there for a very long time. At some point, as sad as this is, I began to mentally pretend that somebody loved me, even the monster. I either lay my head on the monster's shoulder as he walked along, or I pretended in my own mind at the time, as a child of two years old, that he loved me as I envisioned leaning on his shoulder. I am not sure that I actually was moved from the spot where I was laying near the top of the incline; but I seem to favor the interpretation I envisioned being loved leaning against him as he carried me; pretending there was still someone in the world who was alive who loved me, even though I knew there was no one left. From this memory, I believe that my brother was not at this man's home with me, or I might have logically been thinking about my brother; that he was somewhere nearby and loved me.

Later, I remember a wailing cry from the base of my soul, mourning the loss of my precious friend, as I sat on the monster's bed inconsolable. He told me he had put her body in the storage closet downstairs. Said, likely to evoke the very desperation about being completely abandoned again, and without hope, from a broken child that it did.

I have now recovered the memory of this man's face seen as I saw it back then. I saw his face in connection with having remembered he would cut on my body with a sharp implement during abuse in his bed.

The implements this man possessed for torturing children were "highly specialized." During the ceremonies, I have described a device to brace a baby's body as a person violently shakes them designed to not leave marks, a ball with a rope in it that would fit in a child's mouth and be able to be removed later, a horizontal cross that a child could be strapped to that had the capability to spin. From everything I can piece together, the sharp implements to cut and penetrate flesh were rigid, decorated in some cases, skin splitting scalpel-like, with a very thin footprint unlike a knife of any kind. The implements did not leave much scarring, and may not have required stitches to repair the type of wounds they inflicted, but induced severe pain, and precise cutting and penetration of skin.

The specific incident that I have now recalled in some detail took place before the little girl was murdered by him. I remembered that as this monster cut me repeatedly and over long periods of time in his bed, I went into something I can only call a transcendent level of consciousness, a place my mind went during the torture. This transcendent state followed violent agonizing jerking my body did and mental eruptions of agony/fear/screaming/weeping/whimpering in response to being cut repeatedly over a long period of time while in his bed. I have never experienced anything like this transcendent state that I can compare this to; it was different than any of the near-death experiences I have described in this memoir, or any of the simply out of body experiences I endured because of atrocities committed against me.

I also remember that during the time I was in this transcendent state I was aware that the lower portion of my body was engulfed in moisture; my own blood or perhaps urine. The wetness has horror associated with it.

In this transcendent state things got quiet and somehow the pain and suffering diminished, but it disabled me. I could not continue to scream or cry out or cry. Wolsey brought the little girl to this same bed where I lay. She was screaming and fighting him, and flailing her arms and legs. Because of the state I was in, I could not acknowledge her presence and only saw her peripherally. I sense this might have frustrated him. It may be he had brought her to see my reaction to his torturing her. By her appearance (similarity to how she looked at the time of her murder), there could not have been too much time between the ceremony described in the *In Memoriam* section of this epilogue in which she was killed and this session of torture I recall in his bed. The pain I experienced in remembering the incident in his bed is among the worst pain my body has ever had to remember.

I also now remember that I knew the little boy who was tortured beside me on the altar and then was killed. I loved this little boy and was always hugging him. He was smaller than I was, and I viewed him as my baby, with me a two year old "mother." It is as if I can picture us together from a distance, two of God's tiniest little children. His skin was so soft and he was a beautiful little boy.

The monster picked him to die probably because he noticed my affection for the little boy and that I loved him. I can only surmise that I met him under the same circumstances I met the little girl, when I was given by my parents to this monster to stay with him at his residence.

I saw this little boy's corpse buried afterward. I saw that the little boy I loved was literally thrown into a hole in the ground once it was dug. He landed face down and his little feet were crossed at the legs behind him as his corpse hit the bottom of the rectangular grave. I believe it was all done to torture me, as well as to gratify the insatiable need of the monster to destroy children.

I also remember that prior to that I witnessed a woman turn over a baby to Wolsey for payment in the makeshift chapel at his home. The woman had on a faintly plaid shapeless skirt, which was overall light in color. The length of her skirt came to her mid shins and she had socks on and old oxford-like shoes. She was wearing a sweater over a blouse which was gathered beneath the waistline of the skirt which struck me as elasticized. She had on a babushka-like scarf and her overall appearance was disheveled; she was abjectly impoverished in appearance and seemed too old to have a baby that age. I believe she was given money for the baby. I was allowed to hold the baby as I was seated facing the altar. It was magical to have a baby in my arms and I immediately adored the baby.

That baby was then killed before my eyes in the most horrific sight a human being could ever see. She was mortally wounded from the inside out from inflicted stab wounds, and I believe now that the screams of this infant little girl and my own will never stop echoing in my consciousness, for the rest of my days on this Earth. Wolsey finished her off with a knife delivered to her torso. After the baby was killed, I was unmercifully tortured.

This psychopathic man knew me and exactly how to hurt me. After I had seen the little boy killed, Wolsey hit me squarely with the blunt end of a cross to my abdomen. I had a near-death experience then, and what I gleaned from it during the time it was happening to me was that my father did not love me. Wolsey did this in front of my father and he knew it would mean to me absolute evidence that my father did not love me. That is how well that psychopathic man knew his craft of torture.

A similar episode had happened immediately after the little girl's death in which my mother had wrestled me to the ground, and forced part of the child's anatomy into my mouth. I also think that my mother may have used one of the implements I have described to superficially carve a pentagram into my chest then. What I gleaned from that at the time as well was that my mother had no love for me at all. I believe again, that Wolsey added the touches that he knew would have the most catastrophic effect on the child he could not kill.

The memories evoked by finding Wolsey on the Internet have been more than I believed I would survive. I conveyed to Connie McDonald and my husband that I had had enough and wasn't sure how I would get through this. I realized there was only one way, to try to take as much control over the remembering process as I could. That is why I told myself to power through this with all the courage I had ever brought to this process of remembering, and all the experience I had gleaned from these many prior years of remembering what I had to that point, and recovering from the memories. I succeeded in recovering the memories expressed in this section of the epilogue in a matter of weeks.

I have no way of knowing if this man had other relationships that resulted in murder as well or what other circumstances would drive him to want to see babies killed. I only know for certain that he was the manifestation of pure evil on Earth.

Finally, I have to consider now that based on my recent memories whose idea it was to kill me at Beach Grove. It is possible that my parents were influenced to try to end my life as my age progressed and I was increasingly able to verbalize things. It is also possible that Wolsey simply decided it was time for me to die. It would be consistent with what I have remembered that he needed to have that power to destroy the object of so much of his attention, ultimately.

My parents botched attempts to end their children's lives as things transpired at Beach Grove apparently did not result in my parents betraying Wolsey's confidence. Both had reasons to not want their participation with this man to ever be known, and I have some indication that my father may have believed that my mother was protecting my father over the remaining years of their lives together by her allegiance to their marriage, when I believe I saw enough to know that she was only protecting herself.

My mother continued association with the cult even after this. She exposed me to their sadistic practices again, some many months after the failed attempt on my life in Beach Grove. The level of my feelings of betrayal at this late date against her is off the scale. I do not remember any further abuse or seeing Wolsey again after that.

It is possible that when Wolsey fled British Columbia after the *Sun's* damning article on him in 1959 (followed by another in *Time* magazine in 1960), that my parents thought it wisest to leave Canada as well, believing that there might be ongoing investigations into Wolsey's activities in Canada. In the timeframe of the article in *Time* magazine, my parents sat my brother and I down and told us we were leaving the country to go to Australia, to the United States, or to any of other countries they named; just as long as it was outside of Canada.

In all the information available on the Internet, the most confounding outcome of Wolsey's tenure of Satanic practices was that Wolsey eventually set up a church in Santa Cruz County in California, once he fled British Columbia. Over the next twenty years of his life until he died, I suspect he had access to many young people there. I can only imagine authorities in that area were not warned about what I have remembered more than forty years after he arrived there, but I do not yet know.

Only time will tell what else might be learned about this monster, who came into the life of a small child not too long after her birth. A child who went on to become a world famous astronomer, and to describe the beauty and wonders of the universe. Once I remembered that I had known the little girl I saw killed well before she was murdered by Wolsey and realized that I had some special place in the twisted mind of this murderer, I wrote the following to the RCMP in a letter dated June 3, 2011:

"I had a profound connection with this little girl. I feel that there is something about this that will allow me to find justice for her in some way. It goes without saying this man is dead now of course. But, there seems to be something about my ability to have lived that may be part of a purpose I do not yet understand."

I did see this angel buried by Wolsey on the Ceperley Mansion property. I do not even know her name, but she was the sister I lost when I was two years old. We would huddle in dark corners at every moment we could for the human empathy we needed for our plight. She was more my family than my parents ever were. She does not belong on that property, where she was murdered. She and the other children who are buried on those grounds with her must not be forgotten.[4]

---

[4] All together four children were killed in front of me when I was less than the age of three. The fourth child remembered was the second to die. She was the most beautiful child by nature and otherwise that I have ever seen. She was an Asian little girl about the age of one. As Wolsey brought her to the altar the fear in her eyes devastated my soul. We would always keep our foreheads together, leaning on one another with her beautiful eyes in full view. And when she died, Wolsey told me it was my fault and that I would have to pay. I have paid in countless ways for the damage inflicted by William Franklin Wolsey on helpless children, with my parents involved. Although it makes no sense, I want to apologize to the beautiful children I saw murdered and ask their forgiveness. Even though I was so young, I believed that I should have been able to do something to help these tiny children. I would have traded places with any of them. I loved them all so much. Instead, I lived. Perhaps it was to tell you of their existence and the glory of God

William Franklin Wolsey – Archbishop John I of Vancouver
Photo by Henry Tregillis of the *Vancouver Sun* (June 25, 1959)
Taken from the first in a long series of articles –
"B.C. Archbishop Exposed…"
by Jack Cahill – which forced Wolsey to flee Canada in 1960.

Author's Note

EMDR is the process by which I was treated first by Joseph Dickson and then by Connie McDonald. EMDR stands for Eye Movement Desensitization & Reprocessing.

This breakthrough in treatment of unprocessed memories was made by Francine Shapiro in 1987. Without the rapid processing and aid in bringing the memories to the surface through this blessed treatment, I do not believe I would have survived what my parents sentenced me to in adulthood, after only barely surviving my early childhood.

The world owes Francine Shapiro an enormous debt of gratitude for easing so many people's suffering, and to the therapists who use it to help their ailing patients get well.

Retrospective in Photographs

Part 1

[*Left*] I do not know the date of this picture taken of my father Robert Craman. I deliberately chose a picture of my father from a time when a child would not normally remember his appearance. This picture might even be from before my birth. My father changed over the years. He became a compassionate and kind man. Looking back from my perspective now, I believe he was filled with remorse for his actions, in later years.

From Author's Personal Collection

[*Right*] This is my mother Marline Craman. This picture says everything about her ability to project an image that was completely viable and appreciated by everyone who knew her, including me prior to knowing what I know now. In this case, the image was of movie star glamour. Although I have forgiven Marline for her actions, the severity of them makes it impossible for me to want to associate with her. The largest of all reasons is that Marline did not give her allegiance to God but instead to a force that exemplifies that something evil did fill the emptiness inside of Marline.

From Author's Personal Collection

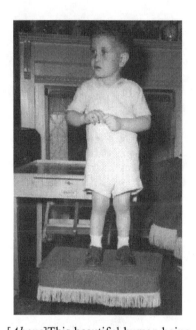

[Below] My mother says once this picture of me was placed in the window of the Valnor Studios on Granville in Vancouver, it remained there for months on end. In the eyes of this little girl are the countless sorrows she witnessed and a level of unimaginable physical and emotional pain that she experienced.

From Author's Personal Collection

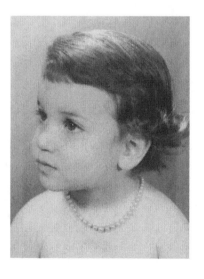

[Above]This beautiful human being is my brother. Within the last year, he had what he calls a vision of traveling with our mother on a train-like vehicle (a reference I think to the location of where many of the atrocities against us were committed as children) and in this waking vision, she turned around to face him and he screamed. He said to quote, "…and then I knew my relationship with her was over." Gary has begun to remember. His hands have locked up just as mine during my sessions of remembering the past, to the point where Gary cannot use his left hand.

From Author's Personal Collection

[*Left*] You can see by the look on my brother's face that this picture in Vancouver was after the blow to his head. Over the years, Gary's appearance and mannerisms improved. This improvement over time would make an instant and sharp reversal in the later stages of young adulthood.

From Author's Personal Collection

[*Above*] That's Becky, my best friend, standing beside Miss Drake at McKinley Elementary School in Pasadena, CA which I called home by the time this 3rd/4th grade picture was taken. We are the two sun-browned students from our time in the sun having fun. It's a tight-knit group from this elementary school and others whose students ended up at Blair High School. One particular student at Blair named Cloe Mayes has kept us all together. My yearbooks were always packed with signed messages by other students about how smart and how little I was.

From Author's Personal Collection.

[*Above*] I was the only girl on the Chess Club at Blair High school, and the only girl on any of the club teams of the other high school we met in competition. By now I knew that I was on my way to my life's goal, which was to become an astronomer and perhaps an astronaut. Although I was shy, I always felt camaraderie for my fellows. In fact, throughout my entire youth, I recalled looking at strangers in particular and saying that I felt love for that person regardless of race, age, gender, and that I would die for that person if they were ever in danger. In retrospect, I do not believe those were my thoughts, but reflected my exposure to the greatest force in the universe years before.

From BHS Yearbook 1970

[*Left*] This picture was taken and given to me by a high school friend who wrote on the back of it, "Two AM before the Physics Final. No wonder Linda gets better grades." My studies were the place where my world of space exploration for the future that I envisioned as my career, could come alive. I spent my young adulthood exploring the universe in my imagination, and made it a reality through my studies.

From Author's Personal Collection

[*Above*] Here I am studying physics in the women's dormitories at the University of Southern California. My roommate and I would go without sleep for long periods of time during finals. That never seemed to bother me. I could turn those nocturnal hours into accomplishments that began with college exams, and continued through my work at The Planetary Society, and of course at Jet Propulsion Laboratory during long hours of spacecraft navigation.

Courtesy Anne Schnee

[*Left*] This is my high school senior picture, in which I have been told, I bear the greatest resemblance to a young Annie Oakley. Because there is so much resemblance to me in some of her pictures, I sometimes think about her. I wonder if she was happy, particularly after she met and married the love of her life. Books allude to a period of her life when she was abused at the hands of a couple she went to work for when she was young. Obviously she overcame her past with a very productive life. I wish that Dave and I had met early in life as she met her husband, and could have spent our entire adult lives together. There doesn't seem to be enough time for David and me to spend making our memories in any one day.

From Author's Personal Collection

[*Right*] Having my son Ryan is the best thing I have ever done. He filled my life with joy as a young mother. Children are gifts from God.
From Author's Personal Collection

[*Left*] This is Ryan's baby picture at a time when he closely resembles his younger son right now. I am pretty sure I dyed my hair blond at that time because people would often remark that they couldn't figure out who the baby resembled.
From Author's Personal Collection

[*Right*] Ryan's half-brother Brett, pictured with Ryan, was 15 when Ryan was born. Brett is married now, became an accomplished drafter, and to my knowledge many of his dreams have come true.
From Author's Personal Collection

[*Left*] Ryan's half-brother Jason pictured with Ryan was 10 when Ryan was born. Jason became a pilot, a skydiver, and a father. I have seen Jason talk God into clearing a very cloudy day so that conditions were such that he could skydive with his older brother. Jason is extremely persuasive. I pray that he is very happy in his life.

From Author's Personal Collection

[*Above*] The boys from left to right, Jason, Brett and Ryan pictured with their grandparents on Brett and Jason's mother Judy's side of the family, Grace and John Dillon. Brett and Jason were young men by then and Ryan a growing boy. Grace was very supportive of me over many, many years of raising her boys and mine.

From Author's Personal Collection

[*Above*] Gibson and Mary Reaves, and their son Benjamin in the only picture of himself and his family Gibson ever gave me. Gibson always said that time spent on people was never wasted. Gibson must have surely believed that. The generosity of their time he and his family spent on my life events was one of the greatest joys my life held during my years at the University of Southern California and for decades after. *Courtesy Mary Reaves*

[*Above*] Gary with his beautiful wife Jeanna (Gina) is actually in our home with us during some rare occasions when they visited for a matter of hours or even once during the Holidays stayed with us to celebrate Christmas. Gina was such a sweet person and had a very strong Christian faith. The person my brother is, is housed in a frame which nearly always defies his catastrophic mental illness and brings him fully out as the caring and insightful person he is.

From Author's Personal Collection

[*Above*] Ryan met his future wife Michelle at his job managing the office of The Royale in Arcadia, CA, a senior care facility. Not too long after this picture was taken, Ryan's appendicitis surgery would end the role he could play in his own future. No one so young it seems should have to lose so much of their life and control over their future because of the malpractice of others. The surgery to remove his appendix was botched by the surgeons and the life he had cherished each day of his youth was gone.

From Hyder Family Personal Collection

[*Left*] I took Ryan and Michelle's picture in front of the garage where Ryan housed his brand new sports car he had bought as part of a promising future before his injury. Nothing, no surgery or any treatment we have found has been successful in alleviating Ryan's pain from the nerve damage caused by the surgeons who operated to remove his appendix, an injury which is called myofascial abdominal neuralgia.

From Author's Personal Collection

[*Right*] Ryan teaches Robert about growing up in Norco as he did, when they visit Ryan's childhood home owned by Ryan's father Jerry Hyder. This was before Ryan's fateful surgery that would change his life forever.

From Hyder Family Personal Collection

[*Left*] This is Dave's and my grandson Robert with his mother Michelle outside my condominium in Arcadia, CA. Ryan's family lived with me once Ryan became disabled. Robert's entire room was a tent the size of a small futon mattress, inside his parent's room. My struggles to give Robert a real home and room of his own ultimately succeeded at a time in my life when it was against all odds.

Courtesy Ryan Hyder

[*Right*] Proud father Ryan when Dave's and my grandson Nathan arrives on the scene. It is the most amazing experience to see your children become parents, and how well they handle it, loving their children and prizing their educations.

Courtesy Michelle Hyder

[*Left*] Michelle, Robert, and Nathan when the littlest member of the family was ruling the house. At age two-and-a-half months, Nathan said to me, "I love you!" The early development was shared by Ryan and was apparently the same for me.

Courtesy Ryan Hyder

[*Right*] From his expressed standpoint, Robert finally has a little brother! Robert lends his name as Nathan's middle name.

From Hyder Family Personal Collection

[*Left*] The precious family as they are today. Life must adjust to the fact that this family's father cannot leave the house without gurney transport.

Courtesy David Meyer

[Right] I firmly believe that God led me to David Meyer as a way of bringing me back to Him. Our wedding, Ryan's birth, and the events of my grandchildren's lives, are the highlights of my life.

Courtesy Linda Jakubek

[Left] Robert bravely walks me down the aisle, standing in for his father. Robert and I spend a lot of wonderful time driving to and from his school each day discussing the universe and Robert's dreams for the future. Robert also spends time learning how to golf from his Grandpa Dave!

Courtesy Linda Jakubek

[Right] Nathan, at just a year old, walks Dave's and my rings down the aisle at our wedding. The rings were attached to the decorated toy lawn mower, which was needed because he could not yet balance without it. He and his brother bless us each day with visits to our room upstairs in the house we all share.

Courtesy Linda Jakubek

[*Right*]　　　Two Associate Professors of Astronomy, life-long astronomers, united in marriage and throughout time.
Courtesy Hal Polner

[*Above*] Dave spent 21 years in the Air Force as an Air Force Fighter Pilot. Dave graduated from the University of Nebraska with a Bachelor of Science in Geology in 1968. He was commissioned a Second Lieutenant in the Air Force and went directly to pilot training at Williams Air Force base near Phoenix, AZ. After graduating near the top of his class in pilot training, Dave was assigned to the latest Air Force Fighter, the F-4 Phantom II as a back seat pilot. He then completed a one year tour in Vietnam, after which he upgraded to the front seat of the F-4. Then, in 1974, Dave volunteered for an exchange tour with the United States Marine Corp flying the Navy version of the F-4. During this tour, his squadron was assigned to the newly commissioned aircraft carrier the USS Nimitz. Pictured is Dave getting his one hundredth landing on the Nimitz! I am so proud of my husband's military service.
Credit: US Navy Photo

[*Above*] Dave's squadron was stationed on the Nimitz from June 1975 to February 1977, flying near Cuba, the North Atlantic, and the Mediterranean. Dave made two hundred landings on the Nimitz during that time! After the exchange tour on the Nimitz was over, back in the Air Force, Dave completed instructor school and safety school and was an instructor pilot in F-4s for the remainder of his career. Pictured is Dave flying his F-4 dropping a fuel tank, while on an alert mission off the Nimitz. *From Meyer Family Personal Collection*

[*Above*] Dave in flight gear by his F-4 on the Nimitz. *From Meyer Family Personal Collection*

[*Above*] Dave and his radar intercept officer, "Cowboy" at their airplane on the Nimitz. *From Meyer Family Personal Collection*

[*Left*] Dave and "Cowboy" with their aircraft before going on alert on the Nimitz.
From Meyer Family Personal Collection

[*Right*] Dave with a brand new F-4E at the McDonald Douglas plant in St. Louis, MO.
From Meyer Family Personal Collection

[*Left*] Dave as an instructor pilot with his F-4 at Homestead Air Force base south of Miami, FL.
From Meyer Family Personal Collection

[*Right*] The entire Meyer Family beside Dave, Gretchen and Robert, then Mark, and parents Ewald and Cecelia. Gretchen and her husband Bob have three grown children and two beautiful grandchildren.

Courtesy Bob Thomale

[*Left*] This picture has special significance to Dave and to me, because it was taken at church for our church directory. At first, Dave was not sure that we should be so revealing about our lives to tell my story. We are private people. My last memory came as a response to that concern. When I was in the presence of God, God considered in a way that I could understand as a two-and-half year old child whether I should live or die. God said, "Live. Die. Live. Die." I responded that I wanted to live, and I thought about my brother. Then God said, "If you live, tell."

From Author's Personal Collection

[*Right*] We lost both of Dave's parents within a year of our own wedding; they went home to God. Ewald and Cecelia Meyer lived their lives as God wanted them to, with each day as Ewald let his friends and family know, holding the joy that knowing Jesus brings.

From Meyer Family Personal Collection

[*Left*] Pastor Brad Viken's guidance in my faith journey has been unwavering. He told me to find out how God could use me mightily in my life. Pastor shares his love of his God with the people of Faith Lutheran Church in Hesperia, CA. His wife Lynda is a Guardian Angel right here on Earth. Her inclination to help others in need is unbounded, and her expertise in all things computers profound. Dave and I are truly blessed they are in our lives.

Courtesy Viken Family

[*Right*] Where ever the journey takes Ryan and his family, they have seen hardship and challenge in unimaginable quantity. Ryan continues his powerful intellectual interests. Michelle shares her passions for cooking and other artistry. Robert is exceptional in everything he does, with a compassion for those who need his help that is beyond his years. Little Nathan has a capacity for understanding the deep issues of life and hardship beyond any possible expectation we could have, as does his brother. They are both brilliant. We pray for God's miracle for Ryan.

From Hyder Family Personal Collection

[*Left*] The future for Dave and I (pictured here with Nathan and camera-shy Walter both costumed for Halloween) includes a cherishing of both our families and the Lord's Promise to us all. The Lord has told me to deliver the message that Heaven is ours for those who believe. Dave and I will share the road that God has paved for us ahead.

Courtesy Robert Wooten Hyder

Retrospective in Photographs

Part 2

[*Left*] Taken as part of a photo shoot for *New West Magazine*.
Used with permission
© *Linda Wolfe*

[*Below*] Original Caption Released with Image: This dramatic view of Jupiter's satellite Io shows two simultaneously occurring volcanic eruptions. One can be seen on the limb, (at lower right) in which ash clouds are rising more than 150 miles (260 kilometers) above the satellite's surface. The second can be seen on the terminator (shadow between day and night) where the volcanic cloud is catching the rays of the rising sun. The dark hemisphere of Io is made visible by light reflected from Jupiter. Seen in Io's night sky, Jupiter looms almost 40 times larger and 200 times brighter than our own full Moon. This photo was taken by Voyager 1 on March 8, 1979, looking back 2.6 million miles (4.5 million kilometers) at Io, three days after its historic encounter. This is the same image in which Linda A. Morabito, a JPL engineer, discovered the first extraterrestrial volcanic eruption (the bright curved volcanic cloud on the limb). Jet Propulsion Laboratory manages and controls the Voyager project for NASA's Office of Space Science.

Image/Caption Credit: NASA/JPL

[*Right*] Original Optical Navigation Image Processing System data product of the Io Plume Pele in the Discovery Picture generated by Linda Morabito on 9 March, 1979. Contour lines by DN range drawn in by Steve Synnott.

Courtesy Linda Morabito

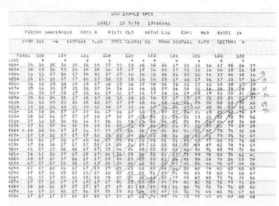

[*Left*] Original Optical Navigation Image Processing System data product of the Io Plume Pele in the Discovery Picture generated by Linda Morabito on 9 March, 1979. Angles of eruptive plume drawn in by Peter Kupferman.

Courtesy Linda Morabito

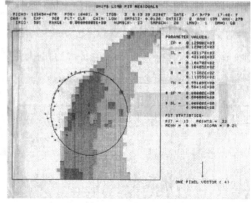

[*Right*] Original Optical Navigation Image Processing System data product of the Io Plume Pele in the Discovery Picture generated by Linda Morabito on 9 March, 1979. Limb fit to edge of eruptive plume performed by Linda Morabito.

Courtesy Linda Morabito

[*Left*] Original Caption Released with Image: Perhaps the most spectacular of all the Voyager photos of Io is this mosaic obtained by Voyager 1 on March 5 at a range of 400,000 kilometers. A great variety of color and albedo is seen on the surface, now thought to be the result of surface deposits of various forms of sulfur and sulfur dioxide. The two great volcanoes Pele and Loki (upper left) are prominent.
Image/Caption Credit: NASA/JPL.

[*Right*] Taken during a visit by Celeste and Bill Peters to Jet Propulsion Laboratory in 1979.
Courtesy Bill Peters

[*Left*] Original Caption Released with Image: Voyager 1 image of Io showing active plume of Loki on limb. Heart-shaped feature southeast of Loki consists of fallout deposits from active plume Pele. The images that make up this mosaic were taken from an average distance of approximately 490,000 kilometers (340,000 miles).
Image/Caption Credit:
NASA/JPL/USGS

[*Above*] Original Caption Released with Image: VOLCANIC EXPLOSION ON IO: Voyager 1 acquired this image of Io on March 4 at 5:30 p.m. (PST) about 11 hours before closest approach to the Jupiter moon. The distance to Io was about 490,000 kilometers (304,000 miles). An enormous volcanic explosion can be seen silhouetted against dark space over Io's bright limb. The brightness of the plume has been increased by the computer as it is normally extremely faint, whereas the relative color of the plume (greenish white) has been preserved. At this time solid material had been thrown up to an altitude of about 100 miles. This requires an ejection velocity from the volcanic vent of about 1200 miles per hour, material reaching the crest of the fountain in several minutes. The vent area is a complex circular structure consisting of a bright ring about 300 kilometers in diameter and a central region of irregular dark and light patterns. Volcanic explosions similar to this occur on the Earth when magmatic gases expand explosively as material is vented. On Earth water is the major gas driving the explosion. Because Io is thought to be extremely dry, scientists are searching for other gases to explain the explosion. JPL manages and controls the Voyager Project for NASA's Office of Space Science. Image/Caption Credit: NASA/JPL

[*Above*] Original Caption Released with Image: This picture shows a special color reconstruction of one of the erupting volcanoes on Io discovered by Voyager 1 during its encounter with Jupiter on the 4th and 5th of March. The picture was taken March 4 about 5:00 p.m. from a range of about half a million kilometers showing an eruption region on the horizon. This method of color analysis allows scientists to combine data from four pictures, taken in ultraviolet, blue, green and orange light. In this picture one can see the strong change in color of the erupting plume. The region that is brighter in ultraviolet light (blue in this image) is much more extensive than the denser, bright yellow region near the center of the eruption. Scientists will use data of this type to study the amount of gas and dust in the eruption and the size of dust particles. Preliminary analysis suggests that the bright ultraviolet part of the cloud may be due to scattered light from very fine particles (the same effect which makes smoke appear bluish). Image/Caption Credit: NASA/JPL

[*Left*] "Discovery of Currently Active Extraterrestrial Volcanism" by L.A. Morabito, S.P. Synnott, P.N. Kupferman, and Stewart A. Collins appeared in the 1 June 1979 issue of *Science*. Credit: From Full cover of *Science* Vol. 204, no. 4396. 1 June 1979. (Image: Jet Propulsion Laboratory, Pasadena).

Reprinted with permission from AAAS.

[*Right*] As noted in the January 21, 1980 issue of *Time Magazine*, *Smithsonian*, *Scientific American* and *National Geographic* showed the same volcanic eruption on Jupiter's moon Io, all in their January 1980 issues, creating a science magazine trifecta with a total circulation of 12,750,000. *National Geographic* wrote, "Morabito knew that an active volcano on Io could be the greatest find of the planetary exploration program. It would mean that some other world in our solar system is still geologically alive. So she and her colleagues checked and rechecked the picture before taking her discovery to the imaging team. By Monday morning the stunned scientists had found not one, but at least half a dozen erupting volcanoes."

Credit: ©2010 National Geographic

[*Left*] As noted in the January 21, 1980 issue of *Time Magazine*, *Smithsonian*, *Scientific American* and *National Geographic* showed the same volcanic eruption on Jupiter's moon Io, all in their January 1980 issues, creating a science magazine trifecta with a total circulation of 12,750,000.

Credit: Reproduced with permission.
Copyright © 2010 Scientific American, a division of Nature America, Inc. All rights reserved.

[*Right*] As noted in the January 21, 1980 issue of *Time Magazine*, *Smithsonian*, *Scientific American* and *National Geographic* showed the same volcanic eruption on Jupiter's moon Io, all in their January 1980 issues, creating a science magazine trifecta with a total circulation of 12,750,000. *Smithsonian's* Don Moser responded to Time by saying, "It just confirms our good judgment."

Copyright 1980 Smithsonian Institution. Reprinted with permission from Smithsonian Magazine. All rights reserved.
Reproduction in any medium is strictly prohibited without permission from Smithsonian Institution. Such permission may be requested from Smithsonian Magazine

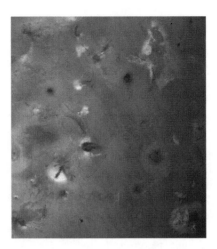

[*Above*] Original Caption Released with Image: Io's volcanic plains are shown in this Voyager 1 image. Also visible are numerous volcanic calderas and two large mountains (Euboea Montes, just above center, and Haemus Montes, at lower left). The plains include some distinct lava flows, such as those of Lerna Regio (lower right), and low mesas, such as Nemeas Planum (bottom center) and Dodona Planum (just left of center). This scene is about 1050 mi (1700 km) from left to right. The composition of Io's volcanic plains and lava flows has not been determined, but they could consist dominantly of sulfur or of silicates (such as basalt) coated with sulfurous condensates. The apparent erosion of the edges of some mesas suggests that they are composed of something volatile, possibly including a component of SO2 ice, which is observed spectroscopically to be widespread on Io. The high topographic relief in some areas, particularly of the montes, suggests that those areas are made primarily of silicate rock, which is much stronger than sulfur or SO2. The bright aureoles around several features probably consist of freshly deposited SO2 frost that was vented from cracks and volcanic conduits. Image/Caption Credit: NASA/JPL/USGS

[*Right*] Taken for the January 1980 issue of *National Geographic Magazine*.
Credit: Albert Moldvay / National Geographic Stock

[*Right*]Original Caption Released with Image: This color picture of Io, Jupiter's innermost Galilean satellite, was taken by Voyager 1 on the morning of March 5, 1979 at a range of 128,500 kilometers (77,100 miles). It is centered at 8 south latitude and 317 longitude. The width of the picture is about 1000 kilometers (600 miles). The diffuse reddish and orangish colorations are probably surface deposits of sulfur compounds, salts and possibly other volcanic sublimates. The dark spot with the irregular radiating pattern near the bottom of the picture may be a volcanic crater with radiating lava flows. Image/Caption Credit: NASA/JPL

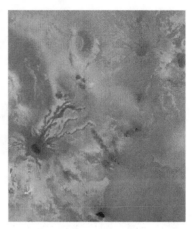

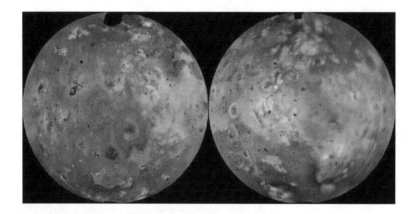

[*Above*] Original Caption Released with Image: Voyager 1 computer color mosaics, shown in approximately natural color and in Lambertian equal-area projections, show the Eastern (left) and Western (right) hemispheres of Io. This innermost of Jupiter's 4 major satellites is the most volcanically active object in the solar system. Io is 2263 mi (3640 km) in diameter, making it a little bigger than Earth's moon. Almost all the features visible here have volcanic origins, including several calderas and eruption plumes that were active at the time of the Voyager 1 encounter. Image/Caption Credit: NASA/JPL/USGS

[*Left*] Taken by Jet Propulsion Laboratory in front of the Voyager 1 model.
Credit: NASA/JPL

[*Above*] Responsible for Voyager Navigation System Design were: Charles H. Acton, Marvin H. Bantell, Carl S. Christensen, David W. Curkendall, John F. Dixon, Jordan Ellis, Donald L. Gray, Tom W. Hamilton, Claude E. Hildebrand, Robert A. Jacobson, Jeremy B. Jones, Charles E. Kohlhase, Tomas A. Komarek, James P. McDanell, Edward L. McKinley, Lanny J. Miller, Neil A. Mottinger, George W. Null, and V. John Ondrasik, Robert A. Preston, Gary A. Ransford, Gary L. Sievers, Richard H. Stanton, Francis M. Sturms, Jr., Richard E. Van Allen, F. Bryant Winn. Members of the Voyager Navigation Team were: Mark J. Adams, Julian C. Breidenthal, James K. Campbell, Robert J. Cesarone, Leonard Dicken, M. R. Dodds, Arthur J. Donegan, Donald L. Gray, Donald W. Green, Jerry D. Hyder, Robert A. Jacobson, Roger E. Koch, Van W. Lam, So Bing Ma, Stanley Mandell, James P. McDanell, Edward L. McKinley, Margaret M. Medina, Linda A. Morabito, Charles F. Peters, Joseph E. Riedel, George C. Rinker, Lawrence E. Ross, Herbert N. Royden, Andrey B. Sergeyevsky, Stephen P. Synnott, Anthony H. Taylor, Edwin S. Travers, Richard E. Van Allen, Donna M. Wegemer, F. Bryant Winn, Tricia Wood, and Robert R. Wynn, some of whom are pictured here. In the back row, second from the left is Jerry Hyder, Ryan's father.
Credit: NASA/JPL

[*Right*] Joe Donegan, Ed Travers, Linda Morabito, and Steve Synnott at the Voyager Optical Navigation Image Processing System taken by Jet Propulsion Laboratory.
Credit: NASA/JPL

[*Above*] OFFICE OF PUBLIC INFORMATION
JET PROPULSION LABORATORY
CALIFORNIA INSTITUTE OF TECHNOLOGY
NATIONAL AERONAUTICS AND SPACE ADMINISTRATION
PASADENA, CALIFORNIA 91109. TELEPHONE (213) 354-5011
PHOTO CAPTION   Voyager 1-98 June 6, 1979
This dramatic view of Jupiter's Great Red Spot and its
surroundings was obtained by Voyager 1 on Feb. 25, 1979, when the
spacecraft was   5.7 million miles (9.2 million kilometers) from Jupiter.
Cloud details as small as 100   miles (160 kilometers)across can be seen
here. The colorful, wavy cloud pattern to the left of the Red Spot is a
region of extraordinarily complex end variable wave motion. The Jet
Propulsion Laboratory manages the
Voyager mission for NASA's Office of Space Science and
Applications. This image was converted directly from digital data to
GIF format.

[*Right*] Original Caption Released with Image: Voyager 2 took this picture of Io on the evening of July 9, 1979, from a range of 1.2 million kilometers. On the limb of Io are two blue volcanic eruption plumes about 100 kilometers high. These two plumes were first seen by Voyager 1 in March, 1979, and are designated Plume 5 (upper) and Plume 6 (lower). They have apparently been erupting for a period of at least 4 months and probably longer. A total of six plumes have been seen by Voyager 2, all of which were first seen by Voyager 1. The largest plume viewed by Voyager 1 (Plume 1) is no longer erupting. Plume 4 was not viewed on the edge of the moon's disc by Voyager 2 and therefore it is not known whether or not it is still erupting. This picture is one of a series taken to monitor the eruptions over a 6 hour period

.   Image/Caption   Credit: NASA/JPL

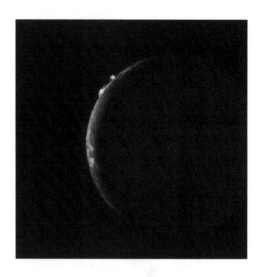

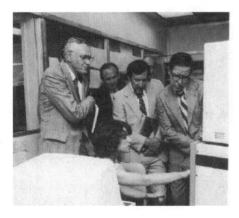

[*Left*] Taken during the visit of Edwin Meese, advisor to President Ronald Reagan, to Jet Propulsion Laboratory.
Credit NASA/JPL

[*Above*] Shortly after the discovery of Io volcanoes, planetary scientist William Hartmann made this painting, which is one of the first to visualize what one of the erupting volcanoes might look like from the surface of Io. The wide-angle view shows colored deposits of sulfurous materials with arcs of erupting ejecta from the volcanic mountain in the distance. (Acrylic painting, 1979, copyright William K. Hartmann, Planetary Science Institute)

"… a place in Canada where I shall go
one day, sit down on the ground, and
weep for what was done to my
brother…"

Beach Grove, Tsawwassen, Canada
Credit: G. Szychter, 2006

"Be still, and know that I am God." Psalm
46:10 (KJV)

Beach Grove, Tsawwassen, Canada
Credit: G. Szychter, 2006

Acknowledgments

There are hardly enough words to describe the contribution my husband Dave has made to this book. As I look back and remember the individual days of anguish and horror I faced as the memories returned, I can hardly believe that *Parallel Universes* has now come into being. It could never have happened; I might never have survived without Dave telling me that he was sure one day everything would be fine, and that I could lean on his love for me. My son Ryan and my daughter-in-law Michelle have always believed in the information age, and by not understanding my fears have moved me forward as though the fears did not exist. At times when I did not believe I would survive, I would look upon my grandsons Robert and Nathan and continue to take the notes that went into this book. I would like to thank Corporal Grewal and Corporal Foster of the Royal Canadian Mounted Police, Mission RCMP Municipal Detachment, as well for their diligence and support, initially, as well as San Bernardino County Sheriff's Department Deputy Sheriff D. Ramos who interfaced with them. My prayer is for justice and peace for my little "sister" who died at the hands of William Franklin Wolsey, and I pray that public opinion will force the RCMP to take up that cause; for the little boy and the baby and the gorgeous one year old, and others like them we may never know about. Connie and Joseph were my lifeline. My literary agent Jack Scovil believed in me throughout and encouraged me steadfastly to put pen to paper. Friends over the years who always believed in me include Celeste, Cathy, Aban, Poonam, Agatha, Terry, Kim G., Lynda, Vern, Gayle, Jane, Gary W., Kris, and Sandy. Pastor Viken is my life's blessing and never doubted the troubles I brought to him from a parallel universe. My brother Gary made this effort a joy so that the world would know about his courage and that he persevered over even more than I could bring myself to share in this book. Be well, my dear brother. Gibson continues to guide my life and efforts through the example he set while on Earth. On August 17, 2011, I remembered the name of my "sister," Pearl. God sent me an angel who gave me the courage to live, and then God took her home. All glory be to God.

For information about having the author speak to your group about
her life in science or her religious experiences:

Send an email to

inquiry@lindamorabito.com

or call

(760) 245-8020

To learn more about the author's presentations visit
www.lindamorabito.com

You are invited to share how you feel about

Parallel Universes
A Memoir from the Edges of Space and Time

Visit the book's website:
http://www.lindamorabito.com

Notes

9886341R0018

Made in the USA
Charleston, SC
21 October 2011